'A fascinating book that uses poker to discuss philosophy, magic, strategy, cognitive science, game theory, deception, biases, risk management and much more. Who knew one book could teach you so much about poker and the best scientific research in so many fields?'

Seth Stephens-Davidowitz, author of
Everybody Lies* and *Don't Trust Your Gut

'*The Truth Detective* is both a riveting read and a call to action. Alex O' Brien intertwines lessons from the poker table with cutting-edge scientific research on human behaviour and the brain, showing us how to understand the world better, and to understand ourselves better. I found myself thinking about *The Truth Detective* long after I read it. Even if you've never played poker, you will be richly entertained and educated by this beautifully written gem of a book'

Jennifer Shahade, two-time US Women's Chess Champion and author of *Chess Queens*

'Captivating, gripping and the best book I've read since *Thinking Fast and Slow*. O'Brien doesn't pull any punches, and examining the bluffs we seek and the bullshit we find in life, [she] combines a number of studies, sources and complex thoughts into a case for critical thinking. This is a book that should be read and savoured in full; it pulls many of the great concerns of the day such as AI, climate change, fake news, pandemic issues, and the power of social media into a riveting page turner. As soon as I started reading, I literally couldn't stop . . . do someone you love a favour and give them the gift of this book. It's absolutely brilliant'

Dara O'Kearney, ultra runner and author of *The Poker Solved Series*

'The challenge of knowing "what is the truth" goes far beyond the poker table [and] I can't imagine a book more perfectly suited to its time than *The Truth Detective*. By using the rules of the game to explore truth and deception, O'Brien makes the topic accessible [and] truly entertaining. The interviews and well-documented research woven throughout give scientific backbone to a much-needed look at a very important topic. This is an exhortation for us all to be more careful consumers of "truth"'

Kara Scott, broadcaster and World Series of Poker anchor

The
Truth
Detective

The
Truth
Detective

A Poker Player's Guide
to a Complex World

Alex O'Brien

SOUVENIR
PRESS

First published in Great Britain in 2023 by
Souvenir Press, an imprint of
PROFILE BOOKS LTD
29 Cloth Fair
London
EC1A 7JQ

www.souvenirpress.co.uk

10 9 8 7 6 5 4 3 2 1

Typeset in Freight Text by MacGuru Ltd
Designed by Barneby Ltd
Printed and bound in Great Britain by Clays Ltd, Elcograf S.p.A.

A CIP record for this book can be obtained from the British Library

ISBN: 978 1 78816 487 0
eISBN: 978 1 78283 671 1

FSC
www.fsc.org
MIX
Paper | Supporting
responsible forestry
FSC® C018072

To the oxygen in my life:
Ava and Jeff

Contents

INTRODUCTION The Cards We're Dealt and the
Hand We Play   1

PART ONE Making Sense of a Complex World:
Critical Thinking and Poker   11

PART TWO Learning How to Read Others:
Communication, Intepretation and Impressions   73

PART THREE Being a Real-Life Truth Detective:
Deception and Patterns   129

PART FOUR Learning to Live with Uncertainty:
Risk, Game Theory and Imperfect Information   199

A Tribute   247
References and Further Reading   251
Notes   254

The Cards We're Dealt and the Hand We Play

A Game of Imperfect Information

People who don't know poker think it's all about bluffing. It isn't. It is a game that forces you to quantify that which is unknown, make on-the-spot risk assessments and come to the right decisions under pressure without the influence of any emotions.

I should know. I learnt this the hard way.

The crowd around the table was four deep and I was sweating beneath the proverbial spotlight. It had been two years since my last live poker tournament yet when I walked back into the poker room it felt like I had never been away. Passing some of the tables on my way to the cashier's desk, dealers looked up with 'welcome back' gestures – a smile, a nod. I waved back, my excitement rising further with the sound of riffling poker chips. I love playing poker. I am not a professional poker player, nor is it my goal to become one. Yet two years earlier, when I was seven months pregnant, I'd finished fourth out of eighty players at my local casino, winning £5,000. And here I was now, back at the tables at the PokerStars Festival tournament in London facing off against over 900 players for a first prize of nearly £90,000.

After eleven hours of play, there were just three hands left and, despite my long absence, I was finishing the day as one of the tournament leaders. At no point had I been at risk of being eliminated. Until William Kassouf sat down at my table.

Unlike me, Kassouf is a pro. His style of play is polarising. He had come to notoriety a few months earlier during the final stages of WSOP (World Series of Poker) where he received a penalty for taunting a player and clashed with another in such a way that the moment captured on a TV broadcast went viral. The player Kassouf locked horns with was Canadian poker pro Griffin Benger, who had been sitting in silence for over four minutes, waiting for him to act. At the poker table that is a long time, and an absolute eternity when you are on the receiving end of Kassouf's speech play: he had not stopped needling Benger in his attempts to elicit a tell. When he eventually did get the tell, he totally missed it. How? Breaking his silence, Benger went on the verbal offensive: 'You're just an abusive person, man, it's not funny.' In the subsequent back-and-forth between the two, Benger repeatedly yelled back, 'Check your privilege!' Had Kassouf paid attention, he would have noticed that – with millions of dollars in play – for Benger to have had the confidence to antagonise his opponent, he must have held the best starting hand in poker – Aces. What made this match-up even more spectacular was the fact that Kassouf was holding Kings, the second-best starting hand in poker. Both players went all in. The tiny 0.4% probability of Kings facing Aces seemed to hit Kassouf hard. Not only was he visibly shaken but he was now also openly calling for one of the two Kings remaining in the deck. None appeared on the board. The studio audience erupted in a deafening cheer as Kassouf got knocked out of the tournament and had to leave the table. Despite losing in front of TV cameras and a global audience, Kassouf didn't change his modus operandi one bit. He maintained an aggressive and bullying table manner. Whenever he was involved in a hand he would launch into an endless stream of verbal pokes and prods to put his opponents on edge and move them out of their comfort zone. And now that was exactly what he was doing to me.

We were the only two players in the hand and the barrage that came across the table was irritating me. 'What have you got? Tell me. I'll tell you if it's any good,' he heckled, trying to elicit a reaction. I tried to tune him out and focus on replaying the actions that had led to this precise moment. He had said, 'All of it!' before smiling and shoving all his chips into the middle after the river card (the last card on the board) had landed.

For him to go all in, his hand had to be good. But how good? And, crucially, was mine better? He acted confident, for sure. But was it bluster?

As the players on the other tables finished, word spread that Kassouf was in a heads-up, all-in hand and a crowd formed around us. Among the spectators were several journalists eagerly jotting down every single exchange:

'. . . *Then she said, "Are you lying to me?" Again it was like a parent might grill a child with chocolate smeared around his chops.*

"No!" Kassouf insisted, about as innocently as the Artful Dodger.'

I couldn't tell if he was lying, but one thing I knew for sure: I didn't have the best possible hand. The best hand, called 'the nuts', would have been a flush, all cards of the same suit.

'Will,' I asked, 'do you have the flush?'

'Nope, I don't have the flush! I DO NOT have the flush!'

I have no idea why I asked him anything at all. It was an act of desperation. He wouldn't have told me if he did. Just as he'd been taunting me, I tried to taunt him. I hoped it might give me a clue. Anything. I didn't know what I was looking for. And I didn't know how to read any answer he might give.

So one more time I tried to remember. How quickly had he called my bet? Had he hesitated? Had he seemed eager? It was no use. I was at a loss. Engulfed by a massive cloud of uncertainty that had moved in over my head, I kept my gaze on the table, trying to blur out the peering eyes around me, desperately seeking a place where I could find the answer I needed. I couldn't catch hold of any clear thought in my head to save me. Instead, I was drowning in a sea of irrelevant questions. Why hadn't I played a few smaller, warm-up tournaments first? Why did I choose my first tournament to be this one – the big one? I cursed my decision-making. Then I reprimanded myself for ignoring my own advice to avoid getting involved in a hand with Kassouf, who was still yapping at me from across the table. I disliked him immensely. Still staring at the board, I tried to refocus my mind on the play, but he did not give me a chance. 'If you got it, you got it!' he jibed. It was the same line he'd used on his opponent a few months earlier during the World Series of Poker clash, the clash that he had lost.

What exactly triggered my decision to call him I do not remember, but I will never forget the crushing feeling that hit me when I looked up at Kassouf, who was staring right back at me like a hyena ready to pounce. I knew right then I was about to lose, even before seeing his cards. I was still moving my stack into the middle when, grinning from ear to ear, he turned to the crowd and announced: 'The coconuts!' smacking down an Ace-High flush. The best possible hand. The absolute nuts.

I was angry and humiliated. What's more, I had given away my tournament life and I had no one to blame but myself.

'Kassouf sat on his knees, his foot shaking in excitement over the edge of his chair. He was silent and offered neither a faux apology nor a rub-down. He smiled still, but reading it would have been poker anthropomorphism: it might have been guilt, sympathy or plain old wicked glee. There was no way really to tell. Kassouf simply stacked up close to 185,000 chips as O'Brien counted only about 20,000 in front of her. About three minutes earlier, it had been into six figures.'

No one cheered, which was something of a comfort. But I knew what everyone was thinking, because I was thinking just the same: why did I call him? The headlines in the poker news the next day summed it up: *Kassouf got into O'Brien's head.*

Looking back now, I know exactly the mistake I made. It began way before Kassouf even sat down at my table. A few months earlier I had watched him on TV during the WSOP. He had bluffed a female poker pro and then zealously celebrated for the cameras, shouting: 'Nine high like a boss!' It was unsportsmanlike and disrespectful behaviour and the scene was burnt into my mind. Kassouf was not just the villain I disliked, but one I badly wanted to beat. When it came to the showdown between us, that moment from the WSOP was replaying in my mind. I couldn't stand the thought of being shown a bluff, of seeing him gloat with the satisfaction of having got away with it yet again. I became so desperate to beat him that my emotions dominated my mind, forcing out any logic or critical thinking. In poker, you cannot make a mistake like that. And when you are uncertain about a move, your best bet is to just fold your cards.

A Game of Strategy

After that public humiliation, I couldn't sleep for days. I'd lie awake in bed, staring at the ceiling, endlessly going over the hand in my mind, reliving the moment again and again. What made this showdown particularly painful was that it had been down to an unforced error. It was on me, and I had to take responsibility for it. By the fourth sleepless night, it was time to stop the self-imposed torture. I couldn't change the past, but I sure as hell could make sure I was ready for the next time I found myself in a similar situation. In the morning, I got up and started studying the game.

You can learn the rules of poker in minutes, but it takes years to truly master it. The game is so complex that the world's best professionals allocate hours of daily study to it. Highly strategic, it requires a number of skills, all of which are used in combination to sleuth for information. Poker players start by asking a range of questions and then move on to interrogating every aspect of the game, meaning they go through a process of stress-testing their assumptions and the information they have at the time.

Using mathematics, statistics, game theory, emotional intelligence, strategy, deception, and verbal and non-verbal behaviour analysis, they detect clues leading to whatever their opponent is attempting to conceal and whatever needs piecing together. Studying and playing the game leads to the development of a strategically sophisticated mindset. What generally happens with beginner players is that they tend to focus on the cards they themselves hold; however, once they gain a better understanding and more experience of the game, their thinking shifts to what their opponent's cards could be.

Nobel Prize-winning mathematician John Nash once described human interaction as being like a poker game; both sides adapt their behaviour to get what they want out of the other person, even if they're not doing it consciously.

When I began my deep dive into poker study, I learnt more than just the equity of a particular hand or the expected value of a certain play. Studying it changed my thinking in ways that saw me approach everyday life as if it were a game of poker. I started assessing and evaluating not just people, but actions and information in my environment, just as I do at the tables. In the process it became clear to me not only that the game of poker was misunderstood, but also that its benefits were being vastly underrated. I realised that the various skillsets one needs to bring to the table are underpinned by proven scientific theories – these structured explanations about how our environment and the phenomena in it work are based on facts, repeated tests and verifications. The more I looked into it, the stronger the line connecting poker and science became. This books details how.

The Cards We're Dealt and the Hand We Play

Our lives are affected by the decisions we've made, and sometimes by those other people have made. Individually and as a collective. To make *good* decisions that lead to *good* outcomes we have to be able to understand and analyse information, including the actions of those around us. No matter how small or seemingly insignificant, every single one of our actions has at least one reaction. Nothing in life happens without this exchange, without give and take.

As a society we *have* to become better at holding not just those in power accountable, but each other too. Everyone *thinks*. We can't avoid it; it's as integral to our existence as breathing. But it seems that left to ourselves, much of our thinking is biased, distorted and uninformed. Yet our quality of life depends on the quality of our thoughts.

The Truth Detective is your roadmap to a more effective mindset. Thinking like a poker player helps us sniff out lurking threats, because none of us is safe from being manipulated to someone else's advantage. This book will transform your thinking and enhance your ability to detect the traps set to exploit us, by people who want to shift our opinions, manipulate our reality and control our thoughts.

Plenty of books teach you how to tell when you're being lied to, and plenty of books will tell you how to play poker. This book will do neither of those things. It's about those hundreds of moments every day when we're faced with an unclear choice or an uncomfortable conversation; the moments where we read or hear something that commands our attention but we don't know how much weight to grant it; and it's a book about how we can help ourselves to find the best way forward. It's about how to react to government policies, how to decode alleged scientific discoveries, how to decipher what our kids say or try to say on the way home from school, how to process this whole crazy post-truth world. Ultimately, I want to show you that we are more likely to avoid the treacherous jungles of the unknown and make good decisions when we use some of the skills that are so important to the game of poker; when we consider that life isn't a bluff, but a game of imperfect information. This book will teach you how to take the skills needed at the tables and apply them in real life. It will show you how to think like a poker player and will tell you why it's important to do so. Learn, as I have, not to look for the lies. Look for what you can verify. Look for the truth. Use your mind and think critically.

PART ONE

Making Sense of a Complex World: Critical Thinking and Poker

Learning about Learning Poker

All truths are easy to understand once they are discovered; the point is to discover them

Galileo Galilei

When we look to verify information, we can minimise the number of mistakes we make and are less likely to get burnt. In doing this, we become truth detectives. But beware: you are signing up for a never-ending quest that requires courage, effort and a healthy dash of humility.

Socrates held that we can only achieve true wisdom by recognising our own shortcomings and lack of knowledge. Looked at this way, the search for truth isn't a destination, it's a life-long process of constant discussion; considering and evaluating the views of others as well as ourselves – or at least that's what happens when it's going well. On the face of it this sounds pretty straightforward, but of course it is not: nothing that involves humans and their many complexities is straightforward. Truth is so coveted partly because most of us want it to confirm what we already think and what we *want* it to be. When we claim ownership of the truth without seeking evidence to verify it, we are failing to engage with each other on a meaningful, thoughtful basis.

There are variables and forces in life that we can do nothing about, like weather or gravity. It is also true that how others react, what they think or what they say and how all this affects us and our environment is an aspect of life that adds both to its infinite beauty and to its occasional ugliness. But just like in poker, there are measures we can take to mitigate negative experiences and outcomes, and skills we can develop to avoid them.

One of the very first lessons I learnt from poker is how to deal with two important aspects of the game: 'variance' and 'luck'. Poker players use these terms to explain outcomes.

When you sit down at the tables, you can expect to achieve a certain distribution of outcomes. Your win or loss is akin to a random draw from that distribution. 'Variance' is a statistical computation on the (theoretical) distribution of outcomes, while 'luck' is the draw from that distribution that is realised. This distribution can be influenced by a number of variables such as the structure of the game, your strategies and skill levels, and those of your opponents.

Therein lies the lesson. And it's two-fold. First: to accept that you are simply not in control of all variables. Second: to understand that you can influence variance.

Life isn't too dissimilar to a game of poker. We don't control the cards we are dealt; how far we prosper or fail depends on our skill, education and knowledge.

Many would not consider poker skills applicable to life. That's mostly down to the fact that poker has an image problem. It holds a dominant position in popular culture (particularly in movies) as a medium to evoke stress and high tension, mostly alongside all the shorthand connotations of gambling (illegal underground dens, smoke-filled back rooms). Rarely do you see it depicted as a strategic game. There are a handful of exceptions, generally provided by storytellers who are themselves avid poker players, like Brian Koppelman and David Levien, the writers of poker cult-classic film *Rounders* and the hit TV series *Billions* respectively.

This popular depiction contributes to the generally held belief that poker is gambling. But it is information, not luck, that is the key to consistently winning in poker. Players will both seek to obtain it from others and actively work on ensuring that they don't leak it themselves. They will aim to conceal the strength of their hand while at the same time paying attention to every detail of the game.

The general perception non-poker players share is that poker is all about picking up on and then deciphering tells. That is *part* of the game, but here's the thing: the detection of verbal and physical cues is only a small part of a poker player's toolbox. The reality is that pieces of information are hidden everywhere, and the best poker players understand what they are and how to look for them.

The significance of the role that luck plays in the game is fiercely disputed. Let me tell you the story of Lawrence DiCristina's underground poker club, and we'll see just how split opinions are and how difficult it is to gain consensus one way or another.

At the time of his arrest in 2011, Lawrence DiCristina's twice-weekly poker nights at his electric-bike warehouse in Staten Island, New York, were making him thousands of dollars a week. The games were advertised by word of mouth or text message only, and seats at the two tables always had waiting lists. DiCristina pocketed a 5% 'rake', or cut, from each hand. But that's not what he got busted for.

The problem was that his operation involved the efforts of 'five or more persons' and had been in 'continuous operation for a period in excess of thirty days' – making it liable for prosecution under the Illegal Gambling Business Act. This law, enacted in 1970 to combat organised crime, covers a long list of gambling operations that includes slot machines, lotteries, bookmaking and poker. DiCristina fought back: his poker nights were not gambling, because gambling is a game of chance. Poker, he said, is a game of skill – a sport.

The courts kept changing their minds. When he appealed against his original conviction in 2012, a district court ruled that poker was indeed a game of skill in which 'increased proficiency boosts a player's chance of winning and affects the outcome of individual hands as well as a series of hands'. In 2013, a federal appeals court reversed that judgement.

To date the US Supreme Court has refused to hear any appeal against this ruling, leaving DiCristina's conviction intact, and along with it the ruling that poker is gambling.

Jessica Welman, a long-time poker reporter who has worked for WSOP, *Card Player* magazine and WPT (World Poker Tour), has told me she believes the sentiment is that the game of skill argument had its moment. The Supreme Court only hears so many cases a year and many parties lobby hard for certain cases to be heard. No one is really lobbying for the 'game of skill' case to be taken up. Why? It seems to come down to money.

Welman tells me that in the greater scheme of things, poker is not a big revenue generator compared with other casino games. At the time of writing, websites in the US states of Nevada, New Jersey, Delaware, Michigan and Pennsylvania – where online poker is legal – each generate on average about $2 million in revenue a month, a paltry sum compared with online casino, which can generate more than 70 times that in revenue a month. In 2023, the New Jersey Division of Gaming Enforcement reported a record $152.9 million in online casino revenue for the month of January alone. Even sports betting, a low-margin industry by gambling standards, generates substantially more revenue than poker.

These are some reasons why poker is still fighting to be taken seriously, as a legitimately strategic game, by those who don't play it. Perhaps another is that in poker you do not have a ranking system that can accurately identify the single best player in the world.

Why? Unlike in chess, where the best player wins virtually

every time, there is no such guarantee in poker. Here the only guarantee is that the best player will win more often than the worst player. In the World Chess Championship only the most skilled get to play for the title. There is no such exclusivity in poker. The most coveted title in poker is open to all – or at least all with a spare $10,000. The Wimbledon of poker is the Main Event at the World Series of Poker in Las Vegas, and anyone who can table the buy-in of $10,000 gets to play it. The requirements are pretty basic: if you've got the money and know the rules, you've got yourself a seat.

Pick any poker room at any one time you will find players with drastically varying skill levels. Recreational players (those who come to play for a bit of fun), semi-pros like me and professional players can all be sitting next to each other at a table. I figured out pretty soon who the pros in my local casino were and then I did what I do best: I asked questions. In the beginning I had mostly been playing on instinct, with some success, but falling short of the top spots. In tournament poker, 'making it into the money' means being in the top (usually) 10–15% of players who get their buy-in money back plus a little extra at the very minimum. Then, as more players get knocked out of the tournament, your prize money increases. In my first three tournaments I just about made it into the payouts, but then got knocked out. In poker you call that 'min-cashing'. As a competitive person (endurance sports are fun for me) not making it any further was seriously frustrating.

How could I get better? What was I not doing right? All the pros had the same answer: just study the game.

Studying Strategy

In many ways poker is quite similar to chess. Both games require you to think about the information you have and then analyse it. Both require you to stay focused for long stretches of time and to plan your actions ahead. In chess you have all the information in front of you, in poker you do not – a crucial difference that adds layers of complexity to the game. In poker you are forced to adjust your strategies more frequently in any one game as the dynamics at the table change throughout. These can be influenced by your opponents' play style and their respective chip stacks. Your strategy can and should change when you're up against one, two or more players, as well as in response to your own position and chip stack. Subsequently, the thought process in poker can increase in complexity, because whether you win or lose depends not just on skill, multiple opponents, field size and game structure, but also on variance and luck. Poker players study all of these elements, all of the time.

I increased my study time. Joined a study group, bought the latest poker books and, when the day job allowed, sat in on online coaching sessions. But the real breakthrough in my learning came in 2021 at a poker study bootcamp. (Yes, there is such a thing!) This was ten days of pure poker study with some of the world's best coaches, set in the glorious Austrian Alps. It was transformative.

From the moment we woke up often until way past midnight, we studied strategies, discussed hands and played online. Our daily study routines included hours at our workstation doing drills: playing against a computer program (a training program based on the outputs of a solver) a hundred hands at a time. Over and over until we hit at least 90–95% accuracy at completing each of the drills, and no longer made big mistakes. The purpose of these drills was to automate decision-making as much as possible. And they worked! It now took split seconds for me to know when to fold, bet, call or raise with a hand in certain spots – patterns were unfolding before my eyes. Like a fog lifting, suddenly things were so clear to me.

One of my favourite moments was during one lunch that had

turned into an impromptu lesson. Our head coach German pro Fedor Holz, one of the world's best players, listened to us discussing hands amongst ourselves and then challenged our thought processes and reasoning. He pushed us to think critically at all times and use logic to assess what properties of the hands are important, then use those to play against others who are not following the correct play (in poker we call this Game Theory Optimum, GTO for short). Assessing the hand in this way then allows us to deviate from the optimal play ourselves and helps us make educated guesses. It may not always be perfect, but so long as we guess better than our opponents, we're still making money. We're still winning.

I'm not sure if it was because I was sitting next to one of the best players in the world, being taught a game I love against a backdrop of majestic mountain ranges, but this moment in time felt surreal and triggered a memory. Leaning back in my chair, I tilted my head to catch the midday Alpine sun on my face and let my mind wander back to those early days when I first fell in love with this game.

Back then, YouTube was pretty much the only place you could find poker lessons by poker pros. In my coaching-related searches, one name kept popping up: Daniel Negreanu.

What singled him out, especially for a novice like me, weren't his coaching videos, but the clips others posted of him playing: Negreanu at the tables, usually locked in a hand with just one other player and a decision to be made. He'd often talk to himself, trying to think it all through and then, in video clip after video clip, he would call out the exact two cards his opponent was holding – right down to the suits, as if he had X-ray vision. It was an uncanny, stunning display of precision, and watching this as a rookie poker player blew my mind. I thought Negreanu had superpowers. I was convinced of it.

I smile to myself as I come back to our impromptu lunchtime

strategy lesson outside on the Alpine terrace. Today, of course, I know that while few players can claim this level of accuracy, all poker pros will deduce their opponent's holding to within a narrow range. 'Thinking in ranges' is a foundational block of poker study, and now here in the bootcamp I, too, was doing just that.

But studying the theoretical aspects isn't enough to win. You also need to understand player tendencies and behaviours and then be able to adjust your strategies accordingly. Poker is a dynamic game that forces you to interact with others, and whenever people interact (be it on or off the green baize) emotions are always in play. Poker makes you pay attention to emotions, both yours and others', and requires you to go one step further and take charge of your feelings.

The game drives you to think in probabilities and make on-the-spot risk assessments. When you play poker you repeatedly find yourself in a position where you don't have all the information; you have a bunch of uncertainties and no choice but to make decisions based on what you do know and plan ahead accordingly. Nothing else teaches you that, says US-based psychologist-turned-writer Maria Konnikova. She is a great example of someone with no prior knowledge of the game, who became a successful player after dedicating time and effort to study.

Konnikova's doctoral work at Columbia University, New York, had focused on the links between self-control and illusory control, and the impact of both of these on risky financial decision-making. She was fascinated by the concepts of chance, uncertainty and risk – and by how our brain reacts to them. She started playing poker as part of her research: she wanted to know what decision-making in a risky environment looks like when the pressure's on, and poker was the ideal arena. The now bestselling author hadn't planned on becoming a poker pro. Yet much to her surprise, she started not just winning, but winning big, picking up a coveted championship trophy in the process. *The Biggest Bluff* – the title of the book she was researching at the time – ended up being a report on her fascinating transformation into a serious poker pro.

With her combined perspectives of psychologist and poker player, Konnikova argues that poker brings real educational benefits, and she goes as far as proposing that it should be taught in schools – as a way of teaching important and relevant life lessons such as resilience, discipline, statistical knowledge, understanding of risk, and emotional awareness and control.

And she isn't alone in her advocacy for teaching poker.

I'm on Skype talking to Avi Rubin, professor of computer science at Johns Hopkins University in Baltimore. He is reminiscing about playing poker with his children some 20 years ago. While other families would bring out Monopoly or Scrabble for game night, the Rubins and their three children (the youngest was just five years old at the time) would sit down with a deck of cards. It was the family's choice of games, which is why a little poker set would always make it onto the packing list for their week-long boat trips. Rubin's face brightens into a smile as he tells me about imparting an important life lesson to his eldest daughter.

During poker games, whenever she had a really good hand, she would remove her sunglasses from the top of her head and slowly slide them onto her nose. It was a behaviour she was modelling after watching poker players on TV do the same for seemingly important hands. But it's a core behavioural mistake – no matter how good or bad her hand, her father told her, she must always act the same. That is because good opponents will pick up on any change of behaviour and quickly begin to correlate it with the strength of your hand. In poker you want to keep your table composure pretty level, so Rubin asked her to try to control her behaviour, to keep her excitement or nervousness under wraps.

Off the table too there is value in keeping our composure, no matter how tense or exhilarating the situation.

Rubin owns a cybersecurity firm, and often finds himself having to negotiate with clients. It may be, he says, that somebody in a meeting says something so surprising that you're caught off guard. But you don't want to show that you weren't prepared. Acting normal, looking like you aren't fazed, is important. He credits poker for his ability to stay cool and tells me that at the tables he would practise maintaining an even keel and not changing his expression, no matter how the action unfolded.

He also draws parallels between the thought processes that he'd use when placing a bet on the poker table, and when negotiating a business deal. When he's trying to figure out what price to aim for, he applies exactly the same steps of reasoning as if he were betting in poker: 'If I go too high, I'm going to scare them off. And if I go too low, I'm leaving money on the table, [when] I could have actually done better.' Both in business negotiations and in poker, who goes first can determine an outcome. In negotiations Rubin will aim to obtain the first bid from the clients, the equivalent of 'having position' in poker and waiting for the other player to act. ('Having position' at the poker table means that you are in a hand with people to your right, so that every time a card comes, they make the decision first – placing a bet, for example – and then you respond to it.)

Microsoft co-founder Bill Gates, who ran a regular poker night in his dorm at Harvard, writes in his book *The Road Ahead* that poker strategy proved helpful when he got into business. It's a belief shared by Jennifer Just, co-owner of a multi-billion-dollar investment firm.

In 2019, Just started her very own poker school, Poker Power. She describes it as a launchpad for girls and women to succeed in school, business and life. 'The skills and strategies that we teach empower women to sit at every table, from the classroom to the boardroom. I truly believe learning poker is a game-changer,' she says in her online biography.

In 2020, Just appointed Erin Lydon and put her at the helm of Poker Power. 'Poker Power was founded because we know there is a strong connection between success and the skills and strategies taught through poker – this isn't your ordinary card game. Poker makes you a better negotiator, better thinker, better at quick decision-making, better at taking calculated risks, better at assessing how power and influence shift,' Lydon tells me.

Through a global network of clubs, tournaments and corporate events, Poker Power utilises gameplay to build confidence, challenge the status quo, learn strategy and assess risk. The goal is to teach a million women to play poker. To help with this mission Lydon has enlisted the help of female pros including Konnikova and a large crew of poker teachers. And one of them is Tamara, Avi Rubin's youngest daughter.

The Rubins and their kids still get together to play poker, only now it's online. 'We don't play for money, we play for pride, but it's so much fun. We open up a Zoom, and with the kids abroad, it feels like they never left,' he tells me. With his kids no longer in need of lessons, Rubin looked for new pupils and found them right under his nose: his college students.

Rubin designed a course that covered poker basics, then went deep into strategy, included guest lectures by poker pros and closed off with a final practical lesson, a poker tournament at his house. Not knowing what the uptake would be, Rubin initially capped the available spots for the course at 100. The spaces filled within record time. In fact, such was the enthusiasm for it, Rubin's inaugural poker course at Johns Hopkins University in January 2020 had to be moved to a much larger auditorium than originally planned. Over 250 students turned up for the course.

Charles Nesson, a Harvard Law School professor, also advocates for poker in the classroom. He founded the Global Poker

Strategic Thinking Society to promote poker as a teaching tool. To him the parallels between the thinking that helps you win in poker and the thinking that allows you to succeed in law school were abundantly clear. Being able to see yourself from the perspective of others, all the while keeping your emotions in check, is a valuable skill in many domains including law and business.

Another Harvard alumnus, former President Barack Obama, is a poker player, too. In December 2009 the *National Journal*, a magazine focused on politics and policy, appeared with the cover line 'Obama as Poker Player'. The article described how the then President of the United States approached issues with a 'poker player's sensibility'. It's not an unusual interest for a president: Harry Truman had the presidential seal embossed on his chips and Richard Nixon was said to have funded his early political campaigns with poker winnings.

Despite such high-profile ambassadors, academic endorsements and organisations such as Poker Power, the game is still struggling to be seen as strategic, and continues to lack the status of a cerebral game, even though it has more to teach people than chess. Because poker isn't fair – and neither is life.

The Bluffs We Seek and the Bullshit We Find

Popular culture tells us that success at the table is all about sussing out the lie or detecting the bluff. No, it's not. It's the exact opposite. As in real life, poker just isn't riddled with bluffs and lies. For deception to be effective, it must be rare – in poker and in life. In reality most people are honest most of the time. Think about it. For the most part the messages we receive, the interactions we have with others and the certainties we rely on in life are true – and that's a good thing. Actually, it's more than that: honesty is essential for a functional society.

Despite their rarity, we devote a disproportionate amount of time and effort to seeking out lies and deceptions. Judging by the sheer volume of literature that is available on lie detection we seem to be consumed by the desire to become lie detectives. Such is the demand that it drives not just book sales but scientific research as well, producing an abundance of experiments and studies dealing with real-time verbal and non-verbal behaviour analysis. But you won't be able to become a human lie detector just by reading a few books and poring over some scientific papers. Sure, some individuals are unsettlingly good at reading people, and their expertise is regularly called upon by national security and law enforcement bodies, but these are people who have devoted their lives and careers to behaviour analysis. They are few and far between.

So why, then, even though most of us won't ever find ourselves in an interrogation room across from a suspect, are so many of us keen to become human lie detectors? The reason is simple and very human: lies hurt us. The pain they inflict fades slowly for some and not at all for others. Lies cause emotional scars that may never heal. It makes sense that we want to avoid being hurt like that. But this isn't as simple as seeing a boiling pot and knowing not to put your bare hands on it.

The reality is that spotting lies is difficult, and we are terrible at it. There are no real cues to deception, and the leading experts you will meet in this book will tell you this. So that's the bad news.

In 1986 a deeply troubled professor of philosophy sat at his desk in Princeton University, New Jersey, staring into the void. Harry Frankfurt saw a crisis looming. He'd long observed the growing lack of respect and concern for the truth. The culprit was a particularly dangerous foe that was creeping into the fabric of our culture. That foe? Bullshit. Something needed to be done. Frankfurt started writing an academic paper which he hoped would begin the development of a theoretical understanding of the phenomenon. The paper, titled 'On Bullshit', would become a cult classic in academic circles and then take on a life of its own when it was picked up by a publisher in 2005. It was reproduced and published as a hardback book, selling more than 600,000 copies within its first year.

We commonly use 'bullshit' when we want to describe something as nonsense. But at its core, 'nonsense' is still vague as a definition. It ducks the question of what is actually meant by bullshit. The term is commonly used to describe both a lack of logic and an untruth. However, these are two distinct notions, which is why Frankfurt took a stab at a better definition in his essay.

He does so by comparing bullshit to what he believes to be its closest relative, the word 'lie'. He finds a clear and important distinction between the two: 'It is impossible for someone to lie unless he thinks he knows the truth. Producing bullshit requires no such conviction.' In short, bullshitters do not describe reality; they make things up to suit their purposes.

In contrast, liars are fully aware of the truth and work actively to conceal it. Bullshitters aren't necessarily liars. What they say may well be true. But they are by no means tied to the truth, either because they don't know it or simply don't care about it. What they say can either be true, false or utter nonsense – their aim is to manipulate, to impress and to elevate themselves in the eyes of others. That is why Frankfurt believes that bullshitters are a more insidious and dangerous threat to truth than liars.

In some ways, Frankfurt warned us about Donald Trump. By the end of Trump's term as President of the United States, journalists would explicitly fact-check all his statements as part of their reporting. Trump may have been the bullshitter-in-chief, but he is by no means the only one who bullshits on a regular basis. Try looking closer to home.

Young Bullshitters

Any parent will admit that their kid has tried to bullshit them at least once, and few would argue against the assertion that teenagers have a propensity to overclaim and display overconfidence. It's a phase they go through, part of their development, part of growing up. In 2019, researchers at University College London decided to study this. They provided strong evidence that teenage bullshitters portray themselves as highly skilled and resilient when it comes to problem-solving, and attempt to give answers that they feel are more socially acceptable.

The study involved over 40,000 fifteen-year-olds from nine English-speaking countries, including Australia, Canada, England and the USA, and focused on maths problems (to avoid any ambiguities, or aspects lost in cultural translation). The propensity to bullshit varied across the nine countries studied. Teens in the USA and Canada were significantly bigger bullshitters than those from Ireland and Scotland, who were the least likely to exaggerate their maths knowledge and skills.

Unlike previous research, this study was able to investigate and dig deeper into the differences between subgroups, as well as look into any possible confounding characteristics between bullshitters and non-bullshitters. The teenagers were presented with a range of maths concepts, three of which were made up – in reality they didn't exist. Yet some teenagers claimed they knew what they were, and within that group teenage boys came out resoundingly as bigger bullshitters than teenage girls. Those teenage boys and girls who weren't truthful also had a striking overconfidence in their own abilities.

The study revealed a further interesting data point: teenagers from privileged backgrounds were more likely to bullshit than their disadvantaged peers.

Experienced truth detectives will note a slight flaw in this study. It's missing something: any teenagers that aren't from

Western, Educated, Industrialised, Rich, Democratic (WEIRD) cultures. Which means that the data, while representative of WEIRD cultures, isn't representative of the rest of the world's teenagers. The influence of culture cannot be overstated: it can drastically affect thinking, resulting in wildly variable behavioural outcomes. Culture plays an important role in the formation of our individual beliefs, ideas and values. It influences both how we express ourselves and how we treat others. (Unless explicitly stated, the studies mentioned in this book will have based their experiments on samples from WEIRD cultures, since unfortunately the scientific discipline of psychology is dominated by Americans and Europeans.)

This is a deeply important aspect to keep in mind any time we review or are presented with data or findings from studies. First, we need to be clear on exactly what is being claimed (teenagers are bullshitters) and what sample size the claim is based on (there is a big difference between 400 and 40,000). Second, we need to look at what and who the information really represents, and be aware of its limitations (teenagers from WEIRD cultures only). When we do this, we are sharper in our understanding and are less likely to extrapolate and make things up. Because making things up is easy to do.

Just like teenagers, adults also make things up – not because they don't know, but because they think they *do*. Adults also regularly overestimate or underestimate their abilities and skills, whether intentionally or not. And no, it has nothing to do with whether people who are unskilled just don't know it: research shows that both experts and rookies who underestimate and overestimate their skills do so in equal numbers. In fact, through computer-generated data and results from 1,154 people undergoing a science literacy test, now retired researcher Ed Nuhfer showed only about 5% could be characterised as 'unskilled and unaware of it'.

Making things up becomes a real problem when people present nonsensical fabrications and made-up ideas as legitimate, valid and meaningful to the outside world. We call this pseudo-profound bullshit – and it is a legitimate scientific term.

On Pseudo-Profound Bullshit

'What's the story and does it make sense?' is a question I have learnt to ask, especially when I am faced with a tricky decision. In poker, it requires me to put together everything I know about the play and the player. I look for logic and credibility. If I can't find coherence in the line of play, I know I am either walking into a trap or I am being bluffed. Either way, if the story doesn't add up, I know I am being played. It's not much different in real life. We believe fake stories not because we're dumb, but because we're lazy thinkers. Making sure what we're being told is true – especially when a story sounds plausible and is told really well – takes effort.

It took no effort at all for Canadian researcher Gordon Pennycook to thank Donald Trump, Oprah, Deepak Chopra, the entire line-up of Fox News, and Rhonda Byrne, author of self-help book *The Secret*, during his acceptance speech of the Ig Nobel Prize for Peace at Harvard University's Sanders Theatre in 2016. Although not entirely serious, he wasn't joking either. His gesture was appropriate nonetheless: the annual Ig Nobel Prizes are awarded for achievements that first make you laugh, then make you think.

His speech summed up the study that had earned the award for Pennycook and his team. Titled 'On the Reception and Detection of Pseudo-Profound Bullshit', it was anything but ridiculous. The researchers were aiming to understand the underlying cognitive and social constructs that determine whether and when bullshit is detected, with the idea of creating a reliable measure for bullshit receptivity. They looked at statements using big words, ambiguity and vagueness that on first reading may come across as profound and insightful, but upon closer inspection are meaningless.

One of the investigations asked participants to rate the profundity of various statements. It used an algorithm to generate sentences such as, 'The future explains irrational facts', 'Consciousness is the growth of coherence, and of us' or 'Today, science tells us that the essence of nature is joy'. In short, the team wanted to see how likely people were to rate bullshit as profound. The researchers then analysed bullshit receptivity, as they called it. They found that those who were less analytical, more intuitive and had lower cognitive abilities were more likely to see bullshit as profound. They were also prone to believe conspiracy theories, hold paranormal or religious beliefs, and were more likely to endorse alternative medicine.

Those who were more sceptical and analytical were more resistant to bullshit. In summary, the study showed that analytical thinking allows us to be sensitive to pseudo-profound bullshit. Hardly a shock, you might think, but the truly shocking thing is that hitherto the subject had not been researched at all. 'Accordingly,' the researchers wrote at the end of their paper, 'although this manuscript may not be truly profound, it is indeed meaningful.'

It's a hard one for a science fan-girl like me to admit, but some scientists and academics succumb to pseudo-profound bullshit, too. You witness it in academic papers, where complexity of sentence structures and the multitude of obscure word choices are intentional and can gloss over a lack of substance. (I could also have written this last sentence as: 'Scholarly writings display intricate content in which lexical composition combined with a magnitude of obscurantist terminology are purposeful and can hypothetically obfuscate with deliberation.') It makes the ability to read between the lines really important. I frequently wondered why academic vernacular often seemed to require stilted language, jargon and overly elaborate writing. Then I came across Daniel Oppenheimer's study.

In 2005, while at Princeton University, Oppenheimer found that a majority of undergraduates admitted to deliberately increasing the complexity of their vocabulary to give the impression of intelligence. Now a professor at Carnegie Mellon University, Oppenheimer suggested that a lack of jargon might be seen as a signal that the author is not an in-group member of the field. Other studies have shown that people are more likely to use big words when they are feeling most insecure. In both instances the predominant conclusion is that complex language is used to mask a lack of confidence.

But before we judge academics, it may be prudent to remember that we are just as guilty. We are all storytellers. With the words we choose, the actions we take and the posts we share we curate what we show and tell others. We manipulate reality as we amplify the good in our lives and omit and actively hide what we don't want others to see. It's a natural human behaviour that has been galvanised by social media. We have created a digital dystopia in which flawless personas and perfect lives are encouraged and celebrated by clicks and followings. These are the perfect conditions for bullshit to flourish in plain sight. The likelihood of people encountering more bullshit in their everyday lives is higher than ever before.

That is why Pennycook's paper called for the 'development of interventions and strategies that help individuals guard against bullshit'. It was a call for teaching critical thinking.

Learning to Think

There used to be a time when the development of the ability to think and ask the right questions was taught in schools as part of the curricula all across the world. Critical thinking was hugely popular in the early 1980s to late 90s. It seems to have lost its standing and popularity as we see it relegated in many places to a mere educational goal.

I wonder if it could be an image problem. Sitting in the auditorium of the 39th Annual Critical Thinking Conference in Leuven (Belgium) I drift off for a moment during the keynote speech by Linda Elder, the president of the Foundation for Critical Thinking. Just what led to the field's unceremonious decline? Was it as simple as failing to adapt to modern times? I ponder as I gaze over the reading materials given to us at the beginning of the conference. The visual cues on these seem to be anchored in the past and the classics, like the conference logo that features an illustrated version of Auguste Rodin's *The Thinker*. Stars of times past grace the covers of multiple A5 booklets in the conference bag. A sort of visual tribute to the genius of Socrates, Albert Einstein, John Stuart Mill and Pierre and Marie Curie.

Binding critical thinking to these great minds can alienate your average person. Let's face it, it's intimidating from the outset. How could one possibly live up to the towering genius of these thinkers? Perhaps Elder is intentional about this positioning, but I fear that emphasising critical thinking as a classical, intellectual art form just keeps it stuck in the past. It certainly isn't helping to assert its relevance in the modern world or, more importantly, to a wider audience.

'You are the ones that are here. You are the ones that matter,' I hear Elder say as she continues to address the modestly sized audience. Is she trying to persuade us or herself? The sadness in her voice makes this sound unconvincing to me. There are plenty of unfilled places. Decades ago, this room would have been packed to its last seat.

An educational psychologist by trade, Elder has been running the foundation for over 25 years. When I asked for an interview, she invited me to join the five-day conference, held at the KU

Leuven in Belgium, suggesting we could find a slot during that time. Among the attendees – some of whom have been coming for years – she is revered; beyond them, Elder and critical thinking have a hard time attracting a wider audience.

Decades after critical thinking was introduced, it has failed to assert itself as a bona fide field of study in its own right and still lacks an academic home. Instead, it sort of blends into the philosophy, communication and science departments. Elder says that this is one reason why it hasn't been able to break away and establish a standing on its own. After attending a number of workshops during the conference, I get the impression Elder is trying to achieve just that. The coursework repeats thinking models and methodologies, but the way it is presented, it comes across as being reserved for those of a certain intellect. At least that's my impression, and it's confirmed when Elder moves on to speak of another reason why critical thinking has failed to assert itself within academic fields. This one is a little tough for me to hear.

In her view, writers of popular science or psychology are trying to make money by writing about critical thinking: 'So now everybody, as it were, and their grandmother has got a book on something to do with critical thinking, and this is only watering it down and making it worse.' Of course, I disagree – I believe that accessible science is an essential tool both for making the case for investing in scientific research and for empowering and enlightening the wider public. But I can understand her frustration. Pop science writers don't typically have a doctorate – I certainly don't. Elder, a cerebral woman with a master's in psychology and a doctorate in educational psychology, may feel cynical about my work. After all, she has lived through the rise and fall of those critical thinking glory days from the 80s and 90s.

The critical thinking conferences that took place back then used to attract more than 1,000 people. There are hardly 200 at this year's meeting. But what the conference lacks in numbers, it makes up for in diversity. The attendees include business people, government officials, researchers, scholars and journalists from an impressive 32 countries such as Algeria, Brazil, Cameroon, China, Czech Republic, Dominican Republic, Ecuador, Palestine, Russia, Somalia and Iran; there are many from the US, and just a handful from the UK. All the more reason to try to popularise it, I think. We think and make decisions all the time. The quality of our individual and collective lives and wellbeing depends on how well and constructively we are able to reason. Why would we not want to popularise it? We should be teaching our younger generations how to challenge and interrogate the information they are given and how to develop their own independent thinking.

We did come close to this once before. Critical thinking had a golden era during the 1970s and 1980s when there was a surge of attention around the development of thinking skills. In the 80s, the US College Entrance Examination Board stipulated reasoning as a basic academic skill needed by college students. And not just in the USA – globally, too, departments of education began to include thinking objectives in their school curriculum guidelines. It was a movement that came on the heels of the 1960s and 1970s social revolutions, a time that saw people becoming more open about their thinking and asking new sorts of questions, leading to the free-speech movement and the fight for universal human and civil rights. It was around that time that a handful of theoreticians used the term critical thinking – before then it wasn't even in the dictionary, let alone in common use.

We still get our definitions for critical thinking mainly from this era, the heyday of the approach. In 1981, during this boom for critical thinking, the first critical thinking conference was held and the approach started to take off in a big way. Those working in the field were deluged by requests for help in establishing and appraising curricula and instruction aimed at critical thinking. From the early 80s, it was taught in classrooms and lecture halls across the US, including on Tuesdays and Wednesdays in the Space Science Building at Cornell University by a real-life human star.

Astronomy 490 was a senior seminar on critical thinking taught by cosmologist Carl Sagan. He was already then widely known for his *Cosmos* TV show, viewed by over half a billion people in 60 different countries. He wrote, too – books that sold in the millions and even won him a Pulitzer Prize. He lived and breathed his passion (being a research astronomer) by teaching, writing, lecturing, being a TV personality, and spending time at the giant radio telescope run by Cornell at Arecibo in Puerto Rico. But he was first and foremost a teacher, and until his death in 1996 remained professor of astronomy and space science, and director of the planetary studies lab at Cornell where he had been since 1968.

Sagan's lifelong goal was to popularise the scientific method, because he saw the growing fallacies of superstitious thinking and blind faith washing over society and threatening to dominate it. He got himself into trouble with religious groups when he asserted: 'The cosmos is all that is or was or ever will be.' He never wavered from his rational and scientific thinking – and he practised as he preached. In one conversation with his young daughter, who had asked him about his dead parents, wanting to know why she had never met them, he told her that they had died. When she asked whether he'd ever see them again, he didn't lie. He told her he would like nothing more but there was no reason to think it was possible, no evidence that he'd be able to do so – it was painful, but he had to accept it.

Neither Sagan's American-born mother nor his father, who had emigrated from Russia, had had any background in science, but they championed and supported their son's ambition with an abundance of love. His bond with them was strong and their memory created a desperate longing in him. He dreamed about them, wishing that it had all just been a horrible mistake and that they hadn't really died, only to wake up and '. . . go through the abbreviated process of mourning all over again.' A part of him was ready to believe in a life after death, and that part wasn't the least bit interested in whether there was any evidence for it. He sympathised with those who mourned by visiting graves and who commemorated their loved ones on anniversaries, but he loathed those who exploited the pain and loss of others: mediums, spiritualists, people who claimed that they could speak to the dead.

He airs these grievances in the opening paragraphs of the most passionate chapter in the last book he wrote. *The Demon-Haunted World: Science as a Candle in the Dark* was published mere months before his death in 1996, and the chapter is headed 'The Fine Art of Baloney Detection'. Both personal and emotional, but no less analytical for that, the chapter makes the case that critical thinking is crucial not just for the scientific method and the pursuit of truth, but also for the wellbeing of a healthy, functioning democratic society.

Concerned by the rise of pseudo-science and conspiracy theorists, Sagan wrote the book not as a medium-bashing and spiritualist-debunking manifesto, but as a book on how science works. It's a manifesto for clear thought in which he writes 'Science is more than a body of knowledge; it is a way of thinking.' He emphasises the need and urgency for sceptical thinking, and warns that the lack of critical thinking in societies and governments can have dangerous consequences, and lead to the erosion of democracy. It's a powerful argument for why science and democracy go hand in hand, and are needed in an advancing society. It's uncanny how much he predicted: not just fake and misleading news but also the polarisation of our world today.

Nearly 30 years after he rang the alarm bells, we remain unable to bridge the divide caused by the differing and radical ideologies we hold. Instead, we have let the abyss grow deeper and wider than ever before. We see both sides trying to own the truth. It's a contest that everyone wants to win, but which no one ever really does. We remain stuck in a loop in which little or no progress is being made. We expect the other side to change. We want them to understand us. We demand that they listen to us. Yet this is precisely why we fail to close the gap and will forever be on opposite sides, trying to outshout one another. We are kept apart by our own inability and unwillingness to actively listen to each other, and we overestimate the level of courage it will take to sit down and genuinely consider the arguments of the other side. If we truly want to defeat the demons that rampage through our societies causing social injustices, if we truly want to dispel the misbeliefs that haunt our world, then we need to find this courage. And find it we must, in order to face those who do not believe that all humans are equal, who will mobilise to take away rights and freedoms from others in order to dominate and dictate, who will erect borders out of fear rather than compassion, and light fires to incinerate laws that allow personal choice and freedom of expression.

It's a big ask when it may seem like we're entering a battle, and when our natural intuition is to avoid confrontation and shy away from situations that can leave us vulnerable and exposed. But not all arguments need to be fiercely confrontational. Arguments can be civil and helpful. The thing to bear in mind is that we all bring our own hurt, pain, emotions, hopes and desires to these discussions. We are not machines. But the rush to reconciliation is a trap to avoid. Eric Liu, former speech-writer and Deputy Assistant to President Clinton, goes as far as calling it dangerous. His view is that the desire for a rush to reconciliation and reunion can end up papering over deep abiding injustices and inequities in civic life.

It's hard work to find consensus, and we saw how difficult this can get during the pandemic. Even though for many people for whom masking (particularly in health care situations) has a very real impact on their mortality and/or health, mask-wearing became heavily politicised with some people feeling government mandates and lockdowns were infringing on their freedoms and their right to live the way they saw appropriate. Liu thinks that there is room for anger and pain and believes strongly that we need to foster a culture in which we can learn to come together by arguing. He admits that it may sound counterintuitive, but in a time of record polarisation and immense vitriol we don't necessarily need fewer arguments, but we do need less stupid ones. The Aspen Institute's Better Argument Project, founded by Liu in 2017, is an effort to help with this.

The project's purpose is to bring two sides together by teaching us how to have conversations we don't want to have, helping us to deal with being uncomfortable and to break out of our echo chambers. The first step is perhaps also the hardest: to enter into a conversation without the first and foremost goal being to be right or get our own way. This crucial step, if done with sincerity, will naturally lead into the remaining steps: active listening (listen to learn and to make the other person feel more at ease speaking); paying attention to context (understanding what cultural dynamics may be in play and acknowledging those); embracing vulnerability (entering what may seem a hostile environment out of our familiar space can make us feel apprehensive and vulnerable) and finally, making room to transform. This again requires a certain level of courage. It means we understand that we may be proven wrong and are prepared to accept this. It also means we are open to having our minds changed and our attitudes adjusted. On this basis we will enter an argument already accepting that we may not reach a resolution, and thus we will then start engaging with one another on a constructive basis that can lead to building a rapport – which, however weak initially, will nonetheless be a step towards coming together.

The key idea is the concept of taking winning off the table (I realise this is a funny thing to aim for in a book that uses poker to understand how we think!). When we focus less on the absolute end goal of winning, we can detach ourselves more easily from our own arguments – and in doing so be able to listen properly and see things from another perspective.

Listening is one of the key skills involved in critical thinking. How? It's simple: we are still communicating even when we're not talking. By nodding and tilting our heads at a slight angle we signal that we are receptive to the other person's comments and imply that we don't have an agenda. In effect, we are signalling to the other person that we are allowing them room to express themselves.

Going one step further entails being genuinely curious about what the other person is basing their information on, what it is that leads them to be thinking in a certain way. Trying to imagine how their views are shaped and why they see the world differently is difficult, but necessary. Being able to empathise enough to step out of ourselves, temporarily disconnect from our own ideas and put ourselves into the shoes of others so that we may understand their point of view is an important skill. It was also one of the things that Sagan taught his students in his critical thinking class. The final written exams he set included a requirement to make a case for both sides of an argument. This exercise alone taught students how to reason better, and that critical thinking is not about finding good reasons for what you believe.

Critical thinking requires you to separate your points of view from yourself and ask different, better questions. This requires you to step back from the issue at hand and slow down your decision-making and judgements. Critical thinking helps you reduce the number of mistakes you make because it requires you to actively look for information that is verifiable. It also challenges you to be courageous. You have to be prepared to admit when you're wrong and when you're forced to re-evaluate something you felt certain about. In essence, if you are a critical thinker you have to be willing to give things up. The solution may not be what you desired it to be, but it will be the solution that is right. As we will see in the following chapters, there are many elements in our lives over which we often believe we have a sense of agency, but the reality and data show that we don't. So our decisions are skewed, biased, misplaced. The task of a critical thinker is not just to solve problems, but to notice problems and reveal the fallacies that may have led to false or inaccurate conclusions. As a critical thinker you are in constant pursuit of which is true, you are a truth detective.

On Believing and Knowing – Conflicts and Differences

Forget about the conspiracy theories for a moment and whether Neil Armstrong really landed on the Moon (he did). Today, anyone with access to a computer and the internet can put their versions of facts and news out into the world. Take any statement, and someone, somewhere will be disputing it.

How, then, do we deal with conflicting statements that don't fit within our world view and go against our existing biases? What do we even do when we're given contradictory information about what's good or bad to eat and drink? Is coffee good for you or not? Does milk reduce the risk of cancer or increase it? How about red meat? Conflicting data creates confusion, and to some degree discord, all the time. We look to science for answers, but science doesn't always have them.

We have learnt this most recently during the coronavirus pandemic. The question about whether to wear masks or not was contentious in the early days of the pandemic because we lacked the data for a consensus. That consensus came when more and better data over multiple studies settled the dispute and made it clear: wearing masks helped reduce the spread of the virus significantly.

Six months before the pandemic swept the world, Canadian researchers Derek Koehler and Gordon Pennycook published the results of an investigation into how members of the public (and scientists) react to scientific uncertainty. People were shown two studies on the same subject – one showed consensus, the other produced conflicting results. They were then asked if they felt they knew more, the same or less as a consequence. In all the experiments, people consistently felt they knew more or the same when the studies didn't show conflict – but when the results were conflicting, they said they felt they knew less. The study also revealed that a lack of understanding of the scientific process can reduce support for science-based policies. Take the climate crisis, for example. People's perception of the issue is linked directly to the overwhelming scientific consensus. Those who believe that scientists disagree on global warming tend to feel less certain that global warming is occurring, and therefore show less support for climate policy.

Scientists, on the other hand, aren't troubled by conflicting data. They know it's just part of the scientific process, because science is a continuing effort for knowledge and truth. It's a method that is based on revising beliefs once new evidence comes to light. So when it comes to conflicting data, scientists see that as evidence that more work needs to be done. That doesn't really help laypeople, whose understanding of the scientific method is further complicated by the emergence of the replication crisis that plagues the science world. Many experiments published now either fail to be replicated when performed by other researchers or there simply aren't enough peers prepared to repeat them in the first place. This is particularly true for psychology studies. But Koehler and Pennycook are optimistic about the replication crisis. 2018 saw the establishment of the Psychological Science

Accelerator, a sort of CERN for psychologists, though unlike the Swiss centre for particle physics it's a globally distributed network of more than 500 laboratories. Before this, in 2015, a group of 270 researchers in the Open Science Collaboration caused a bit of a stir when they declared that they tried to replicate the results of 100 studies published in three high-ranking psychology publications. The results of their cross-checking efforts revealed major flaws in two-thirds of studies, showing results weaker than originally stated. Rather than seeing this as a negative, they considered it part of the process, concluding: 'Accumulating evidence is the scientific community's method of self-correction and is the best available option for achieving that ultimate goal: truth.' The field is seeing a move to right its wrongs via the emergence of large-scale collaborations that aim to self-correct and can improve both replicability and generalisability. This is good news that we can all be excited about. Why? We need to know when we can trust information, especially when it has the potential to drive how we act collectively as a society. And at no other time in recent history has this been more vital than when – thanks to Covid-19 – myriad uncertainties dropped into our lives. These uncertainties included an issue that arguably should never even have made the list in the first place: the benefits or perceived harms of vaccinating. People remain uncertain about vaccines because when the scientific cross-checks eventually came, they were too late – a significant number of people already believed that vaccines caused autism.

Much vaccine hesitancy can be traced back to a single and now discredited study by a researcher and physician called Andrew Wakefield, who was consequently struck off the UK's medical register. But the damage had been done. The now infamous study (see pp.230–31) is generally seen to have reinvigorated the global anti-vaxxer movement.

Now, most of us aren't scientists, and we don't have the means to recreate studies and verify findings. How, then, can the rest of us independently confirm facts?

Just like when a new player sits down at a poker table, so, in life, when we meet new people we use basic inquisitiveness and curiosity to find out more about them. So why do we not treat new information the same way? Adopting a base level of inquisitiveness can go a long way. This means looking for evidence for what we are being shown and told, and watching out for our own existing biases, which will be influencing how and where we take our information from. At its very simplest, it means asking where the information came from in the first place and whether it has been validated. If it has, then by whom or what? The validity of an argument can depend on whether the source of the information is reliable and credible. And what makes a source worthy of our trust? Are the findings validated through careful observation and reasoning? Do sources have a track record and if so, what type? If sources lack a track record, ask why and interrogate further.

When we get into the habit of examining information like this, we are less likely to be taken advantage of or fooled into believing untruths. When we do this, we are reasoning better, not faster. And that's good.

Taking additional steps to verify information takes time – even if it's only mere moments. And so, one of the adjustments you can make to improve the quality of your thinking is a small one, but one that will yield big benefits to your overall decision-making and judgement. It's simple, and it's this: *slow down*.

When we are deliberative, conscious, analytical, and slow in our thinking, we are using what psychologists classify as 'System 2 thinking'.

It is true that not all bad decisions are on-the-spot ones, and not all on-the-spot decisions are bad. Most of our everyday decision-making is done quickly, based on feelings, and mostly unconsciously. This is referred to as 'System 1 thinking'. It is the dominant form in which we all think, because our brains naturally reach out to heuristics (mental shortcuts).

That's why speed and critical thinking are two things that don't work together. Ever. Think about all the bad decisions and poor judgements you've made in your life and try to think about the conditions you made them under. Did time play a role? Would the outcome have been different had you taken time to think whether to agree undertaking another project or respond to an email that triggered you?

In System 1 thinking mode, our cognitive processes are quick, autonomous, intuitive and largely unconscious. It is also where we are most exposed to exploitation.

Let me back this up for you with some science. Pennycook (yes, him again) and his colleagues wondered in 2015 what role deliberation would play in susceptibility to political misinformation and 'fake news'. To assess this, they employed the widely used Cognitive Reflection Test (CRT) as a measure of the propensity to engage in analytical reasoning. CRT is a simple measure of one type of cognitive ability – the ability or propensity to reflect on a question and resist reporting the first response that comes to mind. It is a quick test that consists of three problems to solve.

Here is one of them, and it's a classic example used in economics teachings:

A bat and a ball cost $1.10 in total. The bat costs $1.00 more than the ball. How much does the ball cost?

What was the first answer that sprung to mind? Did you suppress it and think about it a bit more, or use that first answer? Most people's first instinct is that the ball costs 10 cents, but of course that would mean the bat would cost $1.10 and together they would total $1.20. So the correct answer is 5 cents.

The CRT performance correlates with the ability to discern fake news from real news. What researchers have found is that the evidence indicates that people fall for fake news because they *fail* to think; not because of their partisan alignment. The conclusion is that the susceptibility to fabricated, blatantly inaccurate news is driven more by lazy thinking (the researchers' words, not mine) than by bias. The one key takeaway from this study is that analytical thinking is associated with lower trust in fake news sources.

Taking it a step further, in 2018 Pennycook, together with a group of researchers from Yale, Harvard and MIT, looked at just who is most likely to believe 'fake news' and why. In 'Belief in Fake News Is Associated with Delusionality, Dogmatism, Religious Fundamentalism, and Reduced Analytic Thinking', the team analysed data from over 900 participants. The results suggested that individuals who are prone to endorse delusion-like ideas, as well as dogmatic individuals and religious fundamentalists, are more likely to believe fake news.

The success of fake news on social media may have something to do with the change in the way we consume news now – a quick-scroll on Twitter here and a swipe through on Facebook there. We tend to skip right over good news, because nothing grabs our attention as much as the bad, the sad and the negative. It's called 'doomscrolling' for a reason. The term is thought to have emerged in 2018 to describe how our tendency to quick-scroll through our newsfeeds can leave us feeling like we live in an apocalyptic era. Its compulsive nature is self-reinforcing, with platforms optimising their designs and layouts to trigger certain neurological responses that keep us hooked. It feels almost as though we have sacrificed a part of our autonomous thinking in order to connect with many, many others online; we have given way to the fast, intuitive and often emotional processing of messages. Quick-scroll news consumption has made us easy prey for fake and fabricated stories. Some are so well put together and presented that at a glance they are indistinguishable from the real thing. And this attack on our reality isn't all human-led.

45

Non-human intelligence is on the rise. Bots, artificially intelligent algorithms and strings of code are learning and getting smarter and more advanced by the day. The mind-bending sophistication with which AI and 'deepfakes' can mimic, replicate, produce and create 'realities' in a way that was until recently confined to the realms of science fiction is mind-blowing. It used to be thought that some human abilities and skills could never be convincingly recreated by AI. No longer. Chess, poker and even the ancient Chinese board game Go were all domains believed to be safe from machines. Yet in recent years the best human players in the world have been eviscerated in matches against AI. Today, there aren't that many games left at which humans are consistently better than computers. The AI we see emerging can mimic humans more and more effectively, and even be creative in the process.

AI has undergone an explosion in the last eight to ten years, says David Cox, the director of the MIT-IBM Watson AI lab, who started in computer vision in the early 2000s. Computer vision is a field of AI that enables computers and systems to derive meaningful information from digital images, videos and other visual inputs – and take actions or make recommendations based on that information. Cox tells me that some things can now be done with AI and deep learning that he never thought would be possible in the lifetime of his career. Image recognition and description is right up there on the list. For example, a machine can identify a person playing a guitar or a construction worker on a site and then caption the image as such. AI doesn't just recognise and describe imagery, it can create it from scratch, too – convincingly enough that you'd be hard pushed to believe that those artificially created images were figments of an AI. Cox shows me pictures of people. I can't detect anything odd about them. I am floored to hear him say that none of the people in those pictures exist: they were all generated by AI. This is a problem for all of us, as I immediately find out when Cox shows me another picture. This one is of a young woman named Maisy Kinsley, described as a senior journalist at Bloomberg. Her profile on Twitter tells me she 'writes data-driven stories about cars, cyber security & web culture through words, graphics and passion'. Again, I struggle to see anything that jumps out as odd. I can't tell what's not real. But, Cox tells me, she doesn't exist. Even bots need faces, and Maisy Kinsley was a sophisticated scam put together in 2019 to extract personal information from people for malicious purposes. In retrospect, I guess 'words, graphics and *passion*' was a bit of a giveaway. But this is a real problem.

In December 2019, in an effort to police online misbehaviour, Facebook removed nearly 700 accounts that were allegedly using deceptive practices to push pro-Trump narratives to about 55 million users. According to Facebook, itself arguably not *that* reliable here, some of the accounts had used AI-generated profile pictures to pose as real live Americans.

There is more. Video of people used to be harder to manipulate than still images, but now it is possible to literally put words into someone's mouth. These technologies, otherwise known as deepfakes, are becoming pervasive, Cox tells me. He offers some good news, too, even though it's only temporary: 'We are in a stage where it's still largely possible to detect those.' AI still has shortcomings and can make mistakes, and there are many visual cues to look out for (interestingly, it's still terrible at generating realistic human hands). The problem, of course, is that these cues are subtle, and at first viewing my brain had not detected the colour blotches in the background, the position of one shoulder not matching the other or the blurry teeth and double chin in a fake President Obama speech.

There are plenty of online lists of tips and hints for detecting AI-generated imagery and deepfakes. But before we even get to the practical, technical checklists, I want to know if there are any measures we could take or any questions we should be asking when it comes to AI. Are there any thought processes we should be going through? Faced with how easily AI can trick us, I want to know how we can adopt a way of thinking that can help us fend off this increasingly sophisticated assault on truth.

I am hoping for a magic formula, but I'm not getting one. Cox instead tells me that all of the tried and tested signals for judging veracity we learnt to rely on in the past are now basically unreliable. That is decidedly not the answer I had hoped for. The key thing is to understand that these technologies exist, to know that just because a text reads well (yes, AI writes, too) or you saw a video or a picture, that doesn't make it real. It is no longer a signal that identifies something as genuine.

The bottom line, Cox tells me, is that we have to interrogate and be suspicious of everything. Then once again comes the advice about speed: slow down.

This is no doubt a real challenge. We have been conditioned to both create and consume a constant flow of high-speed information through our social media and newsfeeds. Platforms are constantly optimising their designs and layouts to increase user engagement, and in 2022, based on a summary by DataReportal, we spent more time in the virtual world than ever. While there are big variations (ten hours a day in South Africa, for example, less than four hours a day in Japan) on average a whopping seven hours per day is spent using the internet across all devices, equating to more than 48 hours per week – that's two full days, or 42% of our waking lives (assuming an average person gets anything between seven and eight hours' sleep a night) spent online. This surely must directly affect our behaviour. In addition, we become desensitised to what used to creep us out, by which I mean synthetic media – content created by technology, such as artificial intelligence and machine learning, deepfakes being the most prominent form of it. AI-written music, text generation, imagery and video, voice synthesis and more are increasingly entering the main-stream, and repeated exposure softens our perceptions, making us comfortable with 'fake' media and affecting how we create and consume content. The artificial intelligence writing programme ChatGPT that emerged in late 2022 caused great concern about plagiarism when it demonstrated it can produce seemingly human-written text within seconds. We have reached a time in our lives where what is true and what is fake are being blurred by humans and machines alike. And we have good reason to be concerned, because those who wish to exploit or manipulate us are out for one thing: the most valuable asset we have, our attention.

It used to be the case that the attention-grab was limited to only a few media, like printed newspaper headlines and advertising on TV and billboards. Today, methods have not just evolved but have multiplied to the point that our attention can be infiltrated more easily and at any moment at any given time. We are inundated with apps, chats, social media posts and more, all wanting a piece of us, yet we don't possess an infinite amount of attention to share out in equal measure. That doesn't deter corporations from wanting to monetise it, political parties from wanting to leverage it, ideological groups from seeking to capture it and our loved ones from desiring it. After all we live in a world in which our individual success is measured by how much attention we can attract.

Seeing how desired and valuable our attention is to so many, it makes sense to choose more carefully how we use and share it. When we realise that this a precious, much sought-after commodity, then perhaps it becomes easier to think of ourselves as gatekeepers guarding our respective highly prized assets. We can do this by slowing down and assessing the veracity of the information we receive. Only then do we stand a chance of fighting the onslaught of misinformation. It's not an easy task.

*

Thus far we have discovered that a truth detective's methods start with the process of slowing down to allow the time and space to interrogate the source of a piece of information. One of the trickier aspects of this process is learning to watch out for generalisations and assumptions – be they those made by others, or those we may have made ourselves.

'Do you *know* this to be true or do you *think* you know?' That's one question you can ask yourself and others to help you look for precision. Individual words we say and hear are just as important as entire sentences. Being precise can be as simple as not saying 'all' when we mean 'most', 'most' when we mean 'some', or 'some' when we mean 'a few'. I habitually analyse words such as these – though I believe my job gives me an advantage over most people.

As any science writer will tell you, our job is to get the facts right. Being precise and focusing on accuracy is in the job description. Our integrity as writers and journalists rests on our ability to tell the truth without bias. A lot of the time this comes down to knowing when to ask which questions. And that requires paying attention to what is being said. Words still matter and understanding their precise meaning is key.

Developing the habit of seeking accuracy will also provide you with an effective by-product: a behavioural calibration towards facts, evidence and data, and a distancing away from generalisations and assumptions.

Reaching for generalisations when we are unsure of the facts, or making assumptions based on limited experience or a small sample of evidence, can create major fallacies. Continually looking for precision can help. Take the noun 'box', for example. What type of box pops into your head? What shape is it? Is it symmetrical? Are all its sides the same dimensions? A reasonable generalisation would be that all boxes are containers, but this is still imprecise. Was the box you have been thinking of three-dimensional like a matchbox or two-dimensional like the space on a form?

Of course, some generalisations help us navigate our way through the world and understand our environment, because they are anchored securely in evidence. For example, we know not to put our hands on a burning stove. So the following is an absolutely correct generalisation: if you grab a sizzling hot item with your bare hands you will burn yourself. The evidence is solid (extremely painful in this case), and the generalisation justifiable. In poker, when you misplay a hand, that information also becomes anchored in your memory. But we reveal a lack of analytical thinking when we generalise with little or no evidence and allow unvalidated assumptions and prejudices to take hold of our minds. Yet in order to make a point, many of us continue to generalise by making broad comments about things or an entire group of people without sufficient evidence or support. That very sentence is a generalisation itself, which tells us it's easy to do and we cannot completely avoid doing it, but we can begin to exercise mindfulness and caution around the practice.

Fallacies

Sample size is everything here. The larger and more representative the sample size, the stronger the generalisation that can be made – especially when it has been proven through empirical studies, such as the efficiency and reliability of a consumer brand or a statement about women generally earning less than men (which still holds true in 2023). Bad generalisations, on the other hand, are fallacies – errors in thinking and reasoning. Take the following example:

Alex: I think Biden is going to win the election.

Bob: What makes you say that?

Alex: I don't know a single person who's going to vote for Trump, and I have talked to a lot of people.

This is a generalisation based on an unrepresentative sample size. Unless you have spoken to a significant portion of the eligible voters, this is not a statement that can be considered seriously. The general rule is the bigger the sample size, the more accurate the assessment and/or prediction. However, while sample size is key, so is how representative the sample is, meaning we have to pay attention to whether or not the sample has been inclusive and diverse enough to shed meaningful data. By taking a closer look in this way, we become mindful and more precise. Furthermore, if we want to ensure we get an accurate reflection of the world, we need to demand data that are representative of a diverse set of conditions or voices to help ensure we don't live in echo chambers.

Thanks to an increased digital sphere, there are more echo chambers than ever before. That's not necessarily a bad thing. Having more choice to decide which echo chamber you want to live in also presents more opportunity to break out. This may sound a little bleak and may even make you think that we are doomed to live in one echo chamber or another. I would propose to think about it differently. Cultivating diversity in our environment helps to inspire us, of course, but we can also use it to challenge our standing ideas about the world and the generalisations we believe to be true. We are then more likely to scrutinise generalisations when we encounter them, which is particularly important since they are often found in politics and propaganda.

In late January 2015, President Obama sat down for an interview with the online news and opinion site Vox. He was asked by the journalist Matthew Yglesias whether he thought that the media sometimes overstated the level of risk posed by terrorism, compared with other issues such as global warming and epidemic disease. To which Obama replied: 'Absolutely.'

This exchange created a furore in Washington. A month later, Obama's spokesperson reiterated that climate change posed a greater risk to the daily lives of Americans than terrorism. This came on the back of a series of heavy, unprecedented snowstorms and arctic weather fronts that brought bone-chilling temperatures and record-setting snowfall to parts of the northeastern United States. The forecasters had warned that New York City and New Jersey needed to brace themselves for severe snowfalls, too. Only, the NYC predictions didn't happen.

It was red meat for the TV channel Fox News, which jumped in with gusto and tried to show how wrong Obama was. Fox News was arguing that the science was wrong on global climate change: 'They told us that New York City was going to get blown out. We had to give up our freedom and sit in our houses, no cars on the road. Guess what? The models were wrong. They got the models wrong on the science 24 hours before. How about those models 10 to 20 years from now?' Its argument was that the climate models must all be wrong, because the weather models were wrong for the 2015 northeastern snowstorm.

To extrapolate from this that climate change didn't exist was a generalisation that didn't take into account one important fact: climate and weather are not the same. Both snowstorm forecasts and global climate models make predictions about the weather, that is to say, short-term changes in the atmosphere, but climate refers to weather patterns over a long period of time. Of course, having a good dose of scepticism is part of a critically thinking mind – and reasonable when it comes to freak weather conditions (or other situations, for that matter) that appear to be rare, too specific, or not truly representative of the larger picture. What is unreasonable, however, is to purposefully ignore data that might counter our argument or opinion.

This is not to single out anyone (or indeed any TV station) in particular. We all express opinions frequently. The point is that we need to be able to tell the difference between an opinion (or a personal belief) and a fact – and then know how to put those into their rightful places. This becomes especially important when the line between fact and personal belief is no longer clear. And often opinions are left unchallenged.

Rarely are we asked to give reasons for our opinions, and even more rarely do we have to justify or defend the validity of those reasons. It means we are not in the habit of requiring the same of others, and so their opinions are left to stand without any form of evidence or support. But without either of those, an opinion is just a statement, and it doesn't require our acceptance. The same goes for our own statements. So if you would like to avoid speaking in unproven generalisations, look at how you're presenting your opinion and what arguments you can use to validate it. Don't be like Fox News when you argue your case.

Practice, Practice, Practice

We aren't naturally analytical, critical thinkers. It is not something we are born with. But the natural curiosity that we all have in our first years as humans on this Earth lays the foundation for critical thinking. As babies and children, our innate inquisitiveness helps us to figure out tricky situations. Forced to think for ourselves, we work out how to climb out of our cot or how to put a puzzle together. As we grow older, we standardise problem-solving and make more assumptions about environment – and as a consequence become less inquisitive. We experience a stagnation of sorts, if you will.

As we age, we curate a world view in which what we consider reasonable or unreasonable is defined by our own thoughts, and those in turn have been moulded by our biases, values, interests and experiences.

This isn't to say that those are set for life. We know the brain is malleable and so is our thinking. Yes, critical thinking can be learnt, and as with anything that is practised over time, it can become habitual. Getting into the habit of asking the right questions to elicit the information we need is a skill every single person can acquire. Effective questioning starts with thinking about the problem and precisely what you are trying to find out. Ask a vague question and you will get a vague answer. Our question – or questions – should not be ambiguous; they should be designed to yield a clear answer. A question that could result in 'maybe' or 'don't know' doesn't give us any information, but simply leaves us where we started.

We must remember to verify whatever we can, starting with where the information came from, checking the source and questioning its credibility. Truthfulness cannot and should not be associated with those with the farthest reach or loudest voices. Ask yourself if the facts presented are credible, or whether you should question them – and remain aware that the answer to this will be based on existing biases, and those too should not go entirely unchallenged. Look at the information used to present the conclusion, idea or message. Who is it aimed at? What is being highlighted and why? What is being dismissed and why? How can we find information about the perspective that is being dismissed or negated? What is being implied, but not explicitly stated?

Here, too, we can see parallels and learn from the poker tables. A proficient player will run through a poker checklist in their head on each 'street' (the cards that are dealt each round), deciding what to do and what the function of each choice is. Most actions follow a standardised pattern and are effectively automated, but when faced with a tricky decision then an internal dialogue starts a checklist that can sound like stream-of-consciousness muttering: 'Okay, player did X, that means Y, Z is no longer a likely possibility, but A and B are.'

We must stop being afraid to ask questions and feel empowered to do so instead. Do not be afraid to look foolish when questioning the status quo or consensus in the room. By asking questions, we take control of the direction of a narrative that otherwise would be imposed upon us. The ability and willingness to ask questions gives us an advantage over others who don't – and we are certainly privileged compared to those who are not permitted to ask questions in the first place.

At its most basic, any society in which everyone is permitted to ask questions, think independently, elect their government and refute, protest and dismiss propaganda is a democracy. In poker, as in life, much depends on the cards you have been dealt. Any kind of advantage – in either game – can help us win. In poker we call it 'having an edge' over someone. Critical thinking gives you that edge.

Digital Battlefields

> Those who can make you believe absurdities can make you commit atrocities
>
> Voltaire

The social media world is filled with traps laid by bots and AI and those who control them. Social media is not easily compatible with critical thinking: it is set up to play on emotion and instinct, and its addictive quality harnesses parts of our brains.

Writing this during the pandemic, I tried not to succumb to the overwhelming feeling that we had entered a new Dark Age. If there was a resistance fighting for good then it seemed to be losing the fight against a dark side that had unleashed a multi-pronged attack on our planet and its people: racism, populism, xenophobia, sexism and every other divisive -ism you can think of was catalysed by the deadly virus that had been thrown into the mix. Now the negative impacts were not just greater than ever before, the power of social media was also growing exponentially. In 2020 those in power – particularly those in power with a ton of money – were not just running the world, but also controlling how people perceived it. The battlefields continued to be digital news and information and social media platforms. Perhaps we should have listened to the late rock icon David Bowie when the internet was still in its infancy and we used dial-up connections. In 1999 he predicted the internet was going to have 'unimaginable' effects on society and 'change the state of content' forever.

Since the 2016 US presidential elections, the technology writer Kevin Rose at *The New York Times* has been tracking (obsessively, he adds) how partisan political content performs on Facebook, the world's largest and arguably most influential media platform. Reading through his findings a mere 67 days before the 2020 US presidential election, in which many thought Trump could still be re-elected despite languishing in the opinion polls, I felt a chill.

As you will see, opinion polls can be wrong, very wrong indeed. In 2016, they were wrong because they didn't account for people who were too shy to openly admit their political views. When asked in exit polls how they voted, they lied. What they were unwilling to admit to in person, they had no issue with behind the safety of their computer screens – or in the privacy of the voting booth. When no one was looking, they clicked, liked and searched for stuff they would never publicly admit to. Though now it seems it is more acceptable to publicly espouse views that used to be considered 'unsavoury'. Especially within echo chambers. In particular, Rose observes the dominance of right-wing groups and news on Facebook (now Meta), which he warns is something that should not be ignored. It eclipses both in clout and reach any of the democratic and liberal social media communications. 'The reason right-wing content performs so well on Facebook is no mystery. The platform is designed to amplify emotionally resonant posts, and conservative commentators are skilled at turning impassioned grievance into powerful algorithm fodder,' Rose wrote in *The New York Times* a couple of months before the 2020 election.

Staged videos, orchestrated images and fraudulent information are lies, but only recently have we begun referring to them as 'fake news'. It isn't a new phenomenon – the technique is as old as politics itself. It existed way before Facebook was a thing, and a long time before Tim Berners-Lee invented the World Wide Web. Fake news has been part of many of the key moments in our modern history, hasn't needed to depend on digital technology that could manipulate imagery or sound. All fake news needs to succeed is a story told well.

Historic Fake News

Having led his German allies to believe he had no intention of doing so, Mussolini invaded Greece in October 1940. Hitler was furious. Italy had given Germany next to no prior notice, and the surprise move caught him off guard. Germany's propaganda minister, Joseph Goebbels, tried to get a handle on the situation by asking Mussolini to suppress news of the invasion for two days. In this time, Goebbels disseminated an intensive avalanche of fake news about outrageous Greek behaviour, specifically to prepare the German people for the fact that their ally had mounted an invasion.

Goebbels had a controlling grip on what information the German population would receive, and would use violence to maintain that control – as foreign correspondent William L. Shirer recounted in an interview in 1990:

> The Gestapo was so powerful and so good, I would say. I had one other source [who] was an editor of a leading morning paper. And he gave me the daily instructions from Goebbels on what his

paper should print, what editorials they should write and what they should keep out, so I was able, almost daily, to find out what the dictatorship was telling the papers to write and so forth. Well, he got picked up, he was sentenced to death.

In 1944, Shirer reported that American prisoners of war were given weekly newspapers by the Nazis, who claimed it was to allow them to keep abreast of world events, when in fact it was, of course, Nazi propaganda. Shirer headlined his report 'Fake "News" for War Prisoners'.

We know that newspapers, especially ones with a large circulation, can influence sociological and political landscapes. One of the UK's biggest-selling newspapers, the *Daily Mail*, is an example of how a messaging juggernaut can yield great power. Known for its highly partisan reporting, the 125-year-old Conservative paper can influence the thoughts and the behaviour of its readership – and has done so from its earliest days.

On the morning of 23 October 1924, Thomas Marlowe, editor of the *Daily Mail*, arrived at his desk to find a message left for him late the previous night. The message, left in a phone call from an old and trusted friend, read:

> There is a document in London which you ought to have. It shows the relations between the Bolsheviks and the British Labour Party. The Prime Minister knows all about it, but is trying to avoid publication. It has been circulated today to the Foreign Office, Home Office and Admiralty and War Office.

That the British Labour Prime Minister Ramsay MacDonald was actively working to prevent the publication of an ominous document four days before a general election could only mean one thing: the content was explosive. Marlowe had to get his hands on this document. He picked up his phone and started contacting his sources inside government one by one, eager to find out if anyone else knew of the document, and hoping someone would share a copy with him. Later that afternoon he met a source who confirmed the existence of what had been labelled a 'Very Secret' document, but was hesitant to share it for exactly that reason. The meeting was brief, and left Marlowe unsure whether he had done enough to convince his contact to get him the copy.

Within 30 minutes of him arriving back at his desk, Marlowe's phone rang. At the end of the line was another source, who actually had a copy in his possession. He had called to get advice on how best to leak the story. This was Marlowe's chance. Letting his paper – back then the newspaper with the largest circulation in Britain – break the story would ensure that it got maximum exposure, he told his source. He further promised to give it the widest publicity and share it with other London newspapers once the *Daily Mail* had had its exclusive. The source told Marlowe he'd get back to him, and hung up the phone.

The next day, Marlowe had not one but two copies of the document. A second had been posted to him anonymously and was waiting for him on his desk when he returned with a copy already in hand after a meeting with one of his sources. The secret document was a letter. Addressed to the British Communist Party and dated 15 September 1924, it contained instructions to start a revolution. It had been sent by the Soviet leader Grigory Zinoviev, the chairman of the Comintern (Communist International, also known as the Third International), an organisation that advocated global communism via worldwide revolution. Its strategy was to prey on unstable governments, and Great Britain was in its sights.

Britain's first-ever Labour government was standing on shaky ground after only nine months in office. It had been able to secure the keys to 10 Downing Street in January 1924 by forming a coalition with the Liberal Party. Throughout the summer, with parliament in recess, the Conservative Party fuelled a campaign of scaremongering and defamation to turn the public against the government. Through favourable press, it suggested that the government was acting on behalf of the extreme Left – communists no different to the Soviets themselves. In reality, the Labour Party had distanced itself from communism and went as far as banning from the party individuals who identified as communists. But its efforts to improve bilateral relations were viewed with hostility in some quarters. Previous Conservative ministers were supremely suspicious of Moscow, and were now pushing a 'Red Peril' campaign on all fronts, even though there had been no tangible proof of any danger of war or revolution. Until now, it seemed.

Zinoviev and the other leading members of the Russian Communist Party, the Bolsheviks, had been doing everything they could to foment revolution throughout Europe. But attempts to incite an uprising in Germany flopped. They then tried to garner momentum for a revolution against the newly formed Bulgarian government. That, too, failed to materialise. But failure didn't stop their attempts – and here in Marlowe's hands was another letter, this time to the communists of Great Britain.

The timing of the letter Marlowe obtained seemed opportune. The post-war recession, the rising unemployment rate in Britain and weeks of propaganda by Labour's opponents had all contributed to a loss of public confidence and the government's eventual demise.

The letter said the Russians fully supported the recently finalised Anglo-Russian treaties and urged the British Communist Party to mobilise the working class for a military revolution and class war. Marlowe immediately cleared his paper's front page and dictated a new one. He would later describe his haste to print as 'the paper's duty to inform the British public'. The headlines shook the nation:

CIVIL WAR PLOT BY SOCIALISTS' MASTERS
MOSCOW ORDERS TO OUR REDS
GREAT PLOT DISCLOSED YESTERDAY
'PARALYSE THE ARMY AND NAVY'
MR MACDONALD WOULD LEND RUSSIA OUR MONEY!

Marlowe was doing his country a great service: unmasking a spectacular plot to wage war in Britain from within, and exposing the misguided foolishness of the MacDonald Labour government. Except none of it was true. Not the call to war, not Prime Minister MacDonald looking to suppress publication, not even the letters in his hands. Today we'd call it fake news. In simpler terms, it was lies – lies so close to what people wanted to hear that they could be taken as true.

Marlowe had never taken the time to verify the authenticity of either of the documents in his possession. He had noticed that the two copies weren't quite identical (the positioning of the signatures was slightly off). But he took the fact that the letter was given to him by trusted sources – sources he'd known and used for years – as validity enough. Marlowe, the experienced newspaper editor, had been taken for a ride, and all because he'd received something that supported a story he already believed in, one that fitted his own prejudices and beliefs. The letter was published four days before the general election, which saw the Conservative Party gain a sweeping majority.

The Zinoviev letter is history. And nearly one hundred years later, propaganda is vastly more sophisticated, and all around us, all the time.

Sixty-five years later, the British press offered another spectacular example of fake news. On 19 April 1989, the *Sun* newspaper ran a front-page story headlined 'The Truth'. After being forced into an overcrowded caged pen at Hillsborough stadium in Sheffield, 97 Liverpool football supporters died as a result of the crush. The paper ran claims from anonymous police officers that, as people were dying at Hillsborough, their fellow fans stole from them, attacking the police who were trying to help victims and even urinating on them. The stories were initially defended by the paper as vital reporting of the truth, but it later emerged that they were sent in by a Sheffield news agency, White's, and run by the *Sun* unchecked. In 2012, after 23 years, the *Sun* apologised to its readers and the people of Liverpool for its coverage. The stories were completely made up. The source was the South Yorkshire Police.

And so it goes on. In 2003, we heard about Saddam Hussein's 'weapons of mass destruction' – never found – that justified the invasion of Iraq. The People's Republic of China has been more subtle, introducing laws restricting who can distribute news, and requiring the media to show loyalty to the government. As recently as 2022, we have seen the Russian government reasserting state control over the country's largest media companies, placing it 155th out of 180 countries in the Press Freedom Index compiled by Reporters Without Borders. Russia's leader, Vladimir Putin, uses the media to control messages about the war in Ukraine and push his propaganda and lies. He has gone as far as enacting new laws that make saying there is 'war' or an 'invasion' in Ukraine a crime punishable with up to fifteen years in jail. It is information control at the highest level.

Propaganda, fake news, alternative facts, selective information – they all work to distort reality, and they spread faster than the truth. In 2018, MIT Media Lab researchers analysed eleven years of Twitter's archives. They found around 126,000 rumours had been spread by around 3 million people and that false news had reached more people than real news, usually because it seemed more novel, gripping or sensational – and therefore more shareable. Moreover, humans were actually more likely than automated 'bot' accounts to share false news on the Twitter platform. But social bots do play a particular role in spreading articles from low-credibility sources. Also in 2018, after analysing 14 million messages spreading 400,000 articles on Twitter during ten months in 2016 and 2017, researchers at Indiana University Bloomington showed that bots amplify this kind of content at key moments, before an article goes viral. They also target users with many followers through replies and mentions.

> 'Man sues McDonald's for still being
> depressed after eating a Happy Meal'

> 'Man arrested in Florida for barbecuing pedophiles to death'

These are both fake stories that thousands of people shared without questioning. The McDonald's story was completely made up and first published by 8shit.net, which – true to its name – only publishes satire and hoaxes. The second headline twisted the actual events to spin the story into fiction. What was true was that a man was arrested after he poured gasoline all over a hotel room and a car with the professed intent of killing child molesters. He didn't actually kill anyone or set anyone on fire, much less cook paedophiles alive on a barbecue. (Upon arrest, he admitted to the crimes, and when the police officers asked why he hadn't set light to the room and car, the man replied '. . . because you got here too early'.)

A good headline can make or break a story. It is standard practice for media organisations to test two or more different headlines online to see which the audience will engage with more. Half of readers on the page see one headline; half see the other. This allows a newspaper to measure if any one headline gets more clicks than the other. The winning headline then goes on the home page for all readers.

Headlines are designed to hook us. And if we aren't careful, we could be exposed to content that is crafted in such great detail it may make us believe made-up stories.

A Real-Life Truth Detective

Mukul Devichand is an award-winning investigative journalist who started his career at the BBC's investigative current affairs programme, *Panorama*. In early 2013, Devichand noticed that a significant number of political, social and cultural conversations were happening on social media, conversations that were being missed by the mainstream news reporting of organisations like the BBC. When in 2010 the Arab Spring caused a sudden revolution, journalists deployed to cover the news in the Middle East hadn't seen it coming. But it hadn't been hidden. It wasn't invisible. Why did the mainstream reporters miss it? 'They were there talking to certain people in the capital or in their circles,' Devichand tells me. 'They weren't on the pulse of all these younger people who were talking to each other online.'

In 2013, Devichand was in charge of a programme reporting on politics and culture that were going viral online. He called it *BBC Trending*. Anything that was getting traction on the web, in any way, was a story for *Trending*. Some of the stories they featured were light and frothy, like the Ice Bucket Challenge that went viral in 2014. Tens of millions were chatting online about it, but it was the *BBC Trending* reports that pushed the campaign into mainstream news. They were uncovering stories that mattered to people that were otherwise unseen. But what Devichand and his team didn't realise was how much *Trending* would teach them about fakes.

In November 2014, dramatic footage of the war in Syria went viral. In it, a small boy under gunfire falls to the ground, shot. After a few seconds he manages to peel himself off the ground and run through continuous gunfire to rescue his little sister. Millions watched the video of the 'Syrian hero boy' on YouTube. It became a huge international story and soon the printed press picked up the story all around the world. Devichand recounts how his team was under pressure to report on this, too. After all, *BBC Trending* dealt with viral news. He remembers seeing the video for the very first time: 'I was looking at it that day and I just thought, "This isn't adding up to me."' He couldn't put his finger on it, but the fact that the video looked quite slick was one of the reasons he had doubts.

The BBC has a dedicated team that analyses images and information from all over the world for authenticity, as well as a special team of Arabic speakers well versed in Syrian and Iraqi geography. Devichand showed them the video and asked: 'How real is this?' On first inspection the video looked real, but what threw the team were the odd dialects of Arabic being spoken. They just weren't consistent with that region of the Arab world. The team also pointed out that the position of the sun seemed at odds with the supposed time of filming. Even though they couldn't completely dismiss it as a fake, it was clear that Devichand was right to have doubts. While the rest of the media reported on the video as real, Devichand uploaded the story but questioned its veracity. Less than 48 hours later, his questions were answered. A group of Norwegian filmmakers got in touch and told him that the film was indeed a fake. They had shot it in Malta on a movie set that had previously been used for films like *Troy* and *Gladiator*. The whole thing was made up. Lars Klevberg, a film director based in Oslo, deliberately presented the film as reality in order to generate a discussion about children in conflict zones. He told Devichand that they had decided to come clean about the video and reveal it to the BBC, because it was the only news outlet that had questioned the video at all.

Social media has democratised publishing. Anyone, anywhere, can post anything they want, any time. Crucially, social media is built on algorithms that aren't editorially curated, meaning that a post will popularise according to the clicks and views it is getting. The fundamental logic of these systems is to keep people's attention on the social media platform for as long as possible: the longer they spend, the longer they are exposed to advertising. By their very nature these algorithms aren't designed to focus on veracity. They are about popularity. And as the MIT study has shown, fakes, hoaxes, disinformation or prejudice can spread fast, faster than high-quality, corroborated media.

Fake news headlines that are repeated are also more likely to be perceived as accurate. Gordon Pennycook and David G. Rand found indications that a single prior exposure to a headline is sufficient to increase its perceived accuracy when seen for the second time – and that goes for both fake and real news. They found that fake news credulity intensifies with increasing exposure and sustains itself over time.

Judging by how quickly fake news stories can spread, it seems like a big ask to think critically about the stories we read, and to only share news that we know to be 100% credible. Part of what contributes to the success of fake news stories is that most people will trust news shared by their social circle or network. They will then share it without making the effort to verify the content.

It is completely normal for us to surround ourselves with others with whom we share perspectives and ideologies. It even has a name: *homophily*. Similarities in attitude, belief and values lead to attraction and interaction. Simply put, similarity breeds fellowship, and vice versa. Unsurprisingly, adults tend to associate with those of their own political orientation. That also means we run the risk of erecting our own echo chambers where we are only exposed to viewpoints and ideas that we already agree with. This is amplified by social media network homophily. The 2016 UK referendum that resulted in Brexit and the US election that made Donald Trump President are just two examples of 'shock' results that weren't so shocking to people who weren't already in certain ideological bubbles. As such, social media can become a death trap for critical thinking. It inhibits questioning and with its presence and power steadily increasing, navigating social media safely becomes a responsibility few of us can avoid. In fact, when it comes to current events, it is already one of the predominant spaces people go to get their content and information.

A meta-analysis collated in a digital data report published in 2022 showed that 59% of the world's population uses social media. At the time of writing there are 4.7 billion active social media users around the world, up by 500 million from the previous year.

The same global report stated that more than four in five adults now get their news via digital channels, and are two and a half times as likely to turn to social media for news as they are to turn to physical newspapers and magazines. The report stated that over half the world's adult population use social media to get their news and updates on current affairs. There is a danger that opinion pieces and misinformation are taken as news, which is why knowing how to navigate in the online world without falling prey to misinformation and untruths is now a vital tool. Gaining an understanding of how to identify different types of information can help empower us to choose what we take in.

Fake news, disinformation and misinformation are often used interchangeably. But they are actually different predatory beasts.

Fake news stories mimic the form of mainstream news but they are purposely crafted to share misleading or totally fabricated information wrapped up in a sensational, emotionally charged narrative. Such as the completely fake news of the Pope endorsing Trump or the size of Trump's inauguration crowd size or the partially fake reports that take scientific papers then twist or misinterpret findings in order to mislead, either to fulfil a particular agenda or simply to generate more views and shares. Like the story published on 31 August 2014 in the *Mail on Sunday*, which claimed that the rate of decline in Arctic Ocean ice had slowed, when the opposite is known to be happening.

Disinformation is deliberately misleading or biased information, shared intentionally to cause harm. This can be 'news' pushed by extreme political movements with the goal to further an agenda or, for example, phishing campaigns. On 23 April 2013, a tweet by the Associated Press (AP) read: 'Breaking: Two explosions in the White House and Barack Obama is injured'. Within minutes, the tweet had thousands of retweets and went viral. But it was not true: the Syrian Electronic Army had gained access to the AP Twitter account with the intent of causing disruption. It owned up to its hack with a tweet of their own from an account since suspended: *'Ops! @AP get owned by Syrian Electronic Army! #SEA #Syria #ByeByeObama'*. They had achieved their goal: for about six minutes, the US stock market was in free fall. A single tweet sent the US economy into turmoil.

Misinformation, on the other hand, is incorrect or misleading information, presented as fact.

There are now numerous organisations and websites dedicated to fact-checking that one can refer to for help in identifying the truth when it comes to news. If you're unsure or simply want to check you aren't running into a false-story trap, then it may help you to stress test the information against a basic fact-check list.

Avoid the headline trap

Remember newspapers sell because of catchy headlines. Fake news stories often use all caps and several exclamation marks to draw our attention and trigger emotional responses. The more shocking and arresting a claim, the more wary we ought to be about its veracity.

Verify and check the source

Is this a source you trust and is it one that has a solid reputation for reporting accurately? If you're not familiar with the source, then try to find out more about it. Does the online webpage or address look normal? Is the writing correct or are there spelling mistakes or syntax errors?

Check the evidence

Even trusted organisations can get it wrong. Check the sources the article claims to have used and try to confirm that they exist. If named sources are missing or if expert advice is lacking, the likelihood is that it is indeed a fake story, or at the very least inaccurate.

Check the photographic evidence

False news stories often contain manipulated images or videos. And even photos that may be authentic can be taken out of context. There are websites that allow you to reverse-image search and find other versions of the photos online. Admittedly, as AI-generated imagery increases in sophistication, this is becoming harder and harder.

Is the story a joke?

There are parody news publications like *The Onion* that put out satirical stories. However, today in this messed-up world it has become increasingly difficult to distinguish between humour or satire and a genuine story. In 2020 a Facebook group that describes itself as 'a place for political humour and satire, poking fun at those in the government of the day' ran a story saying that British PM Boris Johnson did not have the coronavirus and that doctors who treated Johnson at the hospital said his condition was 'contrived'. Not only did the named doctors not exist but it was also false that Johnson did not have the virus. He did and spent a week in hospital including three nights in intensive care. Nevertheless, this satirical story spread online, with some believing it to be true. Once again, check the source to see whether it is known for parody, and whether the story's details and tone suggest it may be just for fun.

For every minute of 2022, 70 million messages were sent via WhatsApp and Facebook Messenger. Five hundred hours of content were uploaded on YouTube, 695,000 stories were shared on Instagram and 350,000 people were tweeting. In the same time, there were nearly 3 million swipes on Tinder and a total of over $10 million was spent online. That's for every single minute of every single day. The avalanche of information we create each day continues to grow exponentially. A lot of this data is laced with disinformation, misinformation, untruths, distortions and plain lies. It is imperative that we become media literate and think more deeply about what we share and don't share with our networks. The internet has given us the power and freedom to spread our own news. It is our responsibility to make sure that is accurate. Don't be made a fool of.

PART TWO

Learning How to Read Others: Communication, Interpretation and Impressions

Communication

Want to play poker? Lady Gaga will tell you all you need is a poker face, and I would tell her, 'Lady, we got to work on your poker game.' (If you're reading this, Lady Gaga, I'm free whenever you are!) Here's the thing, though: there really is no such thing as a poker face. Or any category of face for that matter. Your face isn't going to make you a winning poker player. If anything, poker trains you to take everything into account, not just the face. I remember the first time I walked into a poker room being struck by the sheer diversity of players of different ages, nationalities, cultural and financial backgrounds (though not gender). You learn quickly as a player to be vigilant when it comes to assumptions and biases about other players. You soon recognise that you cannot predict a person's character traits or behaviour based solely on the way they look.

Face Value

During the Covid-19 lockdown days of 2020, there were those who used the additional hours created by confining us to our homes to learn new skills, like playing the piano, juggling oranges or learning a new language. Then there were others, like me, who did nothing of the sort and instead binge-watched the Netflix series *Indian Matchmaking*.

It was there I encountered the dubious practice of face-reading.

The series follows Sima Taparia, a matchmaker who travels in India and to the US to pair up Indian couples. When I see her pay regular visits to a face-reader to help validate her matches and gain character insights into her candidates, I cringe, remembering my own encounter with a face-reader. It completely mesmerised me.

To a degree I am hugely grateful to Susan Ibitz, the face-reader in question, because she led me into an area that I otherwise would have omitted from this book. Ibitz describes herself as a 'human behaviour hacker', but it was something she said in an interview in 2018 that snagged my attention: 'I can read you without knowing you. I can read someone from a photo.' I wanted to put that to the test and managed to arrange a meeting over Skype.

Even through the screen, Ibitz's gregarious yet self-deprecating manner is immediately endearing and I feel a certain kinship when she tells me that it is difficult to operate in a male-dominated field, which behaviour analysis still is. 'I was a hostage negotiator, I trained hostage negotiators,' she tells me. Today she is founder of The Human Behaviour Lab, where she continues her research and also teaches people how to read others, spot deception and improve on their communication. Ibitz is in the business of catching liars.

Born in Argentina to diplomat parents of Italian and Austrian descent, Ibitz speaks in near perfect English with a slight Latin American accent. She tells me that she's taught a number of poker players. I am not surprised.

A lot of the complexity of poker is down to the individual players. So how well you understand both your opponents and the way you perceive them can help you win. This doesn't require any poker knowledge. And anyone can do it. Observe a bunch of strangers who happen to sit with you around a table: there is plenty of information you can pick up on before the cards are even shuffled and dealt. Not like this, though:

'You have small ears, you're extremely visual, and you take information in your own time, so you don't like to be rushed.' Ibitz had started to tell me about . . . well, me. We had met only a few minutes earlier, but she listed my personality traits as if she had known me for years. She talked about my strong analytical traits and hit the nail on the head when she told me that I am one of those people who likes to review the menu before heading to the restaurant, arriving knowing what I am probably going to eat. She noticed how I was shifting in my chair. Uncomfortable, feeling exposed and laid bare. My eyebrows seemed to reveal a lot, too: 'Your eyebrows – you like facts and data to be straight-forward, you like bullet points. You tend to make lists and cross things off your list because you feel good when you do. You feel like you have accomplished things if you cross them off your list.' Again, this is true about me. I'm not going to lie, I was stunned into admiration. She got all that from my ears and eyebrows.

After our interview, and once my critical mind had awoken from its coma, I couldn't shift the uneasy feeling that came with what I had just experienced. She had told me that I value quality over quantity and place a great deal of importance on family and core relationships. There aren't many people who wouldn't identify with this. As for my analytical thinking traits, well, as a science writer, those are implied by my job title. These things weren't really a great revelation or insights into my personality. They felt like horoscope-style generalisations – and those can be made to sound uncannily specific. Yet, niggling curiosity had been planted in my head. Could one really deduce core character traits about me just by looking at my face? Was it really that easy to determine what made me who I am? I was promised answers in a webinar that Ibitz was hosting a week later. She used it to explain the science she was basing her craft on: physiognomy. I had never come across the term before, let alone any of the 'science' around it. The session didn't answer my questions but instead raised more, leaving me unconvinced about its legitimacy and the soundness of the science. It was time to do my own research and see what I could find out about the history of physiognomy. I knew this was going to be an uncomfortable journey for me. Throughout my school years in Germany, I learnt about the country's cruel, dark past that saw a group of humans categorise and then vilify another group based on what they looked like. This was a past Germany wanted to learn from to ensure it would never happen again – which is why it was taught over and over in all our history classes. Deducing any kind of information based solely on a person's physical features felt inherently wrong to me, and I believed it was feeding into ideologies of extremist groups including, yes, Nazis. As I started my research into physiognomy, the very first story I found was both haunting and utterly disturbing. The alarm bells were now truly ringing.

First Impressions

Solomon Perel was born in 1925, in Peine, a city in northern Germany near Hanover, and died in February 2023 at his home in Givatayim, near Tel Aviv, Israel. In his autobiography he described how as a fourteen-year-old he stood in front of his class, trying his best to stem the rising panic. His teacher, smiling and apparently unaware of the danger he was putting Solomon in, approached him with the measuring tape.

'Science,' he explained to his teenage audience, 'does not lie.' Solomon knew what was happening. Only moments earlier, his teacher had explained to the class that it was possible to identify Jews by their genetically inferior physiology.

'Straight ahead, please.'

Solomon lifted his bowed head and stared into the distance, terrified to meet the gaze of any of his friends – friends who were about to discover that he had been lying to them for years. He considered running, but he knew it was useless – he would never make it out alive.

The students watched in rapt attention as their teacher pulled the tape across Solomon's face, measuring first from his chin to the top of his head, and then from his chin to the tip of his nose. If the professor noticed the beads of sweat forming on the boy's forehead, he said nothing. Solomon held his breath as the measurements were written up on the blackboard behind him.

'Just one more.'

Solomon held his breath as the tape was wrapped around his head and then sharply pulled away. Chalk scratched out the final instalment of Solomon's death sentence.

'The numbers do not lie,' announced the teacher. Solomon closed his eyes. It was over. He felt a hand on his shoulder.

'What you are looking at here,' his teacher continued, 'is the perfect example of a Baltic Aryan.'

For a moment, Solomon thought he'd misheard, but the next thing he knew, he was being sent back to his seat. Somehow, once again, Solomon had managed to dodge the fate that had befallen so many of his fellow Jews.

The Perels had left Germany in 1936 and moved to Lodz in Poland. When the German troops had invaded Poland in 1939, the Jews in Lodz – as elsewhere in the country – were ordered to enter the local ghetto set up by the Nazis. Solomon Perel's parents had suspected this was a place they likely would not leave alive and so they did what they knew they had to do: embraced their children one last time, and told them to run.

The children evaded the Germans but the four siblings were separated along the way. Solomon found shelter in a Jewish orphanage in Grodno, now in Belarus but then in eastern Poland and under Soviet control. One morning, the children woke to urgent voices. The Germans were coming. The children were told to head east. They managed to get to the outskirts of Minsk before the Germans finally caught up with them all. The children, surrounded in an open field, were ordered to stand in a line. Solomon watched as, one by one, his friends were shot dead. When it was Solomon's turn, the German soldier who stood in front of him ordered him to put his hands up.

'Are you a Jew?' he asked.

Without hesitation, Solomon responded, in fluent German, that he was a 'Volksdeutscher' – an ethnic German born in Russia. Later, Solomon would credit his near accent-free German for saving his life. In fact, his German was so good that the soldier didn't even ask Solomon to confirm his ethnicity by dropping his trousers to prove he wasn't circumcised.

Solomon was set free. He adopted a new identity as a German boy named Josef. He was so convincing as a German that he later became a translator for the Wehrmacht on the front line, before being sent to school in Germany. Many years after the war ended, Solomon went to see the teacher who had declared him to be the perfect Baltic Aryan. On being told by Solomon that he was, in fact, a Jew, the teacher looked embarrassed and claimed that he had known all along and had carried out the demonstration to protect him. This story from Germany's terrible past is exactly why I was now deeply disturbed, and struggled to see any validity in physiognomy at all. The more I thought about it, the more shocked I was that this idea of profiling anyone based merely on their physiology could still be allowed to have any breathing room in our world whatsoever. Looking deeper into its history, I found that the Nazis weren't the ones who invented physiognomy. The notion that one could infer character traits from a person's facial appearance is well documented in Ancient Greece (Aristotle wrote about the subject extensively), and it appears to have had a resurgence in the sixteenth century.

In 1586, the polymath Giambattista della Porta published a book entitled *de Humana physiognomonia*, in which illustrations of human faces were matched, side by side, with those of animals. The profile of a man with a beak-like nose, for example, was pictured next to one of a bald eagle. To emphasise these similarities, some of the drawings of humans were distorted to look like caricatures. In the book, della Porta wrote 'Those with large faces should be considered lazy; resembling cows or donkeys, they tend to be stupid and unteachable.' He also went on to say that people with round, stubby noses are 'magnanimous' because he believed people with these facial features shared qualities with the lion that they resembled. However, della Porta's ideas were not only dismissed but the work was placed on a list of forbidden books by the Venetian Inquisition. He had antagonised them by theorising about whether changes to external features could also affect the soul.

But the idea refused to die. In 1746, James Parsons, a medical doctor, gave a lecture at the Royal Society in London called 'Human Physiognomy Explain'd'. In it, he laid out how facial muscles showed the connections between our 'passions' and the body. Emotions engaged certain muscles, he reasoned, creating a physical reflection of our mental states. From this he deduced that looking at someone's face was enough to determine that person's character. He went on to argue that repeated and continual triggering of certain muscles by specific emotions would, over time, tense those muscles perpetually. Therefore, he concluded, passions/emotions would begin to shape the face 'into a consent with the mind'. Some 40 years later, the Swiss pastor and physician Johann Kaspar Lavater came across Parsons' and della Porta's works while researching his theory that signs of the divine could manifest themselves in human form. He took Parsons' idea and ran with it, producing a book in which he advanced della Porta's work, going into much more detail and breaking the reading of the face down to its individual features. His vast collection of essays on physiognomy, *Physiognomische Fragmente zur Beförderung der*

Menschenkenntnis und Menschenliebe was so popular with readers all over Europe that he is now widely regarded as the person responsible for popularising the practice of physiognomy.

One devotee of Lavater's work was Robert FitzRoy, later a vice-admiral and Fellow of the Royal Society. In 1830, then captain of HMS *Beagle*, FitzRoy was introduced to a young geologist who wished to join his upcoming expedition around the world. The voyage was expected to take a minimum of five years, making it vital that all the men on board were of 'sound character'. FitzRoy took one look at the young man's nose and immediately diagnosed a personality lacking in energy and determination. He turned the young man away.

Fortunately for science, the young man – despite his facial shortcomings – did eventually manage to win the captain over. A few months later, a young Charles Darwin set off on a journey that would help him develop his theory of evolution by natural selection. 'I think,' Darwin later said of FitzRoy, 'that he was afterwards well satisfied that my nose had spoken falsely.'

Well aware, then, of its dark history, I kept an open mind about physiognomy while listening to Ibitz, and asked for data that would support the practice and help quash my doubts. Alas, when I looked for solid data to legitimise physiognomy, all I found was that it was just another bogus idea dressed up in pseudo-science garb. The studies that I found in support of it were based on very small sample sizes, and were easily trounced by data from studies using a much larger sample size. Let me give you an example. The following is a study that is both disturbing and dangerous.

In a paper titled 'Bad to the Bone: Facial structure predicts unethical behaviour', scientists from the University of California claimed that they could determine a person's trustworthiness with a simple measurement matrix. Specifically, they used the facial width-to-height ratio (fWHR) to predict unethical behaviour in men. Across two studies, they claimed that men with wider faces (relative to facial height) are more likely to explicitly deceive their counterparts in a negotiation and are more willing to cheat in order to increase their financial gain. Under post-publication scrutiny, however, these findings have run into some problems. Computational psychologist Michael Kosinski at Stanford University in California is one of the people who have reviewed the study. He tells me that he surveyed all the material that had been published on this subject and discovered that the belief of facial width-to-height ratio can predict of a broad range of behaviours such as social dominance, deception or cheating is essentially based on a very small number of studies. And when he started looking at those few studies in detail he found they were usually based on extremely small samples. The paper that resulted from his investigation was published in 2017, and it revealed that about 50% of these studies were based on samples smaller than 25, with an average sample size of 40. Kosinski wanted to know if he could replicate these findings by analysing a larger sample size – a lot larger, in fact. He analysed 137,163 online participants, and found no substantial evidence to support the results of the previous studies.

Kosinski wasn't the only researcher looking for evidence. A team of researchers from the University of Vienna questioned the impact of fWHR in sports. Association football (soccer) provided objective performance data (e.g. goals) and explicit measures of aggression (e.g. penalties) in real-world situations. They analysed data on 472 players: fouls committed, yellow and red cards received, assists and goals scored. Their findings, published in 2018, added to the empirical evidence refuting the impact of fWHR on aggressive behaviour in sports.

Thus far, therefore, there has been little empirical evidence of links between fWHR and real-life behavioural tendencies.

On the flip side, there is plenty of data on what happens when we *look* at a face and how our assumptions, and our conscious and unconscious biases lead our decision-making and judgement about another person.

Most of us believe that our trust is earned over time. Few of us realise that this is not quite true. We decide who is worthy of our trust quicker than in the blink of an eye. What's more, we begin to do so before we can even form our first words.

Research has shown that we form a view and idea in our head about a person from a very young age. What's more, we do this in a single glance. Bulgarian-born scientist Alexander Todorov, whose work focuses on face perception, showed that you need as little as 30 to 40 milliseconds of exposure to a face to form an impression of it. When presented with two images at a time, he has found, toddlers as young as seven months old prefer to look at the picture of a 'trustworthy' face over an 'untrustworthy' one. By the age of four, 75% of children point to the 'trustworthy' face as being the 'nicer' person. (The results were similar when participants were asked to point to the stronger person, or even the smarter one.) Sitting in his office at Princeton University, Todorov explains to me how he and his team came to define 'trustworthiness'. He tells me that faces that look like they're smiling were regarded as approachable. They would be judged by infants as trustworthy, as opposed to faces with somewhat disgruntled expressions. Further, more feminine faces are perceived as more trustworthy than more masculine faces. Todorov's theory about this is that infants prefer the face of their caregivers (and by extension faces similar to those of their caregivers), who are more likely to be women. In addition, women are more likely to be coddling, and tend to display positive expressions. That, he tells me, is why a smiling, feminine kind of face would be more familiar for most infants, and that's how they wrote the instructions for the computer-generated images they used in their research.

*

How and why we deem someone worthy of our trust is worth a closer inspection. Often we think of trust as a conscious attitude towards another person, group or organisation.

Trust guides how we engage with our environment, playing an important role in our day-to-day and long-term decision-making. It influences when we decide to question something or someone and when we do not. It helps form relationships with others. Crucially, it helps build and strengthen cooperation, which is critical for social and economic progress. In a functioning society, institutions are trusted every day to keep their obligations, even if we are not present to monitor their actions. Trust is essential to a democracy.

To trust is to set aside questioning, deliberation, monitoring or challenging and to allow others to proceed without further checks. It also means being willing to run the risk of being vulnerable. Much as I have made the case for stepping up our sleuthing skills and questioning more, the truth is that no amount of critical thinking will protect us entirely from heartache, betrayal or disappointment. We know this because we do not and never will have absolute intellectual autonomy, simply for the fact that we depend on and need each other. We are not completely powerless against hurtful incidences in our lives – but we can minimise their frequency through critical thinking. Because when done well, critical thinking makes us more precise and more able to determine when and whether to question someone or something. Understanding the nature of trust, how it's formed and its various types is essential. And knowing how we decide to trust – specifically, being aware of our own motivations – can help us both avoid placing trust where it is not deserved, and not trusting where we should.

So, why are you reading about trust in a book on how to think like a poker player? Think about trust for a moment. How would you define it? Personally, I would distil it down to the following:

trust is a sort of expectancy about a future behaviour. So, with that in mind, if our process of trusting is flawed, then the outcomes we believe we will get will not match our expectation. If pushed, I'd go as far as categorising trust into two parts – trust in oneself and one's judgement, and trust in the future behaviour of another. This comes into play at the poker tables all the time. Not only do you need to be able to trust yourself and your reads, but you also need to understand that there are forms of trust present that you aren't in full control of: when it comes to assessing your opponents, various trust mechanisms are at work in your subconscious – be they in the form of first impressions or intragroup kinship. And when a betrayal of trust comes from your own community, it can be particularly devastating.

In 2008, the Jewish community in the US was in anguish over the news that one of their own had destroyed the lives of thousands of people by lying, cheating and fraud. A Jew had betrayed the trust of Jews and violated the basic tenets of Jewish law. American financier Bernie Madoff had ruined thousands of people by running the largest Ponzi scheme in history. By promising large returns for their investments, he scammed people out of 20 billion dollars, paying off old investors with money obtained from new ones. Over the course of seventeen years he defrauded anyone who would entrust him with money, including not just charities, but also close friends and family.

Madoff's actions were seen as a betrayal of the highest form, a violation of trust. One rabbi told *The New York Times*: 'He really undermined the fabric of the Jewish community, because it's built on trust. There is a wonderful rabbinic saying, often misapplied, that all Jews are sureties for one another, which means, for instance, that if a Jew takes a loan out, in some ways the whole Jewish community guarantees it.'

When we need to put our trust in people whose track record is unknown, or with whom we have never previously dealt, we tend to look for other information that can guide us to make a decision – such as group identity. Even, as Lisa DeBruine at the University of Glasgow found out, people who just look a bit like us. In one of her studies, DeBruine used software to morph faces to look increasingly (or decreasingly) like a study participant's face. The result: the greater the similarity, the more the participant trusted the person in the image.

Research suggests that intragroup, or community-based, economic behavioural decision-making is in all of us. So it pays to be aware of our own biases about a group or community (be it our own or an external one) as they can support or undermine social trust and thereby influence our decision-making.

In 2011, nearly 300 people took part in a two-part study which tested and scored their implicit (unconscious) race attitude and then asked them to play a trust game. In the game they were asked to give some, all or no money to the other participants. Individuals whose score reflected an implicit a pro-white bias were likely to judge white faces as more trustworthy than black faces, and vice versa. And how much each person gave to the other participants correlated directly with their implicit bias score. Individuals whose scores reflected a stronger pro-white implicit bias were likely to offer more money to white partners than black partners, and vice versa. The study showed that we tend to trust people within a group that we implicitly, unconsciously, favour – regardless of our explicit conscious beliefs. What also emerges from this study is that whom we trust isn't necessarily only a measure of their perceived trustworthiness, it is a reflection of who we are.

When we look at faces, we don't just see faces – we give them meaning, projecting our own assumptions onto them. What gives them meaning are our biases, which influence who we like or dislike, who we believe is happy or not, and who we believe we can trust or not. And this doesn't just come down to conditioning through environmental exposure.

It seems impossible to think that people can correctly identify race in less than 50 milliseconds of exposure to a photograph, yet a study has shown that we do so over half the time. There is no escaping the many categorisations we organise our society into. It's how we make sense of the world. And these categorisations can cause problems when it comes to gender, race, group and culture, for example. Here, even the most liberal and socially aware are prone to thinking in categorisations – because none of us is completely in control of the way we categorise people.

Some of this relates to the functioning of the amygdala. A small cluster of cells tucked deep inside the brain, the amygdala is known to be involved in processing fearful notions, identifying threats and sending signals to other parts of the brain that trigger fight or flight reflexes. Its function has been studied extensively in relation to its function with regards to racial attitudes, beliefs, social decision-making and judgements of trust.

It would be an absolute boon to be able to tell if a stranger is trustworthy just by looking at their face. We know this is not possible, yet appearances still matter to us.

When it comes to sussing out competence and ability by looks, humans aren't that different to animals. The courtship displays in the animal kingdom are loaded with signals to show the other sex that they are a suitable mate, and it's often the case that the males are the flamboyant sex. Take peacocks. When they want to attract peahens, they put on a display. Literally. And peahens have to figure out which of the fancy posers will make a good match and yield good children. Flamingos apply make-up (strictly speaking, this is oil that both male and female flamingos dab into their feathers). This has two messages for the opposite sex: 'Hey, I'm gorgeous and our children will be too. Come and get me' is one. And the deeper the pink the more powerful the bird will look. Researchers have also found that the pinkest flamingos are the toughest; the colour of their feathers demonstrates their efficiency in feeding and dominance at foraging sites. In the animal world, then, signalling is just another word for sharing information.

There is no doubt about it: looks matter. In the human world the judging of suitability and competence by looks is perhaps most aggressively seen online. Every day millions and millions of people pass judgement upon appearance and they do so intentionally. Dating apps are a cesspool for snap judgements of character and background. There is a certain cruelty in the way app users swiping left dismiss potential matches on looks alone. In 2022, the online dating app Tinder boasted over 75 million active users in the USA alone. The app, a self-representation platform, allows each user to post up to six photographs of themselves. Users then choose or discard potential romantic partners by using the app's see-and-swipe mode. There is such an abundance of choice that users rely on first impressions and snap judgements to determine whether they should swipe left (no interest), right (interest), or up (Super Like). What apps like Tinder illustrate is that dating methods have evolved at warp speed, but our ability to make split-second judgements is yet to catch up. Yet, in essence, they trigger much the same decision-making process as print ads or even who you choose to chat up at a bar – using our visual preconceptions about what we believe to be desirable in an ideal partner. Just as animals change their looks to appear more desirable, so do we humans. We sometimes use technology to do so.

The impressions we make can be manipulated by the highly sophisticated photo-editing apps that are now available on most smartphones. A few clicks and taps and we can give ourselves brighter eyes, blemish-free skin and sparkly white teeth. It's still us, of course, just a slightly tweaked version of us, which is perhaps more aspirational than representative of the truth.

Scientists have shown that very subtle differences in images of the same person are sufficient to evoke very different impressions. Changes in lighting will induce different impressions. Without distorting the shape of the face, a mere change in the appearance of the skin surface is enough to manipulate our impressions.

In a study run by Todorov, participants were asked to choose the image that most fitted a particular situation. From a line-up, participants picked pictures of the person they thought most suitable for a small town's local mayoral campaign, for an application for a highly paid consulting job, or simply for posting on Facebook. Clear choices emerged, as did the observation that a biased selection of images led to biased decisions.

David Perrett at the University of St Andrews in Scotland has built on Todorov's work, focusing on one small aspect that turns out to have a profound effect on apparent trustworthiness and perceived dominance. In a study he published in 2020, the data showed that a slight tilt of the head (30 degrees up or 20 degrees down) can alter our perceptions drastically. A head tilt in either direction leads to more negative judgements (less trustworthy and more dominant) than head-level posture. How can a head tilt affect our impression in such a significant way? We should blame our visual system, says Perrett. We tend to think of it as excellent, but it's not. It's actually very poor at estimating the three-dimensional shape of things. He tells me that if you lower your head, tilting your forehead forward, then corners of your mouth will tend to curl upwards and make you look like you're smiling. It's a failure of our three-dimensional vision, a misread. As you change your head posture, your apparent expression changes, even though you might be emotionally neutral the whole time. And it's this apparent expression that counts for everything. 'That's what the point of our article was, to show the power of the apparent expression. And unfortunately, it's driven by the negative aspects of expression. Any part of your face that looks a bit hostile, that's the part we will pay attention to,' Perrett tells me.

So judging a person's character based on first impressions, especially seeing how much impressions can vary when presented with different images of the same person, is hardly accurate. Yet it happens all the time and not without consequences.

A number of studies suggest that politicians who 'look the part' are more successful in elections. In 2010, a group of investigators from MIT showed evidence not just for appearance-based voting but also that judging unfamiliar individuals based on their appearance is a cross-cultural phenomenon. To demonstrate this, they used black and white photographs from political candidates in two countries where electoral behavior has been the subject of extensive research: Mexico and Brazil. Studying real voters, the researchers found that appearance is indeed a powerful arbiter of a candidate's success, no matter the type of election – so much so, in fact, that in some political races looks can account for almost as much influence over candidates' electoral prospects as the strength of the party they represent or their policies. The researchers were surprised to find that despite cultural, ethnic and racial differences, judgements on appearance appear to be universal, as US and Indian study participants responded to the same superficial features of candidates as citizens from Mexico and Brazil did in actual elections. What stood out was the behaviour of voters who knew next to nothing about the candidates or their ideologies: these voters relied on shortcuts, casting their votes based on hunches, gut feelings and stereotypes. Some undecided and swing voters were part of this group of appearance-influenced voters.

We might be tempted to pour scorn on the voters who made their decisions on looks alone, but we should acknowledge we are all 'cognitive misers', and that we constantly reach for shortcuts in our own decision-making.

When we have only an image of a face and no information about it, our brains immediately make assumptions that shape how we see the person it belongs to. In turn, information about faces shapes not only how we *see* images but how we *create* them.

That's why being aware of our tendency towards 'gut instincts' and our own specific biases can benefit our own decision-making.

Using first impressions to predict behaviour really isn't a winning strategy. A more efficient method is to gather facts and knowledge from the parts of the body that transmit information you can rely on and really can trust. Here, too, we can learn from the poker tables.

Good players will observe their opponents' behaviour and try to interpret what it is communicating. Because most of our behaviour happens subconsciously and automatically, the chances are that opponents are giving away free information. Take gesturing, for instance. We develop this behaviour as babies way before we learn to speak. With arms stretched out for a cuddle or pointing at a toy we want to play with, we let our parents or carers know what we want. We don't lose our gestures as we learn to use language to convey our needs. We keep them to accompany our speech. Gestures appear to be an integral part of the speaking process and are not restricted to the use of hands, but often include movements of the head or even of the whole body, as well as postures. What's so important here is that this behaviour isn't learnt by watching others. Congenitally blind speakers gesture despite their lack of a visual model, even when speaking to a blind listener. So gestures are anything but random. They are a strong component of our nonverbal communication. We gesture without consciously thinking – automatically.

Non-verbal signs have to be considered and analysed in context if we want to decode them. Most of us are no better than chance at detecting deception. When we do encounter inconsistencies between what we hear and what we see, we need to ask 'Why?' rather than immediately assuming that we have been deliberately deceived. The problem is that we are very quick to jump to conclusions, and at times this happens without our conscious awareness. Need convincing? Let a spy-catcher tell you why there is no single failsafe method of spotting liars and detecting lies.

Meeting body language expert Joe Navarro is intimidating, even if I am doing it via Skype and he in his study in Florida with an entire ocean between us. It may have been sixteen years since he left the FBI, but he is still every bit the agent. I find this out within minutes of our call beginning. He tells me the number of times I have blinked in the past 30 seconds and that I keep looking to my right, suggesting to him that there might be another person in the room. The window in my study is to my right and looks straight out at a giant eucalyptus tree. On windy days, the rustling of the leaves has a soothing and calming effect on me and I often stare out at it, lost in thought. I realised then that in my nervousness I had subconsciously been glancing over to my giant green pacifier, and Navarro had picked up on it. I turn the camera to show him no one else is in the room and that it was my friend the tree that I was glancing at. We continue with the interview. (A few days later he will email me a link to an article reporting on a small study on how glancing at a plant on their desks helped reduce stress levels in office workers.)

Navarro prefers not to speak about his time growing up. After all these years, the memories still seem to pain him. In my prep for our call, I found out that when he was nine years old his family had fled Cuba and the Castro regime. Fitting in and adapting to their new life in Florida was challenging. The family was mocked for the way that they pronounced certain words, and Navarro realised that to truly fit in he had to lose his accent – and not just in his speech, but his body language too:

'I could tell, for example, when people were being polite with their face, but not being polite with their feet. If you're engaging someone in a conversation, glance at their feet. If they want to get into a conversation, they'll turn their feet towards yours, otherwise they won't. That's "the inclusiveness factor". It helped me to understand if people were genuine.'

Navarro spent 25 years at the Bureau and conducted over 13,000 interrogations. When he left the FBI, Navarro turned to consulting, which occasionally involved TV work. In the spring of 2004, on the set of the Discovery Channel show *More Than Human*, he met Annie Duke, then a professional poker player. They were two of three people the channel had asked to appear on an episode featuring people whose living depended on detecting lies. These three (the third was a psychic) would be pitted against lie detector machines (polygraphs). Each of them was to observe the show's host answering 25 questions, some truthfully and some with lies. The three humans' accuracy in identifying the true versus the false answers, was compared against the success of three lie detection machines: a polygraph, a machine that detects changes in the voice, and a machine that detects pupil dilation. The psychic (perhaps unsurprisingly) was right less than half of the time, but Duke and Navarro tied in their observations, assessing eighteen out of twenty-five answers correctly.

Over the two days of filming, Duke (who has a degree in cognitive psychology) and Navarro spent a lot of time talking. They bonded over the subject of non-verbals and psychology, because at the poker table it is particularly useful to pay attention to a player's body language.

An abundance of cues can help determine whether your opponent at the table has you beat or is trying to bluff you out of a pot. It could be anything from how they lean back or forward (interested in the action), put their hand to their face or how they handle their cards. When they pull the cards towards them it means they liked what they saw, and the opposite tends to be true, too. Players who push their cards away and closer to the muck (the discard pile) are likely to fold them.

Duke, back then known in the poker world as 'The Duchess of Poker', left the Discovery set a friend richer and with her mind somewhat blown. 'I thought I knew how to recognise these physical reactions as symptoms of lying, but Mr Navarro showed me what a neophyte I was in this department.' She went back home and read everything Navarro had written on non-verbal behaviour. In an article a year later, she credits his insights for elevating her poker game to the next level. Because until then, the poker world only ever looked for tells by focusing on the face.

Duke shared Navarro's articles with another poker pro, Phil Hellmuth – one of the most famous players in the poker world, with nine WSOP (World Series of Poker) bracelets to his name at the time (in 2023 that total is now seventeen). Hellmuth was about to start a WSOP academy and wanted Navarro to come and teach there.

In Vegas, the first of the WSOP academy events was attended by a host of successful professional poker players. At one point during his talk, Navarro looked out at the people in the front row and noticed that every single one was taking notes. He wondered how they could play poker and not know about the thumbs, the fingers, the legs? How much money had they lost because all they had thought about was the face?

Professional poker players are known for keeping their expressions in check and revealing little to nothing on their faces (which is where the idea of a poker face seems to have come from), but often players are unaware that they are leaking information from elsewhere. Every body movement (or lack of one, for that matter) can reveal information. Arm motion itself can be a tell. How players place their bets and handle their chips can reveal quite a bit. Watching poker, you will see a whole array of actions: from tossing chips, to lifting them off the felt, to place them into the pot or simply sliding a stack forward – and each of those move-ments can vary in its style and flourishes. The point is, you can't have a poker body. Even people who have no knowledge of poker can pick up on body tells.

To prove this, 78 people who knew little to nothing about poker were shown several silent clips of professional players placing bets at the World Series of Poker in 2009. They were asked to make a judgement on each poker hand, without knowing the number of chips wagered or the individual value of various chips. The participants were divided up into three groups. One watched unaltered clips where the player was fully visible (arm movements plus face), another watched edited clips in which only the player's face was visible, and the third group watched chest-down close-ups of arm movements only. The results showed that the predictions of the face-only group were slightly worse than chance (suggesting that pro players do indeed have a poker face); judgements where both face and body were visible were about 50% accurate; but the arm-movement-only group did statistically significantly better at determining the strength of the hand.

By now, you know that the key to deciphering non-verbals is observation. That's not merely looking around. It is actively taking mental notes. It requires training, but in a world where our attention is constantly split many ways, active observation often takes a backseat. When you walk into a new room, do you check where the emergency exits are? When leaving a meeting do you check your phone immediately and perhaps miss someone approaching you as you walk out? Being a good observer means paying attention to what others think, feel or intend for us. It can help us identify their intentions or their next step. It can help protect and safeguard us from those who are selfish or cruel. If we can see and pick up on the negative cues from others, we can prevent ourselves from being hurt or disappointed. If we don't, we run the risk of being exploited by someone who is not acting in our best interests.

Navarro has written fourteen books on body language. His bestselling *What Every Body Is Saying* has sold millions of copies and has been translated into 29 languages. And he has some advice for us. In many ways, he is echoing the fundamentals of critical thinking when he tells me that no one single behaviour is indicative of deception. To reach the true meaning of a behaviour we must dig deeper and ask more questions. If we detect discomfort, issues, anxiety or tension then we know that something isn't quite right. What we don't know is what or why. We need to see and assess these actions in context. Only by using clusters of non-verbal signals can we infer information to help us accurately assess a given situation and avoid falling prey to misinformation and body language myths – and there are plenty of those.

Body Language Myths

Actions such as nose-touching, mouth-covering, eye-closing, and speaking with a high-pitched voice, for example, are often mistaken as signs of deception. Yet most of the time they indicate something else: pacifiers that calm us and help to relieve stress – just like when my gaze kept flicking from my screen to the giant eucalyptus tree outside my window. Another body language myth is the common interpretation of the folding or crossing of your arms. No, it doesn't always mean you're defensive and uncooperative. Often it's just a self-hug and, yes, again a method you use subconsciously to calm, comfort or soothe yourself. Another reason why crossing or folding arms isn't necessarily about blocking others out is that it can also be used to restrain ourselves or unconsciously signal frustration. 'No question about it, we use our crossed arms when we are upset, but this is mostly as a form of self-restraint and, again, to comfort ourselves. Children do it all the time,' says Navarro. Then there is a prevalent myth about eye aversion being an indication of lying. This can be true, but often is not: looking away can mean that we need to cut the stimuli and help the brain focus. Interpersonal gazes are a very powerful stimulus. And when you're thinking hard, you need to cut down stimulation. When we are driving around lost, and the kids are in the back yelling and screaming, what do we all do? We tell them to be quiet because we need to concentrate, to cut down the stimulation. So looking away is not necessarily a sign of lying or dishonesty – it might be just to help us focus.

Most people assume non-verbal communication is the same across all cultures. Not so. We may be knitted together ever closer, but our cultural differences still remain – so we need to understand them. Eye contact/aversion is one area where researchers have found cultural variations. In some Caribbean cultures, for example, meeting another's eyes can be perceived as rude or aggressive.

Nor are all smiles the same. While Americans smile readily, cultural expectations strongly discourage Russians from doing so in public; once they know you better, they loosen their emotional control and crack a smile. Japanese people will sometimes smile even if what they really feel is disgust, sadness or anger. In this instance, the discrepancy between their behaviour and what they are feeling results from something researchers refer to as *cultural display rules*. And it would be remiss of me not to mention cultures where smiling at a stranger amounts to a sexual proposition, or inversely the 'Cheer up, love' convention in Britain, whereby all women must smile nicely when out in public (I have lost count of how many times I've been told this at a poker table).

One of the first studies on how culture-specific rules can influence where, when and sometimes how experienced emotion may be expressed was provided in 1972 by Wallace Verne Friesen, then at the University of California in San Francisco. He recorded the spontaneous expressions of 25 Japanese and 25 Americans while they were watching highly stressful films. Two scenarios were staged. In the first scenario, the participants were viewing the films by themselves. In the second instance an older, seemingly higher-status experimenter came into the room and asked the participants to watch the films one more time, with the experimenter sitting opposite and taking notes. Americans displayed negative expressions in both scenarios. The Japanese participants were different. They displayed sadness, anger, fear and disgust in the first scenario, just as the Americans had, but with the experimenter present, they forced themselves to smile in order to avoid offending the experimenter. This is a behaviour reflective of cultural display rules.

Collaboration and Collective Behaviour

What these examples illustrate is that non-verbal behaviour needs to be observed in context, especially when cultural differences might be in play. Consideration of what other aspects could be influencing a particular behaviour should be a routine check in your mind. We simply cannot ignore the fact that we are connected to each other; our behaviours, feelings and thoughts are influenced by others as much as others are influenced by us. So we must recognise the dangers of superimposing our own cultural norms and expectations onto the behaviours of others. After all, our success and survival depends on how successfully we collaborate with one another and that depends a lot on how well we communicate with one another. Since over three-quarters of our communication is non-verbal, understanding behaviour is crucial – especially in this culturally diverse world.

While our species perceives the world through our own uniquely tuned assortment of senses with our own uniquely charted evolutionary history in our own unique environment, our behaviour is built on an evolutionary scaffold. And since there is a human–animal link in every area of our behaviour, from cooperation and collaboration to selfishness and deception, a true understanding of our frailties, faults and foibles has to recognise our primate proclivities.

We are, after all, a lot like apes and monkeys. Humans – just like our primate relatives – are intensely social. Take away our ability to get together and socialise with one another and we end up with humans who are stressed because loneliness is tough to deal with. Even before Covid-19 deprived huge areas of the world of social interaction, the World Health Organization (WHO) had that same year declared loneliness as a major health concern worldwide. When the pandemic hit, there were fears of reduced productivity, but these have subsequently been proven to be largely unfounded. People have shown they can absolutely run projects from their kitchen tables, living-room sofas and spare bedrooms. The downsides of the pandemic were not so much to do with our working lives, but our emotional ones. Human beings need each other.

Studies have shown that people with a strong network of friends are less likely to become ill, and that when they do fall ill, they recover faster. They also recover quicker from surgery and live longer. In short, the higher our social net worth the larger the positive impact on our physical and mental health. We are social animals. We need the many everyday interactions that involve touch, such as handshakes and kisses hello, or the more emotionally rich gestures like hugs and caresses.

India Morrison at Linköping University in Sweden studies how social touch influences emotion, motivation and behaviour. Morrison aims to map what happens in the brain and body when someone is hugged or touched on the arm, for example, and how these tactile interactions can act as a so-called stress-buffer.

We have seen that non-verbal behaviour is complex and needs

to be cross-checked and validated through context. A place where we can find some universal non-verbal communication is in the natural expression of emotions in the face. The strong reliability of these cues has even led to an entirely new field that is teaching machines about human emotions.

Affective computing is the study and development of systems and devices that can recognise, interpret, process and simulate human affects, built on the fundamental understanding that solid indicators of information are found on the face. In other words, making machines that can read and understand your emotions. And if we can teach machines to become better at understanding human emotions, then there is no reason why we can't be better, too.

Understanding and being able to regulate emotions can help us stay logical and reasonable. Reading and correctly interpreting emotional cues leads to better decision-making. Just as we have linked trust with betrayal, a similarly knee-jerk link exists between 'emotion' and the term 'weakness'. Emotion on its own isn't weakness, but the failure to acknowledge and then manage it is. When we can't control emotions, we are unable to use our rational and logical thinking, so this understanding is an important asset in our life skills toolbox. And if you want a crash course in developing this skill, then come and take a seat at a poker table.

Recognising Emotions, Within Yourself and Others

'What's a pretty girl like you doing in a place like this?' Any other time this might be perceived as just a mediocre chat-up line. Not in the poker room. Here, it's a deliberately poorly veiled accusation. When I hear those words, I know the speaker wants me gone from the tables as soon as possible. The gloves are off. A battle is on.

The first time a male player took a swipe at me for having the audacity to be female and sit at a poker table was even less disguised and a lot more aggressive. It's a hard memory to forget even after all these years.

It was sometime in early 2014, and I had only started learning to play poker a few weeks before. It was just my third time playing live in a real poker room, which is perhaps why this particular scene is so firmly branded into my mind. The avalanche of emotions I felt when he came for me had such an impact that I still remember exactly what he looked like.

He was wearing a military-style camouflage T-shirt underneath a dark grey hoodie that was unzipped halfway, accessorised with a wide gold chain worn to set off his neck tattoo – a name in script I couldn't make out. His thick brown hair, laden with gel, looked wet and greasy. Every time he was involved in a hand with me, he leant over the black faux-leather padded table edge and into the poker table. His eyes locked on to my face with a smirk, posturing like a jackal ready to pounce and devour its prey. It may only have been my third time in a poker room, but this type exists beyond the poker tables and I'd seen it before.

Guys like him – entitled, chauvinist, territorial and openly misogynistic – are exactly the type of player that drew me to poker in the first place. It is a heavily male-dominated game. But the thing is, I have spent my life proving that my gender doesn't define or inhibit my abilities and skills. If anything or anyone wants to exclude me based on my gender, I want to prove them wrong. Poker provides a perfect environment to do exactly that, because the cards are gender blind. So what the misogynist sitting opposite me did not realise was that I was ready to fight.

By the time Tattoo Neck had lost the third hand to me, the smirk had vanished from his face. Now the jackal was growling. Taking a swig from his beer, he looked across the table and asked me: 'Why are you here on a Friday night?'

He didn't wait for an answer.

'Is your husband boring you?'

I hadn't exchanged a word with him thus far, but he'd gathered I was married from the wedding and engagement rings on my left hand. I looked up, but before I could reply, his smirk was back: 'I'll take care of you.' With that he leant back in his chair, pushed away from the table and spread his legs.

At this I felt the blood rush to my head, my heart pounding through my chest and my hands trembling (I quickly moved them off the table, and sat on them to steady myself). Rage burned inside me, and no support seemed forthcoming.

I was sitting directly opposite the dealer, who avoided eye contact. I looked around the table and a couple of players shook their heads as if to say: 'Don't let it bother you.' No one said a word. I felt exposed, vulnerable and alone. I hadn't before but now I actually did feel like prey. I had to control every single fibre of my body to make sure the jackal could not see I was wounded and in pain. I looked him straight back in the eyes, forced a smile and made sure I spoke in a calm, slow manner when I said: 'I'm here to play poker. So let's do that, shall we?' He let out a grunt, but now I was the one not allowing him to answer: 'And as for my awesome husband, he told me to come here, take all of your chips . . .' with this I pointed around the entire table '. . . and win!' He laughed. He didn't an hour later when I was the one who kicked him out of the tournament by taking his last few chips. Even though I didn't win the tournament that night, I still went home feeling like a winner.

Only 6% of players in live tournaments are female, according to the Global Poker Index. So more often than not, a woman will be alone at an otherwise all-male table. Women are mostly considered to be weaker players and labelled 'too emotional' for the game. In 2017, Dan Bilzerian, a player with millions of followers on social media, told the poker pro Cate Hall in a now-deleted tweet that: 'I want to bet against you because you are a woman and women can't play poker.'

Women are assumed to be less able to cope with tense situations and expected to display 'unnecessary' or 'inappropriate' behaviours because they are thought of as less able to control their emotions. They are also regarded as tight players, meaning that they won't make big, risky plays. Male players use this as a reason to attack. The belief that women are more emotional than men remains one of the strongest gender stereotypes. But the evidence is that this is a misconception.

In 2021 researchers from the University of Michigan and Purdue University studied 142 men and women and assessed them daily for 75 days. Every night, they sent the study participants an approximately 20-minute online survey to assess their emotional state. The researchers were focused on overall variation of emotion – regardless of type or trigger – and whether it systematically differed in men and women, including women in different hormonal states. The lead researcher, Adriene Beltz, explained that they made sure women with 'natural menstrual cycles' and women with a variety of oral contraceptives were included in the study '. . . to explicitly address the notion that women are more emotionally variable – or liable – due to varying hormone levels across their cycles.' What they found is that the emotional fluctuations of men and women are consistently and unmistakably more similar than they are different.

In patriarchal societies, boys are still overwhelmingly told not to cry and are conditioned to tamp down any expression of distress because it's considered a sign of weakness, thus perpetuating the idea that boys are strong and courageous and girls are vulnerable and weak. Not allowing men and boys to cry freely and express their true emotions is just as unfair as it is to prejudge women on their ability to handle tough tasks and challenging situations.

Indeed, there is also evidence that if the conditions were set the same for women as they are for men, the likelihood is that women would take the same risks. It's also important to note that there is a race and class element to the way we assess risk-taking, which tends to be disproportionately rewarded in high-status individuals and unduly punished in low-status ones.

Susan Fisk is a sociologist and associate professor at Kent State University in Ohio. She studies the mechanisms that create gendered inequalities in the economy and works on creating interventions to disrupt them. Fisk tries to identify and understand processes through which broad, macro-level stereotypes about women and men create micro-level gender inequalities in the labour force that in turn reinforce the macro-level gender disparities and stereotypes.

(It's worth clarifying that while so many of us use the terms 'sex' and 'gender' interchangeably, they have two clearly separate functions. The term 'sex' refers to individual biological attributes including sex-related chromosomes, genitalia and hormones; 'gender' refers to social and cultural experiences associated with identifying as female, male or non-binary.)

Most recently, Fisk has been examining risk: the social sanctioning of risk-taking women, the gendered nature of risky decision-making contexts, and how gender differences in risk-taking behaviour can lead to more men at the top of hierarchies. She conducted a study in 2016 in which she proposed that women may rationally choose to take fewer risks, given that risk-taking is less rewarding for them. She hypothesised that gender stereotypes may cause institutional gatekeepers to give women fewer opportunities to take risks. Three years later she deepened that research and looked at whether anticipated gender discrimination – specifically, gendered sanctions for leadership failure – decreased women's desire to go for management and director positions. In her study from 2019, 'Who Wants to Lead? Anticipated Gender Discrimination Reduces Women's Leadership Ambitions', she provided evidence for it.

According to data compiled by Pew Research in 2019, women constitute only 5% of Fortune 500 CEOs, 24% of members of the 115th US Congress, and 30% of college and university presidents. Are women less ambitious than men? Do they not want to lead? There are certainly disincentives. Leadership continues to be seen as a male task and women are punished more severely for their failures than men. More, a woman's failure in male-typed tasks is more likely than a man's to be attributed to low ability rather than to bad luck. This depresses their ambitions for leadership roles.

Fisk concludes that gendered sanctions for leadership failure mean that women leaders have more to lose than otherwise similar men. So these societal reward structures not only create boundaries for ambition, they also have a knock-on effect on women's risk-taking behaviour. Her study highlights that for a woman to go for a leadership position is seen as a form of risk-taking behaviour in itself, because of the sanctions that come when women fail. Women's 'unwillingness' to take risks, she suggests, may actually be a rational response to social contexts in which boundaries and sanctions affect their risk-taking behaviour. (A similar dynamic is happening at the race and class intersectional; it's the same mechanism and the underlying mover is power, or the lack of it.)

And no, it's not all in the mind. It has long been assumed that female/male differences in emotional behaviour were down to female/male brain differences. That female brains were 'wired' differently, with the emotional control centres more likely to be activated in many different situations, including risk-taking. But this argument is undermined by two recent conclusions, says Gina Rippon, professor emeritus of cognitive neuroimaging at the Aston University Brain Centre in Birmingham in the UK. Having spent decades studying the brain, she tells me that there isn't any consistent evidence of brain differences between the sexes.

She points me to a recent survey by Lise Eliot and her team in Chicago. They have reviewed 30 years of brain-imaging findings and concluded that there is no such thing as a female brain (or, by default, a male brain). Men are not from Mars, nor women from Venus; we are all from Earth!

Rippon has a hypothesis she shares with me: could all of our beliefs about sex differences in the brain persist simply because they were established long before we could actually study the human brain, other than when it was damaged or dead? I find some answers to her question in a book published in 2017 called *Inferior*, where science writer Angela Saini meticulously researches and then dismantles the scientific studies on which so many of our misperceptions about gender are based. Most of these studies were conducted by men who sought to confirm existing biases. And those biases go back deep into history. Saini writes about Ancient Mesopotamia (today Syria, Iraq, Kuwait and parts of Turkey), which had a strong emphasis on virginity and women covering their heads in public. Throughout recorded history, in fact, virginity and fidelity have not only been celebrated as female virtues, but have also been rigorously policed. The Mayans believed there to be a terrifying demon that took and raped women who behaved indecently. In Ancient Greece, too, women were taught to dress appropriately and lower their eyes when in the presence of men. The shadow cast over women has never really gone away, and thousands of years later we are still living with these ideas about women and their expected behaviour. It is ingrained into our society and how we see ourselves, so much so that societies continue to punish women who breach these standards.

But, as Rippon has pointed out, we now know that brains, and hence behaviour, can be moulded by experiences, attitudes and expectations – brains can be 'gendered'. So if there is an expectation that women are not risk-takers (which women themselves may also believe) then they (and their brains) will be channelled away from risky situations and risky experiences.

I grew up proving that my gender doesn't define my skills and abilities. Today, I want to instil in my daughter a mindset that has her see a world full of possibility rather than one with socially constructed limitations based on her gender. My husband and I want to normalise what some would consider breaching gender norms. Can boys wear nail varnish? Sure they can. They can also most definitely wear dresses and have long hair. In a world that still mostly sees girls and women as inferior to men, as parents we want to empower our child with the knowledge that her ability isn't gendered and that skills can be learnt, no matter your sex.

And, no differently from any other parents, we want to protect our child from those who wish her harm. While early martial arts classes have taught her how to physically defend herself, to land a punch following a flying kick, we know that the most insidious and hurtful attacks will creep up on her from within herself. Helping her nurture a strong mind means teaching her to understand and control her emotions. It means teaching her how to lose, and how to cope with failure.

But just how *do* you teach an eight-year-old to control her emotions? Like most other things that you teach children, you do it through playing (zero sum) games. Teaching our daughter how to play poker when she was just four years old was a natural development. Arguably, no other game teaches emotional discipline better than poker. It also teaches you to sit down at any table with confidence and be able to take on any opponent, all the while keeping a cool head.

What Are Emotions?

An emotion is not a mood. Emotions are quick and at most last a few minutes, whereas moods can last for hours or days. Emotions are also not feelings, although feelings can be part of them. Emotions are more active in that they often result in an immediate behavioural response, and include physiological reactions to events that have consequences for our wellbeing: your emotional response to drinking sour milk is that of disgust, which leads you to feel, and then be sick. Being sad can increase or decrease our heart rate and skin conductance level, depending on the cause (failure or loss). Emotions guide us. They are functional. When they are triggered, we use them to assess events and surroundings, and we look to them for clues about what may or may not be harmful to us. Emotions describe our relationship to the event that triggered them, and communicate our states and intentions to those around us.

Emotion is key to how we form relationships and bonds. Research shows that the survival of a species depends on bonding, and much of this bonding is enabled by emotion. Humans (and animals) signal intent with emotion. Vital ingredients of intelligent perception, emotions tell humans what to pay attention to, what to ignore, and how to interact with each other. And yet being openly emotional is still generally considered a sign of weakness. Some scholars go as far as saying that emotion undermines the sovereignty of reason. They aren't entirely wrong.

Emotions do influence decision-making. They are critical to our thinking and behaviour. One study showed that people in a positive state of mind overestimate the likelihood of positive events and underestimate that of negative events. People also rely on their affective states as a source of information regarding the global status of their environment. Elections have been won (or lost, for that matter) by the ability of parties to tap into voter emotions and exploit them for political gain. From advertising to politics, our emotions are constantly being manipulated. Knowing when we are being coerced and when we are facing inauthenticity can mean the difference between winning or losing, so the ability to recognise, then read and understand emotions is key to our way of being. By learning how we and others are affected by emotions, we can start recognising and managing them. Rather than wait until kids have meltdowns, marriages fall apart or elections are lost, we must learn to identify emotions better. This can be hard.

An emotionally intelligent decision can be difficult to make when you'd prefer to do the opposite. It takes focused discipline to acquire the high level of self-awareness to know how you're feeling during times of stress. Staying open to another person's anger when it's directed at you without becoming defensive in turn requires self-discipline, and in this increasingly polarised world it's going to take a lot of courage, too.

The evidence is clear: the better we understand each other, the better we do as a collective. When we try to make sense of one another we do so by reaching for a variety of cues to help us decode what we're seeing and hearing. The first place we tend to look for clues is in spoken language. But as we now know, non-verbal communication is just as much of a language and often carries a lot more information than spoken words.

Think about travelling in a country where we do not speak the lingo – when we have to communicate, we look for clues in non-verbal behaviours in the face, body, gestures and even tone of voice. But there's a barrier here. As we have learnt, non-verbal behaviour is complex and differs from culture to culture. Yet most people assume that non-verbal behaviours are universal. And while our assessments will be more accurate within our family and social circle, in an unfamiliar environment where we do not know the person(s) we are often unable to go beyond inferring a certain base level of emotion. We are likely to miss the nuances that are in play. So it makes sense to be a little more generous when it comes to people outside our familiar in-group.

When we find ourselves in unknown social settings, particularly if they are culturally different, it pays to learn about the emotional triggers and norms for that community. This is key, because culture shapes emotion. Anthropologist Jean Briggs learnt this the hard way.

Cultural Differences in Unknown Territories

In the mid-1960s, a particular spot in the northwest of Hudson Bay was a destination for sports fishermen from all over Canada and the United States. Every year in July and August, charter planes would fly in small groups of men (yes, men) for short fishing expeditions to fish for Arctic char and salmon trout in the rapids. The tourist fishermen would camp across the river from a small Inuit tribe of 20 to 25 called the Utku – the sole inhabitants of an area of 35,000 square miles. Contact between the outside world and the Utku had always been rare, and the two groups mostly kept to themselves. Occasionally the Inuits would trade small toys they had crafted out of bones in exchange for tobacco, tea and fishhooks – using mostly sign language. In 1964, the trades increased both in frequency and demand from the fishermen. For the first time they could communicate more directly, because there was a bilingual tribe member among the Utku who would act as a mediator between the two groups: a 34-year-old Canadian woman, Jean Briggs, a PhD student from Harvard University.

Like other anthropologists of her time, Briggs was in search of an exotic world. In the summer of 1963, she went to the Canadian Northwest Territories (later divided into Northwest Territories and Nunavut) to start her field study of a small group of Inuits in a place so remote that for months the tribe would not encounter any other human being. It was '. . . the most remote island I could find on the map,' she recounted during a lecture some 30 years later. Her study of Inuit emotional behaviour would become a pioneering piece of work. She would also be the first to analyse the Inuits' terms (words) and speak about their relationships with one another. When Briggs published her thesis, *Never in Anger*, anthropologists – with the exception of her thesis supervisor – did not consider 'emotions' an appropriate subject for investigation. In fact, Briggs wrote her thesis mostly in secret, because it was unheard of for an anthropologist to investigate emotion, let alone write a PhD thesis about it. Until then, anthropologists had focused on context, behaviour and the causes of emotions rather than emotion itself.

Undeterred, and using an intermediary, Briggs managed to get herself adopted as daughter by Inuttiaq, the religious leader of the group, and started living with his family in their igloo. It was the fulfilment of a childhood dream. She loved the wind, the cold, the snow, and ever since she'd been a little girl she had wanted to know what it would be like to be an Inuit. As romantic as the vision of living as an Inuit was to her, learning the language well enough (the Utku were a completely non-English-speaking community) meant it took over a year to finally start integrating into the family and become part of the group. This integration, however, would be short-lived.

The Utku would treat everyone with extreme courtesy but their mildness would leave them vulnerable to exploitation by others. When the fishermen who came to the inlet asked to borrow the tribe's two large wooden canoes, because their own aluminium boats weren't large enough to take all the men fishing at the same time, the Utku did not refuse, even though they used them for fishing themselves and generally heavily depended on them. Without the canoes, their lives were greatly constricted. Briggs could see the daily strain the absence of the canoes had on the Utku. The tribe needed the boats to complete their everyday tasks, and not being able to go out and bring back fresh fish affected the mental wellbeing of the entire tribe. When, one day, the fishermen returned one of the canoes leaking and damaged, and then asked to borrow the only other canoe the Utku had left,

Briggs, who was there to translate, 'exploded'. Unsmilingly and with an icy tone she told the guide for the group of fishermen that if they borrowed the second canoe the tribe would be left without a fishing boat. She also complained that last time, a previous guide had promised but forgotten to bring the repair materials that were supposed to be part of the exchange, and that the Utku therefore had no means of repairing the damaged boat or even buying repair materials themselves until the strait froze over in November. Without canoes, the tribe would be left scrambling for food and unable to get to their supplies, which were cached on an island. Upon hearing this, the guide responded that if the owner of the canoe did not want to lend his boat then that was of course his prerogative. Briggs turned to the owner of the canoe: Inuttiaq, her adopted father: 'Do you want me to tell him you don't want to lend your canoe? He will not borrow it if you say no.' Earlier that day he had told her in private that he did not wish to lend the canoe, and for Briggs to communicate this – though perhaps this was a bit of a wish-fulfilling fantasy on his part, because as Briggs would find out, he would never really have refused the request of the white men. Such a refusal would have violated Inuit rules of courtesy and obligation, and so Inuttiaq responded in an unusually loud voice, 'Let him have his will!' Briggs writes that her tone was icy when she told the guide: 'He says you can have it.'

She found emotional control was highly valued among the Inuits. Characteristically, gratitude was the feeling the Utku expressed openly. They had full control over any negative emotions they may have had. They saw the ability to stay calm under challenging circumstances as an essential sign of maturity, of being a grown-up. The Utku expected children, especially toddlers, to behave badly and would make allowances for them because they didn't know better. For them, a happy person was considered good and safe. Whereas an angry adult they would consider dangerous, someone who would have the capacity to kill.

In this particular situation (the request for their last canoe), the Utku were fearful of angering the white men and of potential retaliations. The next day, the weather changed again and the fishermen were concerned that new ice would freeze their sea plane and trap them in the inlet. So without a word to the Inuit, they packed up and left. The Inuit assumed they had left in anger.

This had terrible consequences for Briggs, as not just her adopted family but the entire tribe proceeded to punish her. 'Short of murder, the ultimate sanctioning against display of aggression in Utku society is ostracism,' Briggs wrote in her diary. As a form of emotional retribution, she was isolated for over three months.

The behaviour that offended the Utku wouldn't seem unreasonable to anyone in most other cultures, let alone be perceived as offensive. But Briggs came to understand that her action had deprived her adopted father of his legitimate stance of authority and the stance of an autonomous decision-maker. There were cultural norms in play that she had not been aware of. And so her action had taken from him his goodness, and her behaviour caused concern about dangerous conflict with the white men. The Utku perceived Briggs to have un-Inuit volatility and they measured her action against their own standards rather than making allowances for her not being an Inuit.

Briggs' seminal work into the study of emotion has great relevance to our lives today. Unlike her, we do not have to seek out remote tribes hidden away in desolate locations to experience cultural differences. They can be right in front of our noses – on our laptops in Zoom meetings and Google hangouts, and yes, at poker tables.

Few people in the world can see beyond the basic emotions. Even fewer who have studied emotions and their expressions and associated non-verbal cues in such detail that they have developed a kind of X-ray vision into a person's inner emotional state. One of them is the world expert in non-verbal communication, and he lives in San Francisco. I travelled to meet him at his favourite local restaurant, a small German place in a shopping mall in El Cerrito.

The Master of Emotion Recognition

David Matsumoto is professor of psychology at San Francisco State University, where he has worked since 1989. A former Olympic judo coach, he holds a 7th degree black belt and in his sixties is still hard to beat, but that's not why you wouldn't want to mess with him. At six feet tall, Matsumoto towers over most people, yet he doesn't need physical force to pin you to the floor. He does that just by looking at you. He sees *everything*.

But, he tells me, seeing everything can be both a blessing and a curse. There is no off-button, and this ability to see into the inner workings of another's mind can be particularly upsetting when he spots situations he cannot do anything about. I ask him for examples. He tells me he can spot paedophiles, or a husband who is clearly (in Matsumoto's view) abusive to his wife. If I was envious of his ability before, I no longer am now.

Getting to the place where you can see this level of intense detail takes practice, and Matsumoto has four decades' worth of it. Over the span of his career he has published more than 400 academic papers, and nearly 20 books. He is one of the select few recipients of the prestigious Minerva Grant awarded by the US Department of Defense. This grant, worth a whopping $1.9 million, was awarded to fund his study into the role of emotions in ideologically based groups. In one of his early studies, this master of human behaviour and micro-expression detection started from the assumption that culture influences how we produce facial expressions of emotion through cultural display rules, and then looked to see whether culture also influences how individuals perceive emotions in others. He found that Americans are better at recognising negative emotions than the Japanese. Then he dug deeper and found that there were also cultural differences when it came to being able to correctly infer emotional experiences from people's facial expressions.

Becoming the world's leading expert in deception detection was never in Matsumoto's grand plan. It all started with his fascination with babies. He had been wondering why infants could understand their caregivers, mostly their mothers, without comprehending what the words were, because no one understands words when they are born.

The year was 1979. A high-achieving undergrad at the University of Michigan, Matsumoto had started an undergraduate psychology honours programme under the supervision of a giant in the field of psychology, Professor Robert Zajonc. Just before a planned trip to Japan, Matsumoto proposed his idea of studying babies. Zajonc loved it so much that he asked him not to delay and to start the research straight away. And he had an idea of his own: why didn't Matsumoto do a cross-cultural study?

Matsumoto went ahead and studied the reactions of three- and four-year-old American and Japanese kids who were presented with just audio stimuli with no words, and then had to guess what emotions were being communicated. He found the kids could understand and identify the emotions tested for, despite the lack of verbal cues in the stimuli. So started Matsumoto's lifelong career in emotion studies.

Drinking German Beer

Back in the German bistro in El Cerrito, Matsumoto and I sat down with a couple of drinks. He likes German beer. I don't. I am German, but contrary to the stereotype, not all Germans like to drink beer. I felt I had disappointed him somewhat in this regard, and I was sure the panic was all over my face.

Matsumoto smiled and wanted to know more about me: 'Tell me about yourself!' I talked to him about this book and my desire to show that each of us can make improvements to our lives and our thinking by applying a combination of knowledge and disciplines. At this he exclaimed: 'Thank God. Thank God. I am having such a good reaction to that!' (It seemed odd that he was narrating his own emotional state, but I figured he paid attention to everyone's psychological weather – including his own.)

We were off to a good start. I felt at ease and forgot all about being a bag of nerves before our meeting. I continued to speak confidently about my theory, which was that when we think critically we improve our proverbial bullshit radar, so even if we're unaware that we are facing a lie or a liar, at the very least we will more often than not get to a point where we realise something is off, something doesn't quite add up. It is my belief, I told him, that those who are able to think critically will already be doing better than most people. He agreed, and expanded on my thinking.

People, he told me, think there are just one or two signs of a lie or deception taking place, and that's all they need to know about how to spot a liar. The truth is, it's a lot more complex than that. (In this, he echoed ex-FBI body language expert Joe Navarro.) The individuals who tend to be quite good at bullshit detection, Matsumoto told me, are the ones who have to gather and sift information for a living: the police, law enforcement and people who work in intelligence-gathering. He should know. For the past few decades he has been hired by various agencies across the law enforcement and national security spectrum to help train its agents to become better at interrogating and analysing interview subjects.

Of course, it's not helpful to compare ourselves with experts who have received intense training in the minutiae of every part of deception detection. But what can the rest of us do? Quite a bit, as it turns out. And a good place to start is learning about basic universal emotions and how to spot them.

The Seven Basic Emotions

A handful of emotions are displayed on our faces in a universal way, spanning cultural divides across the planet. People from any culture will have the same facial expression when, for example, they're angry. Researchers now suggest that these universal facial expressions of emotion are genetically encoded and not socially learnt. Among a number of studies of congenitally blind people, one compelling line of evidence was provided through a study by Matsumoto and former British judo international Bob Willingham. At the 2004 Olympic and Paralympic Games in Athens, the researchers compared the facial expressions of emotion of blind and sighted athletes. What they found was that there was a near perfect correspondence in the facial behaviours of each group. Most of the blind athletes had been blind from birth so could not have learnt these expressions from others. The researchers concluded that the blind athletes had to have entered the world with an inborn ability to express these emotions.

More than a century before, in 1872, in one of his lesser-known books, *The Expression of the Emotions in Man and Animals*, Darwin argued that all humans, and even other animals, show emotion through remarkably similar behaviours. He was on to something, and since then many studies have confirmed and built on Darwin's pioneering view that emotions such as anger, happiness and sadness are universal to all humans regardless of culture.

A continuing debate remains in the scientific community about the number of basic emotional expressions that are universal – whether there are six, seven, eight or nine. After decades of research, Matsumoto has landed on seven: anger, contempt, fear, disgust, happiness, sadness and surprise. He makes a compelling case for these seven. Now, you may argue that most human emotions are universal. Pride, shame, guilt, jealousy and love, for example, all occur around the world. But the seven emotions Matsumoto has classified are different because they have specific characteristics that other universal emotions do not: they are all signalled by universal facial expressions. Emotions are felt in the body, and so the other characteristic of those seven, Matsumoto explained to me, is that each of them has a universal physiological signature that primes the body for action. (For example, the physiological effects of fear include the release of cortisol and adrenaline; when we are happy, dopamine and serotonin are released.)

Matsumoto invited me to take one of his online emotion detection training programmes. Back in London, I logged on to the course. Several images of a series of people varying in age, gender and ethnicity appeared in succession on my screen. It was always two images: a 'neutral' base image that appeared to show the person displaying no emotion, followed by a second image of the same person with an expression. I was to determine which emotion was being shown. As my score improved and I found it easier and easier to identify the correct emotions, I moved up to the next level. Here, the image expressing emotion appeared for a noticeably shorter time, which made the detection harder and sometimes even impossible. As I progressed through the programme, the images flashed up on my screen for mere fractions of a second. Was that fear or surprise? The eyebrows were raised, but were they drawn together or not? The upper eyelids were also raised, but were the lower ones tensed? What was the mouth doing? The jaw was dropped open, but what were the lips doing?

I would retake entire levels until I was able to read not just subtle expressions but micro-expressions as well – the facial expressions people like to conceal or repress, which are of lower intensity. I did not realise how much I had internalised Matsumoto's training – until I started attending a special kind of virtual town hall meeting that put my new skills to the test.

In late 2021, I was invited by women's grandmaster chess player and poker ambassador Jennifer Shahade to join her and a group of her friends in a bi-monthly game of Mafia – a social deduction 'find the murderer' game centred around vigilante justice and the rule of the mob. The lynching by consensus of suspected mafiosi is a key feature – and an integral part of playing the mafia role lies in the ability to cast suspicion on the wrong party while declaring your own innocence. As a huge Hercule Poirot fan, I couldn't wait to play, and I asked when the next game was taking place. The dates, Shahade told me, were always announced in the WhatsApp group chat. But this was no ordinary group. Among the nearly 100 people were chess champions, famous writers, game theorists, traders, various university professors, lawyers, and then some of the hardest people to read in the world: poker pros.

The roles for each player were assigned via an app. There were two teams, citizens versus mafia. In a round of introduction each of the players asserted that they were citizens and not mafia. Then questioning began during the town hall meeting. The goal was to suss out who the mafioso was before they killed everyone. The game ended when the mafioso was unmasked, or the citizens were all dead. We played over Zoom and across various time zones.

Being in London meant that for me, the games didn't start until 1 a.m. At times this made it hard to stay awake, let alone focus keenly. But on a few occasions I was able to identify a player for certain as mafia solely based on their facial expression during questioning. When you can unmask other players in this manner, especially poker pros who have perfected their poker face, well, those are the moments worth staying up for.

But learning to identify other people's facial expressions isn't enough – not in Mafia, or in poker, or indeed in life. To become more emotionally astute, you need to look inward as well. And that's a lot harder. 'You were emotional. You didn't think critically,' Matsumoto told me in that German bistro, upon hearing about the colossal clash with William Kassouf where I'd blown my tournament life (for a while, anyway). I took a sip of my wine, trying to drown the anger that still bubbles up at the recollection. Having my mistake spelt out still hurt, even years later. I felt he could see the pain in my face, which is why I think he was quick to offer some practical advice.

If I wanted to gain a strong grip on my emotions, he told me, I needed to find out what triggered them. To do this, he suggested a technique he endearingly calls DIE (Description, Interpretation, Evaluation). Essentially this is a post-action review, and requires you to go back in your mind and reinterpret what happened so that if it were to happen again you would make a less emotional move. Used repeatedly, this method will help you to get better at spotting your own triggers. But the real trick to becoming better at handling your own emotions is to be quicker to realise when you are emotional and to understand why.

Since then, I have paid closer attention to my own emotions. While taking deep breaths and regular meditation help, I have learnt that the essence of my mental strength comes more from an understanding that certain events and outcomes are part of life. As I continued to research this book, I found that successful poker players work on their mental game just as much as on their strategy. They are also less likely to get rattled by a bad beat (unless they are Phil Hellmuth and it's part of their shtick . . . see page 191).

Bad beats are those occasions when you're a heavy favourite to win, but you still lose. They're an aspect of poker that you sign up to when you sit down at the tables, and they're part of a certain distribution of outcomes. In other words, they come with the territory. Weaker players tend to become frustrated or angry at a bad beat. They *tilt*, meaning that they deviate from optimal play, which then leads them to playing a losing strategy. Why? Because they neither understand nor accept that bad beats will happen and that, yes, weaker players can and will win against you. And so they let their emotions take over their mind and sacrifice their ability to think clearly in the process.

Irish poker pro David Lappin gives me a further reason why professional players manage to handle bad beats better. He says that a lot of poker players are so committed to the game and game theory that nothing else exists. 'We don't think about the value of money. The chips in front of us are the tools of our business. Similarly, we have severed (usually – this does get tested at times) our emotional link to a situation. It becomes less that we bluffed and "Oh my God, I'm bluffing, please fold, please fold!" and more, "Oh, I have a good bluff candidate here cos I'm blocking the nuts and my range as played is not capped." Therefore emotions don't come into it cos it's just the right thing to do regardless of outcome.' What Lappin is essentially telling me is that proficient poker players are aided by their probabilistic thinking skills. And this, ultimately, is the key to being fine about bad beats.

Learning to look inward and self-analyse is hard, and it takes practice. It is challenging to step away and review yourself in the third person, watching your own actions dispassionately. Think about how many times you've sat down to review an event in your life that didn't go so well. How often did you think about it critically and objectively? If you want to know if this is a winning formula, let me now introduce you to one of the world's best chess players and India's first ever grandmaster, Vishy Anand.

The five-times world champion chess player routinely self-analyses. He attributes wins not to talent but principally to being in control of his emotions. Anand has his mother, Sushila, to thank for this. Not only did she get him his first chess set, she also taught him how to play. Yet her biggest lesson wouldn't become clear to him until many years later.

At first Anand didn't see the point of his mother's insistence that he should sit down after each game and write down the parts where he had blundered. She would not allow him to do anything else until he had done so. After years of these post-game analyses (especially immediately after a loss, while the pain still stung) he began to reap the benefits. This method would help him not only spot mistakes, but also see if there was a pattern of bad moves that needed to be eliminated. Reviewing his actions gave him the opportunity to step back and see if there were better ways to have played. He also found that writing down his thoughts and emotions – good or bad – was a cathartic exercise. (He probably didn't realise it was more than that; in the upcoming pages you will meet a scientist who has proven that writing down your experiences can improve your mental state and health.) Self-reflecting in this manner and developing a high sense of self-awareness proved essential to Anand's winning game.

Anand has made history in India using self-evaluation and critical thinking, but his self-awareness goes beyond strategy. In his autobiography, *Mind Master*, Anand reveals: 'If I've blundered or sensed that I am on my way to making a hash of things, my nails will be gone quite quickly. I'm aware it's a visible cue for my opponent, and I've managed to successfully control this habit over the years in some measure, but I can't seem to be able to help it as an instinctive response.' Chewing his nails is not only a reflection of his emotional state, but also perhaps his biggest giveaway in a tense scenario. (Some non-chess players may not know this, but this slow and deliberate game requires just as much attention to physical behaviour and displays of emotion as poker.) Most of the time, his demeanour at the board appears composed and passionless. Hunkering down and revealing as little as possible is the way he likes to play – and only opponents who have played him often and know him well can even begin to interpret any tiny gestures as signals or coded messages of his mental and emotional state. Anand says paying attention to his emotions and keeping them in control is key to his game.

Chess players will pay close attention not just to the board, but also to their opponents. Even bluffing finds its way into chess. Some players like to mask their true emotions by acting out and pretending to be overly distraught or annoyed about making a mistake, or do the opposite by displaying confidence. In chess, too, deception is part of the repertoire. And just like in poker, players employ tactics to emotionally rattle their opponents, manoeuvring them into making mistakes. Anand habitually takes note of his opponents' little gestures or propensities so he can avoid being distracted before or during a game. He is an example of how staying in control of your emotions is a powerful tool, and how working on improving your self-awareness forges a path to greater success.

There is substantial scientific evidence that effective leadership is related to self-awareness: leaders who are more self-aware tend to generate better outcomes than those who are less so. They are also more confident, and better at decision-making and communicating.

Ginka Toegel has researched how leaders can recognise and manage their psychological preferences and found that executives need to first understand their own natural inclinations in order to modify them or compensate for them. The professor of organizational behavior and leadership at the International Institute for Management Development (IMD) in Switzerland also found that most successful effective executives have had to work hard on themselves, and that leaders need to recognise their outlier tendencies and learn how others perceive those tendencies.

Reviewing the trove of research into self-awareness, I found varying definitions of the term, but one thing became clear over and over: achieving true self-awareness isn't easy, and it requires work. Most of us are far from self-aware. We are conscious and aware, of course, but being truly self-aware requires critical self-reflection as well as the ability to see yourself from the perspective of others.

So how can you start improving your self-awareness? In the process of researching this book, one key point of advice that scientists and behavioural experts alike have kept giving me is to listen. A combination of active listening and active observation will give you a cluster of various signals you can use to interpret any given situation. This can be difficult because active listening does require us to accept criticism when it is voiced. This is especially tricky when we believe we are experts on a given subject.

How to Deal with Criticism

James O'Toole, a research professor at the University of Southern California, says that willingness to listen and take on constructive criticism seems to diminish as leaders grow more powerful. It's even worse in situations where leaders are unapproachable – say, when employees feel they'd be in danger of harming their career by speaking out. Leaders often have few people above them to give them candid and unfiltered feedback, but great leaders listen to managers and employees and actively seek constructive criticism.

We don't have to be CEOs of large corporations to apply this practice to our own lives. After all, we are all decision-makers. The views we hold and the decisions we make about how we run our lives are akin to running our own little corporations in which we are the boss. No matter how small our orbit of influence, being unwilling to listen critically to the opposing arguments provided, refusing to debate and not respecting views that conflict with our own can and does have consequences on a much larger and more existential scale. Toxic polarisation is on the rise, cutting deep into the fabric of society. To be clear, polarisation isn't always purely negative. In fact, potentially polarising practices such as debate, diversity of opinion, and free expression are healthy for democratic societies. But democracy becomes vulnerable in societies in which polarisation starts to affect and limit our ability to humanise and engage with political opponents. Opinion polls in both the USA and Turkey showed that citizens are increasingly reluctant to accept someone who supports another political party as their spouse, a friend of their child, or even as a neighbour. This is yet another version of the 'Us vs Them' mentality. We should all worry when social relationships are affected beyond political discussion. They point towards a future that is so dark, democracy can't survive it.

Varieties of Democracy (V-Dem), an independent academic research body based in the Department of Political Science at the University of Gothenburg in Sweden, works with a vast international network of 3,700 scholars and other country experts to put out a yearly report on the state of democracy worldwide. Its 2022 Annual Democracy report highlights the intensifying trend of autocratisation. Toxic levels of polarisation contribute to electoral victories of anti-pluralist leaders and the empowerment of their autocratic agendas – and these leaders now also seem to be becoming bolder with their use of misinformation to manipulate opinion in their favour. Instances of governments deliberately spreading misinformation are multiplying.

An example of how polarisation and misinformation can place democracy at risk is the violent attack on the US Capitol in Washington DC on 6 January 2021, when Donald Trump falsely claimed that he'd won the 2020 presidential election and galvanised his base to take up arms and storm the building. A couple of years after the event I don't need to look at the report to know that democracy in the US remains under threat. Trump has led the way for open hate speech – and whilst he is no longer in power (at least for now), many of his disciples and fellow Republican Party members confidently walk in his footsteps. Too many to ignore.

The worldwide wave of autocratisation is deepening. According to the report, toxic polarisation got worse in 32 countries in

2021 (up from five in 2011). Across the globe, 36% of the population – 2.8 billion people – are now living in autocratising nations. This includes many countries in the EU, where a fifth of all member states are becoming more autocratic.

If this gives you reason to be concerned, I hope it also mobilises you. There is a lot we can do personally to protect and better our individual and collective lives. We can start with observing others and actively listening to what they say – especially when their views oppose our own. We should continue to try to stay as open-minded as possible, and have the courage to reach out and try to debate with the other side, all the while paying attention to which emotions are in play (both our own and our adversaries'). When done right, applying some rigour to our thoughts will push us to find new and different ways to think about things – as the cliché has it, to 'think outside the box'. And that's difficult for most of us, because our instincts are to maintain our fragile sense of self, and the world outside the box is a challenging place.

It's hard to surround ourselves with people who will push back and challenge us but it's necessary in order to make sure we don't become increasingly narrow and blinkered in our views. To that effect we would do well to actively *invite* criticism, to show we are open to a healthy debate. When our view of the world can be so easily skewed not just by others, but by our own perceptions, it takes real effort to be objective and evidence-based and not give in to confirmation bias.

Decades before online engagement through social media became part of our way of life, Cass Sunstein, behavioural scientist and Harvard professor, saw potential dangers in group deliberations that do not include a range of competing views or differing perspectives on facts and values. In 1999, he wrote that group polarisation helps explain extremism, cultural shifts, 'radicalisation' and the behaviour of political parties and religious groups. He proposed structuring processes in such a way that they break people out of their echo chambers and expose them to a range of reasonable alternative views. The lesson is far from novel, but his point is about the real implications of group polarisation for economic, political and legal institutions, and that is important to all of us.

To think critically means to be aware of these behavioural pitfalls and the limitations of our knowledge. It means to know that our biases and prejudices influence our thinking. It requires us to acknowledge that we aren't always fully in control, even if we think we are. And so, as our emotions affect our perception, we need to accept that they are doing so and not expend psychic energy denying their existence or deluding ourselves about having total control of our thoughts.

Bravery is what's required, as well as actively entertaining opinions and views that aren't aligned with ours. Stepping outside ourselves to enter deliberations with an acceptance that we may be proven wrong. Then we will be more prepared to sympathise with the feelings of others who may be thinking differently from us. But building dialogue is hard. And finding the right words is even harder.

PART THREE

Being a Real-Life Truth Detective: Deception and Patterns

To Perceive Patterns

We are pattern-seeking (and pattern-making) creatures. All day every day, our thoughts and actions are governed by the search for meaning as we look for familiar patterns in the information we receive. We can't help it; our brains are wired to do so. The fundamental function of the brain is to take on information and then generate adaptive behavioural responses, which it does by encoding large numbers of image and sound patterns. We use our pattern-processing capabilities to help us understand our physical as well as social, political, emotional and informational environment. And while this helps us predict our external world and the people in it, it also makes us, well, predictable, and can leave us subject to exploitation and deception. Pattern reading is useful, in fact critical, to most of our reflexive functioning, but these observational and comprehension shortcuts can also be used to undo us.

For a winning poker player, the objective is to maximise your win rate, which makes the ability to exploit your opponents' behavioural tendencies a very valuable skill. Exploitative poker is essentially a strategy that targets imperfect and weaker players who tend to make mistakes under certain conditions because they are inclined to deviate from the optimal play. You can exploit them still further by deceiving them with the occasional bluff. The emphasis here is on the term 'occasional'. While it is certainly a powerful and necessary part of the game, to be effective a good bluff has to be rare, and it has to be seamless. The more naturally and effortlessly a bluff is put together, the more likely it is to be successful, so it must tell a story that is believable. And you do this by creating a betting pattern that is both logically and mathematically sound. Yet, ask anyone who doesn't play poker what they know about the game and they are likely to tell you that poker is about how well you can bluff. This perception that the game is won through deception creates a sort of fascination, which is of course misplaced – as we've seen, there is no failsafe way of detecting deception. In fact, this book goes confidently against the copious amount of literature available on how to detect lies and deception. It is called *The Truth Detective* and not *The Lie Detective* for a simple reason: human beings are terrible at sussing out deception. We miss things all the time – even when we know someone is out to deceive us.

Magic gives us vivid illustrations of how easily you can manipulate what someone sees, what they remember, or how they interpret something. And awareness of these biases and limitations has important implications for the decisions and the judgements that you make both about yourself, and about other people.

Why and how we can miss things has a lot to do with how our brains see the world. Magicians have forever successfully exploited the brain's blind spots.

'This is the routine for the spectator who smokes. The instant the performer sees the spectator take a cigarette, cigar or pipe, he takes the packet of matches from his pocket, tears off one match, and holds packet and match ready to ignite the match. He does these things openly because what he does can only be looked upon as a friendly and courteous gesture. As soon as the spectator is ready to light up, the performer should hold the matches close to the spectator and stake the one match. The matches should be held only as close to the spectator as politeness allows but should, if possible, be closer to the spectator than is the mouth of the glass, or cup, into which the pill is dropped.

This paragraph comes from 'Some Operational Applications of the Art of Deception' – not a set of instructions for would-be conjurors, but a spy manual for agents of the CIA. It was written in 1953 by a magician.

We don't like to think we are easily influenced. We believe that we're in control of our thoughts. When we are forced to accept that we've been fooled, we convince ourselves it was just a one-off. Yet we are repeatedly, and all too easily, manipulated. Not just by the usual suspects, like politicians and advertisers, but by those closest to us, too. Influencing others means asserting power and control, and it's no secret that intelligence arms of governments across the world have long been researching best practices for mind control. Some have been better at this than others. In the early 1950s, the then recently formed CIA was still trying to catch up with the sophisticated spying skills of other nations, so for help it turned to a man whose calling card featured a white rabbit in a hat.

At the elite Union Club on the Upper East Side in New York City, John Mulholland was gazing at his audience. 'Will my signature trick make people faint again?' he wondered to himself. Even though the crowd seemed to be drowning in the cigarette-smoke-filled room, he could still clearly see the anticipation on their dimly lit faces.

He smiled, put his hand into his pocket, pulled out some loose change and stepped towards a woman in the front row, asking her to pick a coin – any coin. She briefly inspected the coins in his hand and made her choice. Next, he pulled out a brand-new pack of cards – still sealed – for all to view, and opened it. He shuffled the cards for a while, then put them back into a neat stack in his palm. Now he began to draw the top four cards in the deck. These he put face up one by one on a small table at the front of the stage.

An Ace. The Nine of clubs. The Three of hearts. Another Ace. He looked up and waited. Absolutely nothing happened. He waited just a few more seconds. Still nothing. There was a nervous cough in one corner and some uncomfortable chair-shuffling in another, and a tension that travelled through the whole audience. No one knew what was supposed to happen next. Finally Mulholland broke the silence. He returned to the lady in the front row and asked her to read out loud the date on the coin in her hand: '1931'. The audience burst into a collective gasp and immediately jolted out of their seats, rising to a standing ovation: the four cards lined up on the table displayed the date on the coin. Mulholland took a bow and left the stage. In his dressing room he found a message had been left for him: a request to meet. Mulholland told no one. Decades later, documents and letters surfaced which showed that on 13 April 1953 at an undisclosed location in New York City, he met with the CIA.

And that was how Mulholland came to work with a certain Sidney Gottlieb. 'James Bond had Q, the scientific wizard who supplied 007 with dazzling gadgets to deploy against enemy agents. The Central Intelligence Agency had Sidney Gottlieb.' So began Gottlieb's *Los Angeles Times* obituary after his death in 1999. However, Gottlieb was the opposite of the positive, likeable good wizard of the fictional Q. The person Mulholland was meeting would later be described as 'Dr Death' and 'Poisoner in Chief'.

No one starts off as evil. Gottlieb's transformation into a deeply ruthless person appears to have been gradual. As head of the Chemical Division of the CIA's Technical Services Staff (now the Office of Technical Service), Gottlieb led a small research team, which produced disappearing inks, poisoned pens and even a single-shot micro-gun hidden in a toothpaste tube. The team went as far as proposing usage and applications for its gear. They developed various plots to discredit or assassinate Fidel Castro, such as exploding cigars or poisoned boots – none of which succeeded. Perhaps unsurprisingly, the then director of the CIA, Allen Dulles, was a huge fan of Ian Fleming's Bond books, and would often walk into the lab and ask his research team to create devices and substances lifted directly from their pages – that is, if they hadn't already built them.

In April 1953, the team's focus shifted decisively towards working on creating weapons and devices – including those using chemical, biological or radiological materials – that would be used 'to control human behaviour'. Anything that could help agents to get people either to give up information or to not talk at all.

Said to have been one of the CIA's most guarded secrets for over 20 years, MKUltra (Mind-Kontrol Ultra) was the codename for nearly 150 projects that researched the effects of drugs and alcohol on human behaviour. Dulles put Gottlieb in charge of MKUltra and he oversaw some of the most disturbing medical experiments, authorised special interrogations and routinely drugged people. His name is linked to the death of one scientist who allegedly jumped to his death from a hotel window while high on LSD. Such was the secrecy surrounding the project that in 1973, Gottlieb tried to eliminate all evidence of his sinister work and is believed to have personally gone to CIA's Record Center to make sure that every single document was destroyed. He failed.

In 2007, rumours filled the halls of Langley that two particularly revealing files had survived the purge – and with their revelation came some of the secrets of MKUltra. Two documents, innocuously titled 'Recognition Signals' and 'Some Operational Applications of the Art of Deception' saw the light of day after being hidden for decades. A spy manual, written by a magician. An actual magician.

Magic and Deception Over the Years

This type of collaboration is not that unusual. History records a number of magicians who answered their country's call in a time of need. In 1856, to avoid revolution in Algeria, the occupying French turned to Jean-Eugène Robert-Houdin to break the spell a cadre of Algerian 'holy men' had on the local people. Performing magic tricks to mesmerised audiences, Robert-Houdin would reveal how the tricks were created to seed doubts about the 'holy men's' seemingly miraculous walking on hot coals, glass-eating and snake-charming. He performed tricks that shocked them so much they believed he was the devil. After he revealed how the tricks were performed and that he was not in fact supernatural, the chieftains praised the magician for his art and pledged allegiance to France.

In 1941, British commandos turned to Jasper Maskelyne, who had made the outlandish claim that he could use his illusions to fight the war against the Nazis and make tanks, warships and even aircraft disappear. The Royal Navy asked him to 'disappear' the entire harbour of Alexandria in Egypt, then being targeted by the German Luftwaffe. And he did, with a classic trick. In just four days, hundreds of soldiers built a decoy harbour at Maryut Bay, a neighbouring harbour, using mud, cardboard and canvas paintings of dummy warships: an entirely believable mirage when seen from a plane high above in the sky. The lights were switched off in Alexandria, keeping it hidden from sight, while Maryut Bay was lit up. It worked. The Luftwaffe wasted their efforts attacking the pretend Alexandria, keeping the real city safe and thereby protecting a vital supply route for the Allies. Maskelyne was using the oldest trick in the magic toolbox: misdirection.

Magicians, it seems, know human behaviour and psychology better than most. So it made sense for Gottlieb to turn to John Mulholland, then America's most celebrated magician and author of several books on magic, including *The Art of Illusion*.

Gottlieb knew that his lab's gadgets would be useless unless agents could get them to their target without being detected. He wanted Mulholland to teach CIA field officers tricks of their own in order to carry out discreet handovers and slip pills and potions to enemies. Mulholland decided the task needed his undivided attention. At the age of 55 he announced his retirement from magic and, in secret, started work on a spy manual for the CIA that would include an introduction to the art of deception.

Some points in his manual were sleight of hand techniques that merely required practice by the agent, such as how a pill attached to the back of a matchbox could easily be released and what type of grip would be required to hold a larger pill and drop it naturally into a beverage. Others were pointers as to how the mind processes the environment. He also discussed how unexpected behaviour would raise suspicion, giving examples like: 'As women do not usually light a match to hold to a man's cigarette, this method cannot be used by a woman.'

There is, in fact, an entire section in the manual devoted to female agents. One of the challenges was the pockets on women's clothing: significantly different in size, number and location to those on menswear. That made it more difficult for women to use pockets as part of their deception. Social conventions of the time meant that a man pulling up a chair, helping a woman don her coat or lighting her cigarette felt natural and expected, but all these manoeuvres were out of the female agent's scope. She was never to act the way a man would, for fear of arousing suspicion. A valuable and easy trick was for a female agent to feign general ignorance to allay suspicions. As Mulholland wrote somewhat apologetically, 'Men are never astonished when she doesn't know something.' When it came to purloining smaller objects, on the other hand, women had a clear advantage over men – it seemed generally accepted that women don't inspect an object just by looking at it, they like to handle it, offering ample opportunity to swipe or swap.

Mulholland knew the crucial element to a trick was this: it's not the eye that is fooled, it's the brain. Magic has more in common with science than with the unexplained, because at the heart of a magician's technique is the exploitation of loopholes in the brain.

Mulholland was ahead of the curve – the science of magic wouldn't become an academic field until nearly 60 years later, when a collection of scientific papers started to raise interesting questions relating to how our brain computes what it sees or doesn't see, and used magic to illustrate them. One of these papers was on misdirection and came from Swiss-born researcher Gustav Kuhn.

Kuhn

I travel south across the River Thames to New Cross to meet Kuhn at his office at the department of psychology at Goldsmiths, where he teaches and runs the magic lab.

As a teenager Kuhn was fascinated by magic, never leaving the house without wearing a blazer with pockets full of conjuring props, so he could be ready to perform at any given moment (he owned numerous blazers for this reason). And he was good, really good. At eighteen, he came third in a prestigious national magic competition in Switzerland. Eager to improve his tricks, he would delve into psychology books, but this had an unexpected side effect: he lost interest in magic and instead developed a passion for psychology. He went on to do a PhD in consciousness, but magic would eventually make its way back into his life. During his studies, some of the researchers he encountered focused on visual attention, and given that directing visual attention is a key tool in a magician's toolbox, it is perhaps unsurprising that Kuhn enjoyed spending time with them the most. These researchers were using eye-tracking to study how people allocated information specifically in the real world, because so much of the other research was being conducted in confined and controlled laboratory settings. Interested in investigating where people looked when they were making a cup of tea, the researchers were trying to ascertain the attentional processes and the memory processes required for such everyday actions. Kuhn tells me he spent a lot of time slurping tea and coffee with that group and eventually suggested, 'Well, why don't we just try and see where people look when they're being misdirected by a magician?' The most obvious connection between magic and psychology is perception. A magician's ability to control visual attention determines what an observer is aware of seeing. In other words, magicians can manipulate our awareness. Magicians define misdirection as the deflection of attention for the purpose of disguise. Visual scientists, on the other hand, would describe misdirection as 'attentional modulation of visual awareness'. While the language may differ, the underlying principles are the same. This was when Kuhn realised that he could study magic scientifically, and that to do so he needed to shift the focus of his own research from general cognition to attention.

At the time there was virtually no psychological research on the science of magic. Studying magic was not considered serious science. At best it was just a bit of fun, and so raising funds for research was challenging.

In fact, Kuhn and his friend Benjamin Parris were once forced to set up a lab in Kuhn's bedroom because they were unable to raise money to fund the use of a proper lab. The pair wanted to discover the parts of the brain that were at work when someone was experiencing magic. And what they found was unexpected.

When you or I see a magic trick, two areas in the brain are activated: one that's responsible for monitoring cognitive conflict (left dorsolateral prefrontal cortex) and another that's responsible for trying to resolve cognitive conflict (anterior cingulate cortex). In other words, magic activates the parts of the brain that are typically involved with both processing *and* resolving cognitive conflicts. The trick creates a cognitive conflict between what we are experiencing and what we believe is impossible. This means everybody experiences magic very differently, as it depends on what you believe to be possible.

The American magicians Penn & Teller view magic as 'an intellectual art form that requires the audience's engagement as well as their suspension of disbelief'. The key word here is 'audience': you can't trick yourself with magic, only someone else. During a magic show, audiences are active participants in their own deception. As Teller often says, the strongest lie is the one that the audience tells itself.

Human nature is predictable, and magicians find ways to exploit this. Magic is designed to appeal to people visually, but what magicians are really trying to do is affect our minds, moods and perception. They want to challenge our maps of reality. And they do so by mere suggestion.

Take hypnosis. Martin Taylor, a British hypnotist practising for 20 years, known for having 'hypnotised' crowds of 100 people en masse, declared at a talk in Oxford that he doesn't use 'hypnosis'. He believes that what we call hypnosis is a combination of the power of suggestion, peer pressure and obedience. He draws upon a personal example to explain.

On a date one night during his student years, Taylor was trying to impress a young woman by telling her that in his spare time he was a magician, and also knew how to hypnotise people. His date immediately asked him to hypnotise her then and there. The problem was that Taylor had been showing off: he had never hypnotised anyone before. But the girl was enthralled – she'd always wanted to be hypnotised, she said. Not willing to lose face, he decided he'd wing it. After all, he had seen a friend who was a hypnotist do it many times before.

Taylor held up her necklace to use as a pendulum. Speaking

in a calm monotone, he started telling her that she was getting tired, her body was feeling heavy and that she was very sleepy. Her eyes eventually shut and she slumped over. Taylor continued to talk to her for another few minutes, all the while repeating how sleepy she was. Then he asked her to sit up and open her eyes and take off her shoes. She did. Later, when Taylor asked her why she had taken her shoes off, she replied that she didn't know. Up to this point, Taylor did not think he had managed to hypnotise her. Then he asked her how long she thought she had had her eyes closed. She guessed about two or three minutes. It had been half an hour. He did it again, successfully making the young woman put all of the jewellery and accessories she had on the mantel-piece, facing the wall.

Taylor was stunned. He had had no training. Where had this power come from?

The Science of Magic

A great deal of research has been done into hypnosis, but exactly how it works is still not known. The biggest enigma for many years was why some people are more susceptible to it than others. Studies have shown that one in ten of us are highly hypnotisable, but some aren't at all.

What various studies into hypnosis have revealed is that it depends on which attention areas of the brain are more active. In decades of research on the subject, only one difference has emerged between those who are susceptible and those who aren't: a higher ability to imagine and disassociate. 'These people can meditate whilst riding a packed tube carriage to work or imagine that they feel cool on a very hot day,' says Amir Raz, a psychiatry professor and researcher at McGill University in Canada. He, too, used to be a magician before he became an academic.

Hypnosis, researchers think, is a psychological process that actually happens all the time. We fall in and out of hypnosis every day. You may sometimes call it going on autopilot.

The brain processes very little information directly, inferring the rest based on assumptions. We go through most parts of our lives on autopilot. In the morning, without consciously thinking about it we put on shoes, turn lights on or off, turn on a tap, lock the door, drive to work. By the time we reach our teens we have internalised these routines based on facts our brain has gathered about how our environment works. Our reality is built on our assumptions: facts we process as unchanging are true at all times. The scientific term is automaticity – the result of learning, practice and repetition without the need for conscious guidance or monitoring.

Take driving a car. When we learn how to drive, we think about all the steps in great detail: press clutch, change gear, lift foot off clutch, step on the accelerator. Automaticity is a process that is fast, one that allows us to get in the car, drive to work and not think about how to change gear every single time.

We are pre-wired to make mental shortcuts. During these highly automated processes our attention and awareness is subdued, and this is when magicians tap in to fool and trick us. The science of magic can show us a lot about how people's decisions can be influenced without their knowledge. It can also help demonstrate how you can convince people of almost anything. You just need enough layers of deception.

David P. Abbott was an American magician at the turn of the nineteenth century, when magicians regularly performed in people's private homes (hence 'parlour magic'). In this setting, Abbott would take a golden ball and seemingly make it float around the room. At the end of the show he would absentmindedly leave the ball on a bookshelf while he stepped out of the room to grab a drink from the kitchen. This was all part of the trick. In fact, he would count on guests to sneak over to the bookshelf and take their chance to examine the ball. They would then find it to be much heavier than any fine thread could support. What they didn't know was that they had picked up a far heavier duplicate of the ball, left out intentionally to fool the audience. The ball they had seen swirling in the air was only a five-ounce ball. Stumped and amazed, the audience was completely taken in. The success of the trick relied largely on the audience making assumptions.

Abbott was showing rather than telling that the ball was too heavy for a thread, which made this far more convincing. And by not making explicit statements or offering guests the chance to hold the ball, he avoided potential further scrutiny or suspicion. Letting the audience make assumptions is an integral part of every great magic trick, and its power should not be underestimated. We are making assumptions when, either consciously or subconsciously, we believe things to be true without the need for any supporting evidence. And powerful assumptions can make all kinds of things happen right in front of our eyes. It all depends on how well you construct the story. Magicians are exceptional storytellers, and like all great storytellers they follow an important rule: show, don't tell.

In a more recent example, a magician-cum-scientist used this technique in real scientific experiments.

Jay Olson was known as a child star in the magic world. At just seven years old he was hired to perform at a sixteen-year-old's birthday. By the time he was ten he was standing on stage at a conference on magic in Reno, Nevada, performing tricks in front of several hundred people. And like many we've met in this chapter, he became a psychologist. He completed his PhD with Amir Raz at McGill.

Raz's lab is located on University Street in Montreal, near the bottom of Mount Royal. When I arrive for my interview with Olson, I find him already waiting for me at the entrance of the building. He suggests we do the interview while taking a stroll up Mount Royal. I am excited about a walking interview. It ends up being a hike and within a few minutes my enthusiasm for the idea evaporates in the glaring October sun. I failed to check the weather forecast and I am dressed for a full-on Canadian snow-storm. But it's worth the effort, as I get to hear first-hand how Olson managed to make people believe that a machine could read their minds.

There was a lot of prep and planning work involved, he told me. Ahead of the study, participants were told that 'The Neural Activation Project' was a collaboration across different universi-ties and that the researchers at his lab were testing how effective the machine was on different people. This was all a lie, including the name, but it was necessary to give the project credibility and build the base for the cover story. Olson and his team needed participants to assume that the technology was credible, because stating this explicitly would have raised suspicion. So to truly lure participants into feeling that this wasn't fake and that there really was a machine that could not only read their minds but also implant thoughts, every single aspect and interaction on the day needed to communicate legitimacy.

It began the moment participants stepped into the build-ing. The study was conducted at a long-established institution – the Montreal Neurological Institute. The main foyer is a visual homage to neurology, with a tall white marble statue in the middle of Nature unveiling herself before Science. Designed in art deco style, almost all of the foyer's motifs represent different parts of the central nervous system. Two leather sofas are placed against walls facing each other. On a side table is a cardboard model of a brain profile. It's here that participants were greeted by research assistants dressed in white lab coats and holding clipboards, who led them to the lab in the basement of the build-ing. On the way to the lift, the participants were given a brief talk about the Neuro – as the institute is known – it was both a working hospital and a research centre, it first opened its doors in 1934 . . . all true. They then walked past a stretch of doctors' offices, one bearing several real institutional logos and including the name of the fake project. 'This is part of the Neural Activation Mapping Project – have you heard of it?' they were asked, in order to make the project seem better known. Some participants even believed they had. To minimise suspicion, Olson focused heavily on making sure that participants drew their own conclusions about the process. As they exited the lift, a sign reading 'McConnell Brain Imaging Centre' was clearly visible. A secretary sitting behind a computer greeted them with a smile and handed over a keycard. The research assistant then swiped the keycard on a pad to gain access to a restricted area – passing under a yellow safety sign warning of a strong magnetic field. They were now in a doctor's surgery-style waiting room where researchers explained the process. Once done, they entered the lab, which required another swipe of the keycard.

A second set of doors slid open with an audible swoosh. The room was dimly lit. The only other light emanated from several computer screens, which displayed rotating brain scans. A hospital bed was placed against one of the walls. A muffled, repetitive sound came from behind yet another door, and another sign read 'Warning: Powerful Magnet'. The door looked heavy and was framed by stainless-steel bolts, like a high-security vault. The participants were told that was where the scanner was. They walked in and saw the source of the repetitive humming sound – an MRI machine. As each participant entered the study room, the lab technician wrote down a number on a piece of paper and placed it face down on a table. Then the participant was moved into the MRI machine and told that the machine would be calibrated to insert this number into their mind by attempting to manipulate the brain's 'natural electromagnetic fluctuations' to influence their choice. After the participant exited the machine, the experimenter asked for his or her chosen number, then turned over the paper to reveal that their number matched what the lab technician had previously written down. It appeared as though the machine had influenced the participant to choose the number that was written down from the start. In another condition of this experiment, the participant was asked to silently think of a number between 1 and 100 and the machine would then attempt to read the participant's mind. What Olson and his team showed is that with an elaborate set-up, they were able to really convince people they no longer had control over their own thoughts. When asked, participants described feeling their head was getting hot and swelling, or feeling a voice or force was dragging them to a number that they didn't want to choose, or that a number would pop into their head and they would try to change their mind but couldn't. They said that their mind was just stuck on that number. They all believed that the machine was controlling their minds.

In reality, the machine did nothing at all. It was unplugged, and Olson was playing the humming sound on a loop through speakers. The researchers used a magic trick, Olson said. When I heard this, I literally stopped in my tracks. 'How does that work?' I asked him. Had they planted cues in the environment to make participants think of a particular number? I mentioned Derren Brown, who once explained a trick in which people had been exposed to subconscious cues, so that when he eventually asked them to pick a visual, they picked exactly what he wanted them to. Olson told me that participants had a free choice of numbers and that no kind of method was used to influence them. 'There was no psychology involved there, it was purely a magic trick. So, basically whatever number they chose, they believed it was on that page the entire time, although it actually wasn't.'

I asked him again, 'How does that work?'

'I mean, it's a magic trick, I can't share that,' he replied and started walking off, signalling quite clearly that there was no way

I was going to get that out of him and he wasn't going to break his magician's code. I guess once a magician, always a magician.

In a variation of this study and as proof of concept, Olson together with his colleague Samuel Veissière, a professor in psychiatry at McGill, introduced the MRI scanner as a healing machine to children who had been diagnosed with ADHD, Tourette's Syndrome, chronic skin picking and migraines. One of the kids was a twelve-year-old girl called Maria. For two years she had been constantly picking the skin on her arms and face, even in her sleep, leaving it raw, sore-looking and prone to frequent infection. The angry-looking skin made Maria so self-conscious about her appearance that she was no longer comfortable going out in public. After two sessions in the scanner, her skin picking decreased, including when she slept. Encouraged by the results, Veissière gave her an additional session in the scanner, telling her that her skin would heal faster and faster and that her hands would no longer want to pick her skin. Her skin started to clear up. Maria's mother told Olson that after the session her daughter's skin had remained intact, well hydrated, free from scaling and even largely free from itching. Again, the scanner used in this experiment was switched off and did nothing at all. In addition, the parents were in on the ruse. They knew it was a placebo. And this time there was no magic trick involved, merely the suggestion that this was a legitimate healing machine. 'We actually told them that the machine was based on the power of suggestion and can help the mind to heal itself,' Olson told me. At a one-year follow-up meeting, Maria's family reported that she no longer picked her skin. It is hard not to think of this as magic.

By the time Olson took his first class at university, he already had a strong foundation in human psychology. What struck him were the big overlaps between the science and magic. A lot of what he was being taught he had already known from performing. They just used different terminology. What magicians would call 'misdirection', psychologists would refer to as 'attention orient-ing'. Where magicians talked about 'forcing', psychologists called it 'nudging' or 'persuading'.

Olson looked at one of the most common tools magicians use: a deck of playing cards. He approached 119 people on the street and on university campuses and asked them to pick and remem-ber a card they saw while he flipped through the deck.

He raised the deck to just under the participant's eye level and riffled through it. The entire thing took around half a second. The trick was that one of the cards – the target card that Olson *wanted* the participant to pick – was intentionally shown for longer than the rest; it was likely the only card that was clearly visible. When asked, nine out of ten participants would report complete freedom of choice when picking their card. But in reality, Olson successfully controlled their decision.

With both these studies, Olson showed how magicians can manipulate us into believing we act freely and that we are in full control of our decision-making, when we are not. But we know magicians are hardly the only ones that have figured out how to nudge us into thinking and acting in a certain way, because life is a game, and we are all players in it. Every task we set our-selves, be it as simple as making a cup of coffee or as challenging as running a marathon in under three hours, requires interac-tion with the world. Meaning that even though our goals may not be the same, to achieve them depends, for all of us, on how we retrieve and encode information from our environment. We rely on this feedback at all times. You could think of it as being under constant influence, which makes whether we have true free will or not debatable. One thing is for sure, though: there will always be those who will seek to increase their influence on us and manipulate us for profits or their own gain. And they are becoming increasingly sophisticated in their methods.

Online Manipulators

Want to get your ex back? Or get your husband to have kinky sex with you? The Olson study showed how easily and quickly our subconscious can be infiltrated and then used to manipulate our thoughts and actions. And, inevitably, someone set up a company to help you to do just that. Selling targeted manipulation campaigns to individuals who wished to change another person's action, online service The Spinner prided itself on providing a highly effective and individually tailored advertising model – until, that is, Facebook and Instagram blocked it in January 2020. For as little as $49, any individual could launch a targeted campaign to influence a person of their choosing. Then a form of subconscious propaganda would be unleashed onto the target, who had no idea that they were being exposed to wilful manipulation by someone else. It was an approach that many would find sinister. If you were the target, you would be sent a link to an innocent-looking page such as a holiday destination or an item in an online store. When you accessed that link, cookies were placed onto your browser. From then on, over a specified period of time (usually about three months), the intended person was exposed to messages aimed at coaxing them into a specific action.

'The reason it is so effective is that the initial attack comes from someone you know,' the company's COO Elliot Shefler told me in a phone call we had before the ban. Interesting word choice, I thought to myself. He seemed happy to use the word 'attack', despite his continued efforts to focus our conversation on the positive, 'happy ending' stories. The site has tailored campaigns specifically targeting 'Loved Ones' to get them to stop drinking, eating meat, smoking, riding motorcycles or doing drugs. Want them to accept you for who you are? Why not send them a campaign to get them to 'Accept my gaming habits' or 'Accept my pot-smoking habit'? Even your children can be involved – one of the available preset campaigns promised to influence Mom/Dad to

'Get your kid a dog'. If you wanted to get rid of a co-worker, there was a campaign for that, too. Want your friend to lose those extra pounds? Buy them a campaign. A person in a bitter divorce battle could buy a preset campaign called 'Settle. Don't go to court', which would seed their ex-spouse's screens with links to articles that discussed the benefits of exactly that decision. Shefler tried to focus attention on the benign and the positive, and mentioned the many thank-you notes the company had received from those who successfully got engaged and parents who were able to stop their children from quitting college. But when I pressed him on the moral and ethical implications of manipulating unsuspecting people, he deflected by pointing out that the company was operating within the law, just like any other marketing and media advertising company, including social media giants Facebook and Google. Back in 2019, when this conversation took place, the laws were still insufficient to prevent companies such as The Spinner from placing cookies on your computer and infiltrating your private sphere. And it's not hard to see how this could be abused by those who wish to go further than just preventing us from drink-driving or getting divorced. Shefler admitted that they used to do campaigns for politicians but '. . . after Cambridge Analytica, we only now do brands.'

The autonomy to make decisions according to our own will and choice is foundational to our idea of freedom. Wars have been fought to protect this freedom. But how do we protect ourselves when we don't know we're being influenced in the first place? With pattern recognition. That's the first step. The better we can identify patterns, the better we are at understanding our environments. When we're able to notice them, we not only notice irregularities within them but can predict what can/should/will happen next. But it's a two-edged sword. On the one hand, pattern-making leaves us open to deception because as we've seen, these mental processes are often automated, with us paying little cognitive attention. On the other hand, we can use pattern-making behaviour to our advantage.

Take chess. Knowing that a move is possible is often enough to raise your awareness and sensibility to exploitation and attack. An ability to predict what others *could* do next can give you reason to pause and think through your decisions more carefully. And in a way, life is like a game of chess. Your life is the result of a sequence of decisions you have made. They make you who you are. The quality of your decisions relies on our ability to understand and analyse information, including the actions of those around us and indeed on our understanding of the circumstances around us.

Researchers studying decision-making through the medium of chess have shown how the quality of decision-making changes with the time available, the skill of the decision-maker and the difficulty of the decision at hand, as well as the time of day that we are making it. (Remember from Part One we are also less likely to fall for fake news when we slow down and deliberate.) Looking at over a million chess games in an online database, scientists could see that those playing later in the day made riskier choices, often taking quicker but ultimately less successful decisions. The results also indicated that we have greater control over our decisions in the mornings, irrespective of when we prefer to sleep. The assumption is that as we grow tired, the need for sleep influences the quality of our choices, even if we think we are focused, and we don't consciously feel tired.

Another chess study from 2006 looked at how novice and experienced players differed. What made the more experienced players, specifically grandmasters, winning players wasn't their ability to think eight, ten, fifteen moves ahead. Their winning edge came from examining their own proposed moves and discarding bad ones. Novice players were more likely to convince themselves that bad moves would work in their favour. That was because the novices would only take into account countermoves that would confirm and justify their strategy, rather than also considering countermoves that would weaken their position. Experienced players have not only studied and taken part in more games, they also look for reasons *not* to take a move more than reasons to do so. And this is actually the root of the scientific method.

The philosopher Karl Popper wrote that what makes science *science* is the way that scientists begin with a bold new hypothesis that can be tested – or falsified – by evidence. Rather than looking for evidence to say, 'This is true', scientists go out of their way to find evidence that it is false. The difference between a scientific and a non-scientific statement lies in its falsifiability. The usefulness of this to you and me comes in the idea that for anything to be considered scientifically sound, it has to be *testable* (Popper said, controversially, that if a theory does not make a testable prediction, it is not science) – in other words, capable of being proven incorrect through observable, measurable experiments.

Popper was adamant that you can never prove that a theory is true, because that would require you to prove every single circumstance, which is impossible. But just a single instance of a counterexample is enough to blow up the whole theory and disprove it. If you live to see only white swans and never once see a black swan, you may theorise that all swans are white. But spotting just one black swan will falsify your theory.

Take the following two statements 'Water evaporates at boiling point' and 'Jesus is God'. Only one is falsifiable.

If we want to avoid being made fools of and be sure about the truths that seem significant to our actions and our view of the world, then we should all be trying to disprove them.

This can be hard. Truth isn't always self-evident. It may be intentionally or unintentionally hidden, distorted or obscured. Magicians have shown how what we believe to be truth is in fact a deception of the mind, and we've seen how. This is at its strongest and most powerful when they steer us to believing they had very little (if anything) to do with our decision-making. Step away from the magic show and into real life, and we see how all sorts of nudging and forcing lead us to think and behave in a particular way. If you're now wondering if we should be going through life cross-examining everything, the answer is no – not everything. As we all learn more about how our brains are influenced and our behaviour directed, we become more sensitive to nudges, and as a result will become better at discerning when to question things. We will recognise truth clues everywhere – and many of them will be hidden in the words we say and hear.

Word Power

Anyone anywhere can find information in words, right down to the smallest, most innocuous parts of speech. What makes word sleuthing so interesting is the difference between those words that are intentionally used or omitted, and those that are part of our individual patterns and markers, and which can therefore reveal a lot about our intentions and mental states – even when we think we aren't spelling those out. Once you have learnt what to look out for, all it takes is one simple method: paying attention.

You don't have to become a poker player or a body language guru to get reads on people. The best and easiest method of getting reads is and will always be through closely observing what people say and how they say it.

In the late 1970s, in a heads-up, 'winner takes all' poker game at the Las Vegas Hilton, two of the world's best poker players were chatting across the table before the game. Amarillo Slim took a sip of his coffee and looked at his opponent – a fierce, aggressive player by the name of Betty Carey. She was having tea. 'Betty, how is your tea?' Slim asked her. 'Oh, wonderful. This is really good tea!' she replied. Slim knew she liked it. She had no reason to lie. At the time he didn't know that this little exchange would help win him $100,000. About an hour into the game, Carey went all in with her chips. Slim thought she was bluffing, but he needed to be sure: 'Betty, how do you like your hand?' he asked her. 'Real good hand, Slim!' she shot back. But he noticed a difference in tone and manner to when he'd asked about her tea earlier. He deduced that she must be lying, so he called her with a pair of Fives and won. The next time the two played, Carey wore earplugs and beat Slim. In his autobiography, *In a World Full of Fat People*, Slim doesn't mention the date of the second encounter, or perhaps he simply didn't remember when this match-up happened, but he did remember precisely how he felt after his defeat: 'Boy, that was hard! Talking to my opponents is my secret weapon, and I couldn't get much of a read on her or pick up any tells from her voice.'

Live tournament poker is great fun – if you have the stamina for it, that is. Your endurance will be put to the test, especially at larger tournaments that run over multiple days and where play sometimes lasts twelve or more hours each day. The hours will stretch and test your patience as you can easily sit there for what will feel like eternity, folding hand after hand, playing only a few hands if at all. A professional tournament poker player wants to take advantage of the many mistakes her opponents will make throughout the tournament. She will be protecting her chip stack and be unwilling to take unnecessary risks by committing a large amount of chips with a marginal hand. She is often biding her time before her weaker opponents lose their patience and get their money in with the odds against them.

Some players wear headphones to cut the boredom. Others, like me, use them to tune out the table chatter and focus on the play. I often have nothing playing through my headphones. I use them as a deterrent. People are less likely to chat to you when you signal you don't want to engage. Headphones also help to avoid distraction from table talk, and mean I am cutting my risk of giving anything away in the process. I have watched pros make huge (and at times impossible-seeming) all-in calls based only on what the other player revealed to them through idle talk, like the time in 2006 at The Golden Nugget Hotel and Casino in Las Vegas.

The High Roller Suite at 'The Nugget' has been host to some of the most exciting games in poker history. In 2006, Daniel Negreanu had just put his opponent Antonio Esfandiari all-in. Esfandiari was now facing a tough decision. A call could potentially double him up, but the flip side would see him lose all of his cash, more than $70,000.

The action up to this point had been pretty standard. The initial round of betting saw Phil Hellmuth put in a raise of $3,200 and Negreanu calling, but then Esfandiari placed a re-raise of $12,000 into the pot. Hellmuth folded and Negreanu stayed in the hand. The two players went to the flop (the first three cards on the board). The players saw a Queen, a Six and a Ten being revealed. Negreanu was first to act but didn't add any money to the pot and checked instead. Esfandiari opted to put in around $15,000, over half of what was already in the pot. Negreanu responded by pushing all of his money into the middle, placing Esfandiari – who had about $50,000 left in his stack – all-in.

You could see the agony on Esfandiari's face as he tried to figure out whether or not Negreanu had paired a Queen. This was the crucial bit of information he lacked. Queens would beat the two Jacks he was holding in his hand.

Shortly before and after shoving his money into the middle, Negreanu had projected a lot of confidence with his speech, which is what made Esfandiari think that he had Queens. At this point Esfandiari was speaking out loud and asking Negreanu questions in the hope that it might coax him into revealing any type of clue. It worked. Negreanu said something he shouldn't have: 'I will show you a card after you fold.' That was a mistake.

In effect he was asking Esfandiari to fold, potentially an indication that he didn't have a strong hand. Esfandiari now knew that his Jacks were good and put the rest of his stack into the middle.

It wasn't Negreanu's posture that revealed the truth about his hand's strength, but his words. There are numerous situations in life where the only place we have to gather information from is in the written and spoken words. Some of us are better at it than others. And a few of us have developed our word-sleuthing skills to such a high degree that we can help, protect and even save people. Like Chris Voss.

In the late summer of 2000, a young American, Jeffrey Schilling, was taken hostage by Islamic militants in the Philippines, who broadcast his capture on TV and demanded $10 million from the US government for his release. This was a job for the FBI's elite Crisis Negotiation Unit, a type of 'special forces' of negotiation. The US put Chris Voss on a plane to Manila.

Voss was one of the best hostage negotiators in the field. He had started his career talking people off the proverbial and actual ledge, working the suicide hotlines. It was a tough job – and it provided him with the best training he could have received before getting involved in hostage negotiation. It also taught him the core element of any successful crisis management: active listening.

Paying attention to what words were being said – and how – and then responding with positive affirmation gave him the foundations he needed to face hostile negotiators. Over time, Voss worked himself away from the phone lines and right into the heart of high-profile standoffs.

Once on the ground in the Philippines, Voss encountered an unexpected issue that impeded any progress in the negotiations: he was not allowed to negotiate directly with the kidnapper. Instead he had to go through an intermediary. And that intermediary was the head of the Philippines National Police's Special Action Force, a military officer by the name of Benjie. And Benjie had his own ideas about how to deal with the kidnapper, a rebel leader called Abu Sabaya. He wanted to take a hard line with him and objected to any suggestions by Voss to establish a rapport-based working relationship with Sabaya, who was personally negotiating the ransom for Schilling.

Weeks passed. Little progress was made. There was no prospect of getting closer to freeing the hostage. Then one night during a break, Voss and Benjie were sitting in the library of the US ambassador's residence, working on a negotiation strategy. Voss took a sip of his drink and sat there deep in thought, trying to figure out why Benjie wasn't playing ball and was resisting so strongly the idea of building a rapport with the rebel leader. Then it dawned on him – he had to negotiate with Benjie, too.

Voss went straight to the point: 'You hate Sabaya, don't you?' Sabaya was a murderer and rapist, Benjie replied. But this was personal. Benjie went on to reveal that he had encountered the kidnapper before – twice. Once, when Benjie had been leading an assault on one of the terrorist's hiding compounds, Sabaya came on the radio and proclaimed that he was unfazed by the mortars. They were music to his ears, he had nonchalantly told him. On another occasion Sabaya, again on the radio, had told Benjie that he was standing over the corpse of one of his officers. Recounting these moments was too much for Benjie. Yes, he did hate him, he told Voss, and with that outburst, Voss had achieved a breakthrough. It was the equivalent of: 'That's right.' These specific words are like a key that unlock and then transform a negotiation.

After the breakthrough, Benjie seemed to control his anger, and the next time he negotiated with Sabaya, he followed a list of instructions Voss had put together. Schilling was freed not long after. It seems that a key component of a strong negotiation strategy is to get into your opponent's head and understand what they are feeling.

Whether you're dealing with a terrorist or your own child, difficult conversations are part of our daily lives. Knowing *when* you have been successful in your negotiations is important for the future of any relationship and positive outcomes, because the subtly different expression of 'You're right' as opposed to 'That's right' is a trap. It's an illusion that may give you the impression you've succeeded, when in fact what you have done is failed, because it can mean you're being palmed off. So being forensic and identifying the true issues can not only help pinpoint how to frame your questioning, but can also signal to the other side that you have now understood something you hadn't before. The respondent feels 'seen' and therefore becomes more open to considering other viewpoints. This is crucial in any debate or negotiations. Another lovely example comes from a personal story in Voss's book *Never Split the Difference*, which illustrates why getting to 'That's right' is so important.

At six foot two and 250 pounds, Voss's son Brandon was naturally built to play in one of the toughest sports there is: American football. Brandon loved the game and in particular being a lineman. For those unfamiliar with the game, lineman is the most physically challenging position: playing at the line of scrimmage. The players here are known as defensive linemen and their role is to charge into the offensive line and try to disrupt the opponents' play. These so-called blockers display Herculean power and strength and often (especially in the professional National Football League) look like descendants of Thor.

When Brandon moved to a new school, the football coach there took him out of the line of scrimmage and placed him behind it. Players here are called linebackers. Their job is to try to avoid offensive blockers and rush to tackle the ball carrier. Brandon went from charging into the opposing scrimmage to having to avoid it. This he did not like one bit. So he didn't do it. Instead, he continued to ram into opposing blockers head-on, much to his coach's dismay. His coach pleaded with him to focus on getting to the ball carrier instead of flattening opposing blockers. '[It] was a source of pride,' writes Voss. Every time his coach tried to talk to him about it, Brandon would respond with 'You're right', but then would go right back onto the field and carry on tackling offensive blockers.

Step back for a moment and think about the times we use the phrase 'You're right'. The chances are that it's when we want to shut down a conversation, not because we've actually embraced whatever it is we are being urged towards. This dynamic has been scientifically examined and indeed researchers have indeed found that when we use 'you', it indicates distancing and separation from an issue or person. It's a form of deflection, in which the person saying the words does not fully accept the conclusion or the facts at hand. It doesn't signal agreement; instead, it reveals a lack of understanding.

Back to Voss and his son. After the coach failed to get through to Brandon, Voss had a go. He, too, got the 'you're right' treatment from his son. The FBI's lead international kidnapping negotiator, a man who successfully negotiated with murderous hostage-takers, was at a loss. He couldn't even get through to his own kid? In his mind he went back to the Philippines and remembered Benjie, where his pleas had also fallen on deaf ears. Now, too, he knew he was missing something. What was it that made Brandon defy the logic of his new position in the team? Then came Voss's lightbulb moment, as the underlying reason for his son's behaviour finally dawned on him.

'You seem to think it's unmanly to dodge a block,' Voss told his son. He pressed further and asked whether his son thought it was cowardly to do so. At this, Brandon stared right at him, paused and then said: 'That's right.' In that moment what seemed to have happened is that once Brandon felt seen and understood, he was willing to be less stubborn. After that chat with his dad, Brandon changed course, avoided blocks and became a star linebacker. His team won every game.

There is no exact map to a successful negotiation, but the path there is made easier when we take a step back, put ourselves into the shoes of the other person, and think about what they might be feeling and thinking. And when we're then able to ask questions that show we understand their feelings, we give them the safe space and confidence to reveal their true thoughts. The more people feel understood, the more likely they are to act in a constructive and collaborative manner. Such is the power of words, however ordinary they may seem.

A wealth of compelling evidence shows that the words we use have tremendous psychological value. Our beliefs, fears, thinking patterns, social relationships and deceptive behaviours are all reflected in the ways we use words. The evidence that words provide rich information comes from those who study meaning in human language. These people are called semantic analysts.

James Pennebaker is an eminent figure in the field of language analysis. When I met him over Skype he told me about how he'd got into this research area. He'd always been interested in mind–body problems, chiefly in how psychological factors influence physical health. Could keeping secrets affect you physically, he wondered? This led him to the world of secrecy. Secrecy is, of course, very close to lying. If you're actively keeping something from being revealed that you're embarrassed or upset by, or you're keeping secret about being a victim of a traumatic experience, you're living a kind of lie with other people, even though you're not actually actively lying. You're holding back, the so-called 'lie of omission'.

In the early part of Pennebaker's career, he was studying the body's physiological response to stress and found that keeping secrets can make people sick. He wondered what would happen when people shared their secret. Would their health improve? At about the same time he was invited to give a series of talks at the FBI. There, polygraphers told him that people usually felt liberated after confessions, despite facing severe punishments.

This called for an experiment. Pennebaker brought people to the laboratory and had them talk or write about a big secret. He ended up running several experiments on how writing about secret bad experiences was associated with health improvement, which then led him to start to look at *how* people wrote about these bad experiences. Could analysing what people were saying and how they were saying it be used to predict whether their health would improve? In other words, he was trying to see if there is a 'healthy' form of writing. It turned out that identifying 'healthy' writing was really difficult, which is how he came to develop a computer program. He describes this as a kind of birth of all the work that he has been doing since trying to understand how we use words and how the words we use in everyday life can tell us about people.

The program he developed is called LIWC (pronounced Luke, short for Linguistic Inquiry and Word Count). It takes any given text, counts all the words, and categorises them. It searches for groups of words that have been predefined as matching the various categories of interest; for example, it counts words that are related to the construct of anger ('hate', 'kill', 'angry', 'outrage', and so on). The 80 different word categories include one that contains the first-person singular pronouns 'I', 'me' and 'my'. The algorithm counts all occurrences of 'I', 'I'm', 'I'd', 'me', 'myself', 'mine' and then calculates the percentage of total words that are first-person singular in a given text. It does this for all positive and negative emotion words. 'I' is a marker of depression, insecurity, self-focus, says Pennebaker. 'It's also a marker of authenticity, and so we've done experiments that show that when people are telling the truth, they use the word "I" at higher rates,' he tells me. Language analysis as an authentication method can also be hugely useful when it comes to documents whose origin or authorship need verification.

Over 200 years ago, one man accused another of lying. The problem was he couldn't prove it. Nor could the accused defend himself. He was dead.

Between 1787 and 1788 *The Independent Journal* in New York and two other newspapers published a series of essays that came to be known as the Federalist Papers. It is generally accepted that these papers helped ratify the US Constitution. Each of the 85 short essays was signed with the pseudonym 'Publius', a nod to Publius Valerius Publicola, one of four Roman aristocrats to lead the overthrow of the monarchy and found the Roman Republic. So who was using the pseudonym Publius? Not one, but three great minds who helped to sell the Constitution to the American people: John Jay (a lawyer and diplomat who became the first Chief Justice of the Supreme Court), James Madison (who would go on to become the fourth President) and Alexander Hamilton (the first Secretary of the Treasury). They were three of the Founding Fathers, a group of revolutionaries who led the war for independence from the British monarchy.

Hamilton died in a duel. On the day before he departed for his fatal meeting, he wrote a note revealing the authorship of the Federalist Papers. In fact, Hamilton declared he had written most of the essays. That was a problem for Madison. It is largely agreed that 51 of the essays were indeed penned by Hamilton; Jay had contributed only a handful (five); Madison and Hamilton had collaborated on three, but that left twelve papers whose authorship was disputed. Madison left it fourteen years after Hamilton's death before he decided to dispute his account. With his word against a dead man's, there was no definitive proof. It would take nearly 145 years, a pair of statisticians and multiple computers to work it all out.

In 1962, two professors, Frederick Mosteller at Harvard

University and David Wallace at the University of Chicago revealed the results of their long and thorough analysis of the Federalist Papers. They had sleuthed for linguistic patterns and markers, looking to identify subtle patterns of word choice that were characteristic of either of the Founding Fathers. It took the two professors three years of combing through their known writings.

Using the frequency of key words (they boiled those down to 30, which included words such as 'also', 'vigor' and 'this') they built a mathematical picture of Hamilton and Madison's respective writing styles. They compared the frequency of non-contextual words (propositions, conjunctions, articles, adverbs) in the disputed papers with the range of frequencies with which the same words appeared in other works known to have been written by Hamilton or Madison. Non-contextual words include some of the most used words like 'the', 'and', 'of', 'to', 'by' and so on, but their frequency of use can differ from author to author. The researchers concluded that Madison was the author of eleven of the twelve disputed papers, and suggested that he was likely to have also written the remaining one.

The case seemed settled. Indeed it was for a time. But a myriad of new methods have been developed since then. These new methods go beyond the analyses of function words that Mosteller and Wallace used. Computers can now analyse texts using the mean length of a word, frequency, richness of vocabulary, and characters (character count and long-range correlations), in addition to syntactic and semantic information and text format. In fact, the Federalist Papers have become a sort of analysts' sport. That said, the studies that have since emerged mostly concur with Mosteller and Wallace.

A more recent case of 'Who wrote it?' came in 2013, when the crime novel *The Cuckoo's Calling* was published. It caused controversy when a Twitter user didn't believe that its stated author,

Robert Galbraith, was a real person – insisting instead that it was written by Harry Potter author J. K. Rowling.

The *Sunday Times*, a UK broadsheet, hired a forensic linguist to get to the bottom of the allegation. It took Patrick Juola at Duquesne University in Pittsburgh, Pennsylvania, less than an hour to analyse several books Rowling had written (for comparison, it took Mosteller and Wallace three years to analyse 85 essays). Cross-referencing the books, Juola saw that the linguistic fingerprints matched those of Rowling. He found similarities in word length, overall vocabulary, and the use of word pairs (two words regularly in close proximity). A key indicator was the 100 function words Rowling used most frequently.

Of course, our brains are incredible and fast in many ways, but for certain types of task they lack the speed and efficiency of a computer. So how can we process word cues? There are tells in language and they can be just specific words.

Even our word sleuth Pennebaker seems to have a tell word, which he found out by chance. He was surprised when a friend thanked him for a review he had given anonymously. Pennebaker needed to know what had given him away. His friend laughed and told him it was just one word: 'intriguing'. Now, this isn't a particularly unusual word. But if, like Pennebaker, you make a habit of using 'intriguing' and its variations, then it becomes a tell, no matter how subtle. I ask Pennebaker if everyone has a tell word. In all likelihood, yes, he responds. Even Madison and Hamilton had theirs. Hamilton used the word 'readily' whereas Madison never did. Madison used the word 'consequently' in nine out of fifteen papers whereas Hamilton – who had written the majority of the papers – only used it in three of them.

(This notion of tell words has been corroborated by my editor, who informs me all authors have linguistic tics and that one of my own tells is the word 'misperception'!)

Sometimes words are so obscure or unusual that they can

stand out like a beacon. In 1996, three words helped end a seven-teen-year manhunt.

Writing Style – the Capture of the Unabomber

On 25 May 1978, Terry Marker, a security guard at Northwestern University, Illinois, opened a letter that exploded. Marker, the first victim of a serial killer who came to be known as the Unabomber, survived with only minor injuries. Over the next seventeen years another fifteen letter bombs were sent to universities and airports, killing three and injuring 23 people. A $1 million reward for the Unabomber was posted. At the time it was the FBI's biggest-ever manhunt. But the eventual capture of the killer didn't come down to the many DNA samples, partial fingerprints, or the thousands of tiny pieces of shrapnel that had been collected at the bombing locations. Ultimately, the Unabomber gave himself away – through his own written words.

David Kaczynski was busy helping his mom clear out the family home after she decided to move from Chicago to New York. There were still some of his older brother Ted's belongings in the house, including piles of old writings. Kaczynski skimmed through them and noticed something odd. There was something unsettlingly familiar about the language used. It reminded him of a piece he had read not too long ago: the Unabomber's manifesto, which had been published in papers nationwide including *The New York Times* and the *Washington Post*.

Could his own brother really be the serial killer the authorities had been hunting? David's wife had had her suspicions all along and had shared them with him, but Kaczynski ignored her and wouldn't even entertain the idea that his own brother could be responsible for the horrific attacks that terrorised the nation. It just couldn't be Ted. David had idolised him growing up. He loved him. Yet the more he read the boxes and boxes of Ted's writings, the more he could see the Unabomber's writing style in them. The suspicion was now gnawing at him too. He grabbed a copy of the manifesto and started to re-read it. Three words delivered a crushing reality: 'Cool-headed logicians' – it was a phrase his brother used.

Torn between love for his brother and duty to his country, David Kaczynski contacted a family friend in DC, a lawyer, who then called the FBI. The Bureau's semantic experts examined the writings and matched the rhetorical language patterns to the Unabomber manifesto. Ted was arrested at a remote mountain cabin in Montana in April 1996. He later confessed to his crimes in court.

Still, there aren't always these stand-out word tells. (That would be too easy, wouldn't it?) Instead, information often comes via word patterns.

We each have a way of speaking and writing. My fellow writers out there could take the very same content you are reading right now and retell it very differently, in their own style, and with different choices of emphasis. The art of storytelling is as much about style as it is about content. Just as there is more than one way to bake a cake, there are plenty of books that cover the same subject. Writers weave their voices into their writings. Their writing style is their fingerprint. It's what sets them apart.

Fewer than 200 words in the English language make up 60% of all the words that we regularly say, write, hear or read. Most of the rest? We pay zero attention to them, neither as listeners nor as speakers. These are the little words like 'to', 'the', 'at' and 'on' that we use with content words. Linguistic analysts have a name for them: function words.

We may believe that we are in control of our words and even, perhaps, that we choose them carefully. And that may be true for some words, like nouns and verbs, but not for function words. Not only do we not pay attention to function words, we use them completely unconsciously. Language analysis tools indicate that we have little agency over this, and in the process of using them we are creating unconscious linguistic patterns. Because they vary less with changing topics and genres than other words do, the analysis of function words is considered to be the most reliable method for attributing literary authorship.

Think about how to describe where the cutlery is placed in a table setting. From left to right, a basic standard table setting typically starts fork, plate, knife. The description of the location of the fork, for example, can vary: it can be *to*, *on* or *at* the left of the plate. These terms all clearly describe the position of the fork and it seems to make no difference which one you use. This, perhaps, is why function words are often overlooked: at first sight they don't seem to be adding anything material. Yet they can provide powerful insight into the human psyche. The choice of words can define a style of language. It can determine how our online dating prospects view us, distinguish which rap artists are honest about being true gangsters, diagnose whether our therapists are just as depressed as we are, or expose which of our colleagues secretly think they have a higher status than we do. They can also reveal if there are issues in our relationships.

On What We Don't Say

There is a long list of ingredients to any successful relationship. Most of us know that how we speak to each other is key. But few of us know that the nuances of word choices can reveal a lot that we want to keep hidden, whether consciously or subconsciously.

In a study from 2009, a seemingly innocuous part of everyday speech provided an important window into the inner workings of intimate relationships, the qualities of the connections between partners, and the ways that emotions are expressed and regulated when couples have to deal with conflict and challenges. In this study, 154 married couples were observed during a fifteen-minute conversation, and researchers determined the quality of a marriage purely by assessing the individual words they used. The core finding was that couples who spoke using mostly 'me' and 'you' had a rockier relationship than those who used 'we'. Separateness in language, researchers said, implied a greater sense of independence and distance in the relationship. Behind the study were two researchers from the University of Texas in Austin, Cindy Chung and James Pennebaker – yes, him again. It was because of this study that I decided it was time to meet him.

When we met over Skype in October 2018, it was a month after *The New York Times* had published an anonymous opinion letter about life in the Trump White House. Pennebaker – recognised as the US's leading word expert – had been inundated with calls to analyse the letter and reveal the identity of the author. He never did. At least, not publicly.

Privately, he did indeed analyse the letter, and had pinned it to one person and one person alone, he told me. I felt giddy with excitement. I was about to find out the identity of the author who had had the inner circle of the US President rattled and desperate to find them. My excitement lasted only a few seconds. Pennebaker made it very clear that he would only tell me the name under the condition that it was strictly off the record. Of course, he was right to guard the identity of the whistleblower. But he had no issue with my sharing his view that the popular notion that the letter had been penned by Vice President Pence was wrong: 'First of all, he is just not a good writer and that piece was written beautifully. It was logical and had a sly sense of humour to it. It showed real sophistication. And Pence isn't even on that planet.'

This wasn't the first time Pennebaker had been asked to assess the speech of leaders and government officials. In early 2000, Pennebaker started looking into the changes in leaders' rhetoric over time, analysing how language use changes before going to war, after being attacked and as leaders lose their grip on the reins. After 9/11, the FBI commissioned him to study Al-Qaeda communications – videotapes, interviews, letters. Pennebaker and Chung found that Al-Qaeda leader Osama bin Laden used 'I' words very little but 'we' words frequently. This indicated overconfidence bordering on arrogance, the researchers stated. Perhaps the most valuable finding came from the technique known as the meaning extraction that Chung applied. This revealed bin Laden's obsessions and intentions: rage against his homeland, Saudi Arabia, but little interest in Israel compared with other Al-Qaeda operatives.

Today, the pool from which analysts can extract meaning has grown exponentially, and way beyond the rhetoric of leaders, terrorists and 'persons of interest'. Billions upon billions of words are produced and freely shared online. Anyone using the internet, putting likes, dislikes, shares, tweets and posts out into the digital space, can be subject to analysis.

From our political opinions to our support for groups of people and our likes or dislikes for a brand, public opinion has never been so public. And never has it been so easy to find and assess. Once, pollsters and newspapers would send out swarms of people to interview and survey the population to gather insight. Of course, this methodology was imperfect: the number and the types of people that could be reached was extremely constrained. In addition, it took far too long to go through the responses manually. Those constraints no longer exist. Automated and computerised tools help measure and summarise vast amounts of content. The dramatic increase in the volume of digitised text readily available online is matched by more and more analysis algorithms that are popping up by the dozen. And wherever there is an opportunity to gain insights into people's psyche, the desire to monetise this is never too far off. Companies increasingly look to algorithms to get an idea of whether their interactions with their target audience are positive, negative or neutral. And of course insights into people's general morale or feelings are of great value to political entities, too.

The desire to find solid links between the way people feel and how they are likely to act as a consequence has spurred on researchers in a range of areas. One group thought they could exploit the emotions on display on social media to predict the financial markets. 'Twitter mood predicts the stock market' is the title of a 2010 paper by researchers who claimed to be able to correlate mood to the behaviour of the Dow Jones stock market index. They said they could predict with near 90% accuracy how the stock market would behave next.

It would be quite something if it were that easy. To pin down the movement of the market to 'mood' alone is to ignore the fact that the Dow is influenced by a number of criteria, such as policy, trade wars, international and national conflict, climate and, yes, pandemics. It came as no surprise that the results didn't hold up when other researchers tried to replicate the findings.

To be fair, it is perhaps not an unreasonable thought that AI could be powerful enough to make these types of prediction, considering how large language models such as ChatGPT have demonstrated an impressive ability to mimic human language. However, we are still a long way away from algorithms, machines or robots fully understanding the nuances that humans use to convey messages – not least because what we say isn't always what we mean. We use nuances that come in the form of indirectness, or misleading statements disguised as polite excuses and civil justifications, or simply as a way to avoid making a statement at all. Nuances are often missed by humans, and even when we pick up on them, we don't quite know how to interpret them. But, a researcher in Chicago had a go.

Forensic Accounting

Anastasia Zakolyukina is an associate professor at the University of Chicago Booth School of Business. She analyses accounting and finance using natural language processing and machine learning. In other words, she is a word hunter. Her hunting grounds are conference calls, where she analyses the linguistic patterns of senior executives.

To investigate a method that could help predict when senior executives are being deceptive, Zakolyukina reviewed the quarterly financial statements of the companies whose conference calls she was analysing, to see whether their financial records had been manipulated. Prior research had used a variety of accounting-based models to identify and predict accounting manipulations, but the results of these methods had been modest.

Instead of studying their financial statements, Zakolyukina analysed the language CEOs and CFOs used during conference calls – assuming that the executives knew when reports had been intentionally manipulated. To help with her forensic analysis, Zakolyukina used Pennebaker's LIWC program. It let her categorise positive and negative emotion words, certainty and tentative word and speech hesitation. Additionally, she segmented out self-references (I), first-person plural (we), third-person plural (they) and impersonal pronouns (such as 'everybody', 'anybody', and 'nobody').

By classifying words, she could predict with up to 66% accuracy when senior executives were lying. This may not look like an impressive number, but scoring better than chance meant that this method gave an additional forensic tool to investigators. They could now also use the linguistic cues of CEOs and CFOs in conference call narratives when trying to identify financial misreporting.

The use of first-person singular pronouns implies that the person is taking ownership. And so when CEOs were being deceptive they used fewer self-references, more third-person plural ('we', 'they'), and fewer certainty ('always', 'never') and more hesitation words ('ah', 'blah', 'eh', 'um', 'ehhh', 'hm', 'oh', 'ugh' etc). So when they were lying, they would use the pronouns 'I', 'mine' and 'me' little or not at all, and would overuse terms like 'we', 'us' and our 'team'. They spoke in significantly more general terms ('you folks know', 'shareholders would agree'), distancing themselves from the subject while at the same time trying to gain credibility. They also used fewer extreme negative emotions ('adverse', 'despair', 'fail', 'difficult') and fewer references to shareholders' value and value creation ('increase', 'enhance', 'unlocking', 'delivering').

We see a good example from Enron CEO Ken Lay, addressing his employees around the time the company was about to go bust: 'I think our core businesses are extremely strong. We have a very strong competitive advantage. Of course, we're now transferring this very successful business model and approach to a lot of new, very large markets globally.'

In one of her subsequent studies Zakolyukina looked at the methods CEOs used to *not* answer questions. She found they did this using blockers: non-answers – answers that didn't contain the information they were asked for. They would say something like: 'I am not going to answer/comment on that' or 'I don't have the information to hand/can't share the details'. They also employed what Zakolyukina calls the *interruptor method*: when a speaker interrupts the person asking the question midway, never allowing them to finish their question. Then there is the method of responding to a question with a question, allowing the original question to be dodged entirely.

In a 2019 study, Zakolyukina looked at explicit phrases used to avoid giving out information, with the aim of developing a measure for disclosure. To do this she scoured through a huge data set of nearly 3 million question–answer pairs from corporate conference calls from almost 3,000 firms. Why corporate conference calls? These are company results calls, which occur quarterly, and typically have the CEO and CFO of the company present, as well as investors and analysts. A key part of these calls is the Q&A section: what is or isn't disclosed in this section becomes very important, as analysts will then compile research including recommendations on whether to buy, sell or hold securities in the company, which can affect its stock price. In an interview with *Forbes* in March 2022, Zakolyukina explained: 'We do not really have a good measure of how forthcoming executives are in their disclosures. Extant approaches that, for example, count the number of press releases or the number of words in press releases do not really get to the information demanded by investors. The interactive nature of earnings conference calls allows us to capture non-answers to the questions asked.'

She found that in a typical conference call, 11% of all answers were non-answers. Further sleuthing showed that across various industries, an average of one in ten questions were left unanswered; it also indicated that those questions tended to be more negative in tone, more complex or trying to extract more detail or specificity. Questions that contained more uncertainty words, and questions that weren't clear and were difficult to understand, were also left unanswered.

Choosing not to answer a question does not automatically indicate deception. It may be a strategic withholding of information ahead of a product launch or a merger. It may be active avoidance or simply due to ignorance. But the very nature of non-answers means that they raise suspicion and interest and can cause tension. This in turn can have a range of consequences. To investors, silence is a negative sign. It signals no news, and to them no news is bad news. As an example, in the May 2018 conference call held by Tesla Motors, CEO Elon Musk repeatedly interrupted analysts before they even finished asking their questions. Musk's combative nature was considered the number one reason why Tesla Inc stocks took a nosedive that same day, losing over 5% in value.

Zakolyukina's work comes on the back of several other corporate investigations, which also used algorithms to sleuth for information. LIWC was used by a number of research groups when an unusually rich semantic hunting ground became available in 2004.

That year, hundreds of thousands of internal emails from the managers at Enron were released. With assets of more than $60 billion and nearly 30,000 staff, Enron had been the seventh largest corporation in America. The company had risen to stratospheric heights. It was a juggernaut, which is why its collapse shook Wall Street to its core. The investigations that followed were looking to decipher why the lies and failings hadn't been spotted much sooner.

Deception theory suggests that deceptive communication leaves behind linguistic footprints. As a method of communication, email is a hybrid between informal speech and formal writing. The enormous cache of Enron emails that were made public supplied the first large-scale collection of real-world emails – and thereby provided unprecedented data points for researchers.

The Enron emails revealed that people who use fewer first-person pronouns may be signalling that they're trying to dissociate themselves from their words. A further indicator that a message may be fabricated is the lack of so-called exclusive words, such as 'but', 'except' and 'without', which signals a less cognitively complex 'story', one that is easier to create and remember consistently. Also, people who feel guilty tend to use more negative emotion words when they're being deceptive. Using standard models of deception, researchers have been able to apply them to emails and demonstrate which ones are likely to be deceptive.

Today, corporate forensics relies heavily on algorithms and AI to hunt for fraud. And PwC, one of the world's largest professional services firms centred around everything accounting, uses word-analysis software. 'Searching the data used to be a case of using certain key words and reviewing the hits,' Jonathan Holmes, partner at PwC's forensic services practice in London, tells me. Now, PwC's standard practice is to collect all the data it can get its hands on from email, financial information, instant messages, shared drives and so on, which is always way too much for any human or groups of humans to process manually. Gone are the days when forensic accountants had to analyse reams and reams of documents. Today they have the power of technology at their fingertips to help them with the surgical work and the hard graft of searching the data and overlaying sources to derive chronologies of what has happened. Artificial intelligence and machine learning can use a single term, phrase, or an entire paragraph, and then map out related concepts. Even more so these technologies make it possible to tell a computer that a certain email is relevant, then ask it to provide all the emails that it thinks share characteristics with that specific 'hot' document. These technologies can show complete networks of communication, revealing who is talking to whom, and quickly identifying persons of interest and related conversations.

That's how the Libor (London Interbank Offered Rate) scandal was brought to light in 2012. Several financial institutions colluded with each other to manipulate the banks' lending rate for profit. Bloomberg Terminals used to be the preferred chatrooms for traders to arrange trades on stocks, bonds, currencies and commodities outside an exchange, and by analysing these chats, investigators connected the dots and were able to charge three traders with fraud.

Of course, not all investigations can or should be digital; sometimes you just have to find the physical evidence – or lack thereof. Muddy Waters is a short-selling hedge fund that prides itself on sniffing out accounting shenanigans at listed companies, and then betting against them. The fund is so good that when it bets against a company, it creates a tsunami on the stock market: given Muddy Waters' track record, others assume its investigations have given it good reason to do so. The company made headlines in 2011 when it investigated a Toronto-listed company, Sino-Forest, which at the time was the most valuable forestry company on the Toronto Stock Exchange. The timber firm was based in Ontario but did most of its business in China, where it claimed it owned acres of woodland. Only, Muddy Waters struggled to find the trees. It released a 40-page report claiming Sino-Forest was a multi-billion-dollar Ponzi scheme and labelled it a fraud. Sino-Forest's stock price plummeted 95% within a week of the report's release. The company ultimately ceased to exist a few months after that.

Deception is a popular field for study, but it's also one of the hardest. For the most part, deception studies are set up in the form of an experiment, mostly in a lab, often at a university and using students. But even when they're not in a lab, they are still planned and staged. The problem is that these studies lack an important component: the real-life consequences of being caught. This can and does affect lying and truth-telling behaviours, and so the results cannot be presented as iron-clad proof. That's why, when real-life scenarios present themselves, as in the case of the Enron emails, researchers jump at the chance to study them. As technology has expanded not just our ability to communicate in writing but also the frequency with which we do so, it has extended the semantic hunting grounds into everyday communication. Researchers find plenty to study in our casual communications with each other.

Butler Lies

We lie. We all do. Daily and often. Out of necessity. Sound like an excuse? It's not. Even though lying can be bad, we do it to shield and protect, because the alternative would mean hurting feelings or causing offence – and so lying becomes an important and frequent part of our daily lives and social interactions.

For thousands of years, human communication was predominantly face to face. Social media introduced a new channel of communication, and the sheer volume of information we create every day is staggering. We send written messages constantly via email, Facebook posts, tweets and WhatsApp messages. Instant messaging (IM), rather than voice-calling, is the single most used feature on a smartphone. In fact, messaging is the preferred method of communication across generations and nations. In 2020 the messaging platform WhatsApp saw 100 billion messages being sent through its platform every day. Communication via messaging-based platforms has had a significant impact on how we talk to and trust each other.

Sure, being able to connect with others instantly and easily is of great value, but there are downsides. The pressure to conform and to respond to messages by always being 'on' and available can affect us negatively. Plenty of studies have shown that the constant pinging from devices calling for our attention has brought a set of problems that previously had not existed. Some of us feel overrun by the email load and unable to work uninterrupted for long periods of time. So how do we deal with it? We lie, kind of. We routinely use a specific type of deception as a tactic to avoid having to respond right this minute. In 2009, researchers at Cornell University in Ithaca, New York, led by Canadian communication and psychology researcher Jeffrey Hancock, coined a term for this deception: they called it a 'butler lie'.

The term refers to the butlers of old, who as one of their roles would act as social barrier between their masters and people who wanted to have access to them. They were trained to make polite excuses and civil justifications as to why their employer was unable to meet or see a person. A butler lie can be used to avoid a new conversation or a continuation of an existing one. It can look something like this: 'Okay, sorry, gotta go; I have to dash out and run some errands.' Or it can be used to smoothly exit an ongoing conversation: 'Okay, back to work for me!' (My favourite is 'Must go, my phone is about to die.') Or one can be used to explain other communications behaviour, such as why there has been a long pause in between conversations – for example, 'Hey, just saw your call. My phone wasn't with me.'

Hancock and a group of researchers examined this behaviour in detail. They found that one in ten of all instant messages qualified as lies, and of these, one in five were butler lies. Clearly, lying is an important social practice, and it has become acceptable to lie when we want to enter or exit ongoing exchanges. It's a means of managing social interactions.

'You name it, man, there [are] as many ways to lie as there [are] to tell the truth,' Hancock tells me. We sit in his office overlooking the Oval at Stanford University, where he now works. Until the 1930s, sheep used to graze the patch. Today it's a pristinely manicured lawn. The moss-green grass is so rich in colour that the flower bed pops like a kaleidoscope against it. Palm trees stretch tall into the sky, bathing in the rays of the ever-shining sun, swaying softly in the gentle breeze. What a lovely place to come to work or study at, I think.

Hancock's career started nowhere near a university, but at the Canadian customs agency. He remembers thinking at the time how crazy it was that there was no way to tell if someone was lying to them. He has been interested in how people communicate ever since those days at the agency. He went on to study psychology, and for his PhD he wanted to focus on how people talk when using the internet, and how they form impressions of others. His advisor at the time was worried. This was 1997. The internet was still relatively new tech, and no one knew whether it was just a fad or something that was here to stay. Now, of course, the internet and spin-off technologies such as messaging and other social media apps have increased the speed and quantity of information that is shared among humans and organisations exponentially. And what's most interesting is how the internet has made it so easy to lie, to the extent that online misinformation and disinformation have become a common part of the internet. From populists to click-baiters and from deepfakes to hoaxes, the internet is rife with lies and liars alike. Hancock clearly had a finger on the pulse when he chose to focus on online communication. For nearly three decades he has researched everything from fake reviews to deceptive online dating profiles to how online misinformation can influence beliefs about elections or how social media can affect our psychological wellbeing. It's an impressive archive of work, which has turned him into one of the most sought-after experts on deception.

Not every lie is the same. Lies can cover a wide spectrum. This is why we hear terms such as 'not quite true', 'false statement' or 'incorrect', rather than the more loaded word 'lie' itself. Exaggerating or underestimating numbers is an example of lying in ranges. How far these lies veer from the truth can affect how much we then perceive these as lies. For example, Donald Trump's repeated assertion that 3 million people voted illegally in the US elections, when the real number is very close to zero. Trump's claim is not incorrect or even not quite true: it's a point-blank lie.

I look at Hancock and ask him the question I've been dying to ask since I stepped into his office: Does he analyse on the go, and can he tell if someone is lying to him? There was a period when he did, he told me: 'I was thinking about it all the time, and in fact I started playing poker just to see if I could apply those skills, and I was actually pretty good.' He was better at the maths side than the deception side of poker, he tells me, but quickly adds what poker is fundamentally about: 'Figuring it out.' It's an important aspect to remember: in poker as in life, there is no universal cue. There is no Pinocchio nose. Deception is contextual.

There we have it once more. Yet another expert telling us that there are no real-world, one-size-fits-all cues to deception – but there are cues to believability, and those cues you have to piece together yourself.

Culture and Behaviour

We have heard that to truly understand and assess the meaning of words, we need to view them in context, which includes under-standing the person who says them and where they come from. Why is this key? Because we're not all playing by the same rules.

Each and every one of us carries our own communication rules. These are defined both by culture and by context, and thus cultural differences can affect communication style. A lack of cultural awareness makes us more likely to misread, and also mislead, others. So it helps to have an understanding of a person's culture before we try to interpret what is being said. This becomes increasingly important in a world knitted tighter together by an ever-growing digital network, where being aware of cross-cultural differences is a valuable asset.

All cultures have rules of speaking and their own versions of indirectness and politeness. Misunderstandings can occur when we transfer the rules of our own culture to people from differ-ing cultural backgrounds. Think about these following examples.

Chinese spoken communication is governed by the notions of politeness, respectfulness, self-denigration while elevating others, and extreme modesty. For example, responses like 'No, I'm not pretty at all' and 'My English is poor' are likely to be expressed out of modesty. In Chinese culture, respectfulness will also be communicated through greetings. 'Professor, where are you going?' or 'Aunt, what are you busy with?' are examples of the speaker showing respect and care towards the hearer.

In a further example, Korean English professor and director of the Korean Language Program at Columbia University, Joowon Suh, explains how English speakers may have missed out on some important nuances in the popular Netflix survival drama series *Squid Game*. The fictional dystopian show, in which desperate contestants play deadly games for cash prizes, was subtitled for non-Korean speakers.

She explains how the on-screen translations didn't capture the nuances that would have highlighted important emotional details, particularly focusing on how Korean speakers use address terms. They use honorifics a lot when speaking to each other, and in the show, the evolution of the relationships between the characters is signposted by the changing terms of address.

As an example, Suh picks a scene between Sang-woo, a stockbroker and Ali, a Pakistani immigrant, who had been addressing him as sir ('Sajangnim'). According to the subtitles, Sang-woo asks Ali to call him by his first name, but he actually uses the term 'Hyung'. Koreans don't customarily call each other by their first names. 'We are not really a first-name-based society,' says Suh. 'Hyung' means older brother of a man. It signifies a close relationship.

Later in the show, just before Ali is betrayed by Sang-woo, you see Ali walking around calling out for him, using 'Hyung! Hyung!' By now Ali believed he and Sang-woo were close – as close as brothers, even. That's why this particular scene is so heartbreaking, if you know the distinction between 'Hyung' and 'Sajangnim' in the Korean language, explains Suh. For a Korean speaker, the betrayal is much more tragic than for non-native speakers who will have missed the nuance.

In Japanese culture, the word *Hai* can have various

interpretations of both 'Yes' and 'No'. It is an expression used to show that you are listening and paying attention to what the other person is saying. Contrary to Western misperception, it does not necessarily mean agreement, or 'Yes'. Arabic speakers tend to be more indirect than Americans. Germans are known to not mince their words and can be very direct, which can make them seem impolite – they don't have an actual term for 'small talk', because they don't do it.

Being encyclopaedically knowledgeable about every single culture on Earth is an unreasonable proposition. What is not unreasonable is to develop an attitude that assumes that cultural differences could always be in play in any engagement with others. If you adopt this attitude, you're handling your interactions with others with a sensibility and respect that allows for better communication. If you do not, you run the risk of judging others by imposing your own standards and cultural norms onto them. And we are judgemental enough as it is.

Linguistic Profiling

'Yo, where's table seventeen?!' The shout rang across the room, piercing through the white noise of 200-odd murmuring players and the riffling of chips. The lost player was a short, black-bearded guy who looked like he was in his late twenties and about to pop into a 90s hip-hop video (although his coordinated outfit of white Nike baseball cap and white balloon-like Puffa jacket paired with sparkly white trainers made him look more like the fictional satirical character Ali G than Tupac Shakur).

The tournament director showed him to table seventeen, my table. As he sat down to my left, he announced: 'Let's play some fucking poker, people!' With that I knew just what type of player he was going to be. I call them 'firecrackers'. This is a type of player who doesn't take poker seriously enough to study it – yet it remains a game he feels entitled to win. He is a textbook loose cannon. I knew I was in for a treat, and I was not disappointed. In my head I gave him an hour before he lost all of his chips, but he proved me wrong. It took him just three hands to spew away his stack.

We all make assumptions about people based not only on what they say, but how they say it and what they sound like. We use these linguistic markers to make judgements. When we encounter someone speaking with an accent, we will deduce that their native language may be different to ours. It immediately anchors our perception of the other person and can affect our behaviour and our subsequent interaction with them.

A group of researchers led by Patricia Bestelmeyer at Bangor University in Wales scanned the brain activity of study participants while they listened to voices reading numbers with southern English, Scottish and American accents. When participants heard voices that were similar to their own, the researchers observed increased activity in the bilateral amygdalae – the pair of small, almond-shaped regions deep in the brain that are linked with emotions. If we are familiar with it, an accent can give us information about a person's background in terms of geographic location, and we can even pinpoint people to different parts of one country simply based on audible differences – when a trained ear hears a Liverpudlian or a Glaswegian, it'll know one is from England and the other from Scotland. But the impact accents have on us goes further than that.

While we are effective at distinguishing accents, we are terrible listeners. Many of us fall back on stereotypes and negative value judgements about a person's socioeconomic status and characteristics based on accent. In the UK, researchers cite this as one of the main reasons for the lack of social mobility. The Accent Bias in Britain project goes as far as saying that language may well be one of the primary cultural practices through which mobility and socioeconomic success is obstructed. In 2019, the project specifically looked at accents and investigated whether unconscious accent bias played a role in how job candidates were evaluated. Eight hundred participants were asked to rate each one of 38 different British accents (on a scale of 1–7) for its prestige and pleasantness. Received Pronunciation (also known as 'BBC English') remains top rated and the accent of prestige (even though less than 10% of the population speak like this). Historically industrial urban accents (Birmingham, Liverpool, Essex) and ethnic varieties of English such as 'Asian' and 'Afro-Caribbean' all received poor ratings. The project's findings showed accent bias to be pervasive and, more remarkably, that the hierarchy seems to have remained consistent over the past 50 years. It seems that a sort of standard language ideology continues to be used to judge those who fit it more favourably. Those with an accent from working-class, regional and ethnic minority backgrounds are placed at a disadvantage, creating an immediately uneven and unfair playing field.

In 2022, researchers complemented the earlier study by surveying thousands of college and university students in the UK, as well as early-career and senior professionals, and reported that the same categories – social class, region and ethnicity – affect whether a person feels anxious that their accent may impede their professional progress, feels a compromised sense of belonging, or has experienced mocking or singling out of their accent in workplace and social settings.

The mental shortcuts we use all the time are useful, of course, but they can potentially skew our ability to judge fairly. To avoid unduly discriminating against others, we would do well to pay attention to relevant cues (like experience, skill, knowledge) and not rely solely on social stereotypes. We now know that a mere accent can influence our perception and affect our decision-making. How others use grammar and pronounce words sets off yet another round of verbal cues. It's worth being cautious about our decisions when we catch ourselves making assumptions based on what we hear.

While racial profiling is based on visual cues, linguistic profiling uses auditory cues that may well dip back into our ideas of where someone is from and what their background is.

In 1999, a black man was convicted in Kentucky based not on eyewitness evidence, but because of a voice on tape that 'sounded black'. Testimony by a white police officer who had never seen or met the defendant before was accepted by the court because the officer stated that he had heard the voice of the defendant. The allegation was that during a drug deal, the defendant, Clifford, was the one who had handled the drugs. The issue was that an informant named Vanover had already testified that the crack cocaine actually belonged to *him*, that it was he who'd made the sale to an undercover cop, and that Clifford had not been involved in the transaction. There was no video evidence, and the recording from the wiretap was deemed inaudible and thus was neither admitted into evidence nor played to the jury. The prosecution needed to prove that it was the defendant who had sold crack cocaine. The officer providing testimony, Officer Smith, hadn't been at the scene but had been listening in to the transaction via the wiretap. The following section of the cross-examination is a good example of Socratic questioning, which as it unfolds unearths the fallacy of the officer's thinking.

Defense Counsel: Okay. Well, how does a black male sound?
Officer Smith: Uh, some male blacks have a, a different sound of, of their voice. Just as I have a different sound of my voice as Detective Birkenhauer does. I sound different than you.
Defense Counsel: Okay, can you demonstrate that for the jury?
Officer Smith: I don't think that would be a fair and accurate depiction of the, you know, of the way the man sounds.
Defense Counsel: So not all male blacks sound alike?

Officer Smith: That's correct, yes.

Defense Counsel: Okay. In fact, some of them sound like whites, don't they?

Officer Smith: Yes.

Defense Counsel: Do all whites sound alike?

Officer Smith: No sir.

Defense Counsel: Okay. Do some white people sound like blacks when they're talking?

Officer Smith: Possible, yes.

Officer Smith never saw the transaction taking place; he simply heard it. This is an extreme example, but sadly race identification based on voice alone isn't a rarity.

Housing discrimination is illegal. That doesn't mean it doesn't still happen. John Baugh proved you could be discriminated against based purely on your accent.

In 1988, Baugh accepted a fellowship at the Stanford Center for Advanced Study in the Behavioral Sciences (CASBS), which meant he had to move to Palo Alto for a year. He travelled ahead and looked for an apartment that was big enough for his family. This was the pre-internet era, so house-hunting required scouring through the classified sections and picking up the phone to call ahead to enquire about availability and viewings.

On the phone, Baugh would explain that he was a visiting professor at CASBS and looking for a space for his family. No landlord had asked about his 'race', but in four instances when he went to see the places he was denied a viewing, and either told that the apartments were already let or the owners had decided to take it off the market. Baugh suspected that the refusals were a direct result of the way he looked. Baugh is African American. He wondered whether or not you could be discriminated against purely based on your accent, so he did what any scientist would do: he put it to the test and devised an experiment.

In March 1999, Baugh and two colleagues, Thomas Purnell and William Idsardi, published their study into what sort of cues might trigger discrimination. In the inner-city communities of Philadelphia and Los Angeles, African American Vernacular English (AAVE) and Mexican English, also known as Chicane English (ChE), are spoken widely. Baugh, who grew up in these communities, was able to speak these with ease.

In one experiment, he called landlords three times at 30-minute intervals. Each time he started with the exact same words – 'Hello, I am calling about the apartment you have advertised in the paper' – but used a different speech pattern and accent. Baugh noted reactions and answers, and a pattern became apparent. He was invited for a viewing nearly two and a half times as often when he spoke in Standard American English. He proved that a majority of people made snap judgements – racist ones. In a second experiment, study participants seemed able to deduce origins just from the single word 'Hello'. How was this possible? Accents.

Nearly 50 years ago, James Emil Flege at the University of Alabama found that it takes just 30 milliseconds of speech for a listener to identify an accented speaker's ethnic or cultural background. And we know that even when listeners do not recognise an accent they tend to make snap judgements anyway. An accent can trigger social categorisation in a prompt, automatic and occasionally unconscious manner, says Ze Wang, associate professor in marketing at the University of Central Florida. Wang focuses on consumer behaviour and customer experience analysis. She has built on Baugh's research and that of many others since, to see how accent stereotypes can have bias on customers' evaluation and interpretation of their service experience. In short, she looked at customers' accent-induced prejudices.

In a series of experiments that either required participants to listen to taped phone calls or make phone calls to a pretend bank's customer call centre, Wang and her colleagues made the same findings over and over again. Even in cases where service scenarios and conversation scripts were identical, customers rated the performance of employees with an Indian accent way lower than their counterparts who had either an American or British accent. When the service outcome was a bad one (i.e. the customer's request could not be fulfilled), the negative associations with the Indian accent were even more pronounced.

American Standard English is now the form of English predominantly taught across the globe, which is why you may find non-native English speakers from the Pacific to the Far East and even Europe speaking with an American accent. It is believed that the rise of American English started with the Second World War, and its spread is further heavily attributed to its dominance in popular culture, movies, information technology and the internet. American English may have bumped British Standard English off the top spot. Even so, when it comes to accents, the British version is still perceived as 'better'.

To better understand the reasons why we do what we do and why we think what we think, we need to go beyond which action causes which reaction. We need to seek out the root causes – the *why*. So why is the British accent perceived as sophisticated and pleasant to listen to, and why do people associate it with professionalism, ambition and competence for higher-status jobs? Just how did it come about that the British accent, and particularly Received Pronunciation (RP), enjoys such great positive bias, not just in the UK but across the world? Money and politics have something to do with it.

The standardisation of the English language in Britain is believed to have begun around the end of the 1500s, with catalytic factors including the invention of the printing press and the emphasis on classical learning that led to Latin and Greek becoming the languages of the educated.

Three hundred years later Britain was a highly divided nation, chronicles linguistics professor Urszula Clark in her book *Studying Language: English in Action*. She details how the country was divided not just geographically by regional dialect and accent, but also socially by the growing rise and influence of Standard English as a national language. Standard English had become the language not only of government and administration, but also of a cultural elite.

By the end of the 1800s, when compulsory education had been introduced nationwide, learning to read and write Standard English had become part of the state school curriculum. Any deviation from the 'proper' speech was regarded to be incorrect: using 'superior' and 'refined' language was a sign of belonging to a 'superior' class. Clark, who is one of the UK's leading experts on English regional dialects and accents, writes that spoken as well as written Standard English was regarded as a model of refinement, and with the expansion of the British Empire, a carrier of political power worldwide.

Accents can evoke positive qualities, too. Which accent people like most, and associate with positive qualities, will vary from person to person (it's the Irish one for me). Ask linguists and they will tell you that French-accented English doesn't tend to be stigmatised; instead it is generally romanticised and associated with charm and sophistication. Positive accent biases are less well understood, because of the widespread belief that they are less harmful to society. There are plenty of accents that don't enjoy quite so much positivity – like German. My faint accent is enough for people to enquire about my country of origin. When I reveal that I'm not a native Brit, but someone who was born and spent her formative years in Germany, I get surprised looks. I am generally met with an expectation that I should be speaking with at least a modicum of a German accent, because '... most Germans do'. It's a stereotype that is disguised as a compliment ('You don't sound German'). The 'Don't mention the war' jokes (yes, still those) are also never far behind, nor the assertions that Germans love rule and order, or that German efficiency and German cars are unsurpassed.

The associations are so powerful that even the most liberal people will have harboured some stereotypes about my nationality, which is then used to define or justify who I am. Friends will put my insistence on punctuality down to my German-ness, and people I have just met will proceed to paint for me a picture of what I'm like without asking any further questions. I find this difficult to accept, yet my nationality remains something I am regularly measured against.

I keep seeing this at its clearest at the poker table: learning my nationality can change how players act towards me. German poker players enjoy the reputation of being the best in the world. The moment other players find out I'm German, they will assume I am one of those brilliant players – and let's be honest, I definitely am not (well, not yet anyway). The play will change, and my opponents will start playing more cautiously against me and bluff a lot less.

Yet stereotypes and cultural norms are part of how our brain sees the world. We think on an 'if A then B' basis; this is how we make sense of our environment. The point here is to be aware of the many pitfalls and biases that could negatively affect our judgement and actions. For example, I am aware of my own strong bias when it comes to swearing. I want to preface this by saying I am not afraid of hearing profanities and swear words, nor do I refrain from using them myself. I swear a lot, but I am mindful of my environment and one place you will not hear me swear is at the poker tables. And certainly not after a bad beat.

Having your premium hand beaten by a lesser one can feel like a punch to the face, particularly when the stakes are high. A swearing rampage isn't going to help you, but it will give your opponent and everyone else on the table an opportunity to come for you: they can see you have lost control of your emotions and are rattled. This is why having a firm grip on yourself is a vital skill at the poker tables. Everything is a piece of information, and information is valuable.

About Swearing

One of the most recognised players in the game is Phil Hellmuth. With numerous titles and (at the last count) a record seventeen World Series bracelets (more than anyone so far by a wide margin) he is a bona fide top poker player with one foul mouth. Whenever he plays, he attracts the attention of the media, which seems to be one of the reasons tournament organisers have been turning a blind eye to his swearing. Now it seems the poker world is getting tired of his antics. There have been calls to discipline him, especially after a televised meltdown in 2021 where he was audibly frustrated about losing repeatedly, and over the span of four hands unleashed over 40 F-bombs. Personally, I believe Hellmuth's swearing is at best all roar with no bite. These are tantrums he throws whenever he feels entitled to win, and judging by the frequency of his swearing, that's a lot of the time. But he isn't the only one swearing at the tables. Even though casino and tournament rules forbid it, these are not strictly enforced. There seems to be a general understanding that it helps players to vent and swearing is overlooked so long as it is not directed at another player. This is where the line tends to be drawn, and if a player crosses it, a penalty will be issued – at least according to the World Series of Poker rule book. It's a clear line, but often in real-life situations we are left to decide how we deal with what we hear, and whether or not we deem it to be menacing.

The way I deal with swear-boxes at the table depends on what time of day it is. Literally. During the day I tend to ignore them, as more often than not when you hear swearing it's someone self-flagellating, voicing frustration about their misfortune. It's usually not directed at another player. In the evenings, on the other hand, if you do happen to encounter verbal aggression, there is a higher probability it is directed at other players, which makes it harder to ignore, especially when these players are not just rude but drunk, too. I'm not going to lie: I feel uncomfortable in these situations, however infrequently they occur. I am always on edge a little because without fail, these players will amp up their intimidation roar when they come to play against me. It's textbook behaviour of asserting dominance over a female, and even the fact that I can see right through it doesn't make it feel any less menacing. Like the drunk Russian I once had a tense exchange with at a cash table at The Vic, a casino on Edgware Road in London.

He had sat down, swigging on his beer. It wasn't his first – his clumsy attempts to stack his chips in front of him gave that away easily. Immediately after he played the very first hand he was dealt and then won it, he started to posture by berating the other players, his speech littered with swear words. When players berate other players during a game, what they're really saying is 'I'm so much better than you' (often they aren't). And Drunk Russian wanted us all to know he was really good at poker. The next hand was dealt out. Drunk Russian had re-raised a bet from a player in early position. It's a move that is used to signal strength. The action was now on me, on the button – the most powerful position at the poker table. I looked down at an Ace-Jack. A pretty good holding. Not the best, because there were still a number of hands that could beat mine. Ace-Jack is behind any Ace-King or Ace-Queen and behind any pair. I needed to know how much I would be risking if it were to come to an all-in situation, because by re-raising a player in early position, Drunk Russian was trying to tell the table he had a strong holding.

'How much are you playing?' I asked.

'Ten thousand!' he shouted back.

He didn't have anywhere near that. Looking from across the table, I estimated his chip stack to be around £220. I had over four times that in front of me, so I covered him easily. Perhaps he was insulted but it was clear he was annoyed because the stare he was giving me said as much.

That escalated quickly, I thought to myself. I have lost count of how many times men have talked down at me at the tables and tried to degrade me for daring to intrude on what they no doubt see as a male space. Moments before, I had been planning on folding my Ace-Jack; now there was absolutely no way I was going to fold.

Without shifting my eyes from his, not even for a moment, I responded:

'Sure.'

I paused for a second, our eyes still locked in the stare-off, and calmly added:

'I call.'

I grabbed a large-domination chip and flicked it into the middle, still holding his gaze. The table chatter had already died down. Everyone else was now following the action in utter silence.

When the player in early position also called, Drunk Russian started dropping F-bombs. The three of us went to the flop (the first three cards that landed in the middle of the board). Early position player checked. Drunk Russian checked too. I did not. I reached for my chips and pushed a large bet into the middle. Early position folded. Drunk Russian stared again. I stared right back. After about 20 seconds he folded. His subsequent swearing was drowned out by the table's collective cheer. (I realise my anecdotes mostly depict moments of anger and frustration, but these are just an illustration of aspects of the game that are also part of life. We can't avoid unexpected and unwelcome situations. We must deal with them, ready or not.)

Emma Byrne has spent years researching the effects of swearing on our mental, physical and social conditions. As observers we all react differently when we hear or use swear words. It all depends on context, says Byrne, who wasn't the least bit fazed when in a packed restaurant her then two-year-old daughter shouted at the top of her voice, 'Mummy, get me out of this fucking high chair.' She tells me how heads turned, but she didn't care. Instead, she stared right back at the other parents and at their kids in the high chairs. Those kids were also expressing their displeasure at being strapped in and not allowed to run around the restaurant. Unlike her daughter, they were throwing food or dropping their cups on the floor, screaming, rocking their high chairs, or wriggling and trying to escape. 'My daughter used this expletive in the most instrumental way. She gave me such clear insight into her emotional state without having to hurl everything at me.' And in that context, Byrne was okay with her toddler using the F-word. She understood that her daughter had had as much as she could stand. So she took her out of the high chair and outside for a little walk together. 'I'd take that over a tantrum any day,' she tells me with absolute clarity.

Byrne, a computational neuroscientist turned science communicator who has written a book called *Swearing Is Good for You*, wasn't looking to become an expert on swearing. That happened by accident.

In her research days Byrne spent a lot of time looking at how the body deals with reward and pain, and how we learn from positive and negative reinforcement – which is what got her into swearing. Pain and swearing go together like toast and butter. 'Yeah, pain and swearing, it's hard to imagine one without the other,' she tells me.

Swearing can also be a sign of aggression. There is the perception that people from lower classes swear more often than the upper-middle classes. Byrne grew up on a housing estate in Yorkshire (northern England) in a working-class family and didn't go to private school, but earned her doctorate in computer science at University College London and has a middle-class accent. She reckons the perception is down to a sense of entitlement. In British culture, she says, there is a difference between lower-class swearing and upper-class swearing. 'So we have this kind of U-shaped curve. In the United Kingdom, the middle class is really abused for swearing, and the working class or people on benefits swear about as much as very posh people. The difference is whether or not you feel you need to apologise for it.' She makes a further observation: posh people don't have to swear at you, they just instruct their lawyer: 'You piss me off, I'll evict you from my property.' 'You piss me off, I'll fire you from your job.' Whereas most of the rest of humanity has to be content with 'If you piss me off, all I can be is impotently serious.' And that is when people quite often say things they regret. So swearing as a display of aggression has something to do with how people feel they can access a slight amount of power when they are frightened or angry. Aggression among people without financial or legal resources tends to be either linguistical or physical.

Most people don't use swearing to intimidate. When you look at copious amounts of swearing, it's usually used for solidarity or to be jocular. Particularly in workplace cultures that tend to be more male dominated, like IT, engineering and factory work, swearing is used more as a form of social bonding than in more female-dominated workplaces. Some of that has to do with the social risk that women take when they swear, because research shows that women are judged more harshly than men for swearing. In female-only groups, or where encountering men is not going to be as much of a problem, women do get to swear as much as men. We tend to moderate our language around the opposite sex. And women in all cultures tend to adopt a slightly more indirect register than men.

In all the cultures that have been studied, swearing tends to be used to dissipate tension rather than to increase it. It also seems that what we think about swearing is at odds with the pragmatics, the reality of swearing. When asked, we tend to think of swearing as aggressive and abusive. Actually, there are many ways of being abusive or aggressive that don't involve swearing. Equally, Byrne says there are far more ways of using swearing to be friendly than we tend to think.

On Sharpening the Focus of Our Mental Lens

There can be more to words than first appears. We now know that even the functional basic words we often overlook can carry deep meaning, show us patterns. There is power in words. They can affect us. To take the simplest of examples, we might find a 'no' when we really want to hear a 'yes' devastating and hard to recover from. Importantly, though, the same situation with the same responses could trigger vastly different reactions in different people. That is because what we pay attention to or not, deem important or worthy of our emotion comes down to the infinite variety of our experiences and learnings, which have shaped how we think, see, hear and act. These are the things that make us different from one another, that make us unique.

In many ways, we are similar and predictable, which is what makes us vulnerable to exploitation or to misguidedness. We have heard about why not everything is as it seems, and that we can all fall prey to deception and hidden meanings, especially ones that happen right in front of our eyes. Being sure of facts requires us to verify them, sometimes by trying to disprove them. This includes stepping outside our echo chambers and having the courage to sit down with others who we don't agree with. We have learnt about some of the tools that can help us be better prepared to enter debates that challenge our views or our thinking. We have heard over and over that listening carefully and paying attention to what's actually being said, then putting all that into context (cultural and otherwise) is crucial. And so, a first step towards a productive discussion is to ensure we are not batting away every single counterpoint but truly engaging with the opposing side.

That's quite the to-do list, and it may seem like a lot to hold constantly in our minds. However, our reality is one that is wrapped in layer upon layer of complexities, and it is up to us to peel those back to reveal the facts and hidden meanings. We can choose to live a more inquisitive life, because those who want to take advantage of us rely on our lack of motivation to ask difficult questions. What feeds their power over us is our own mental sluggishness. Let's not allow others to manipulate us this easily. Let's sharpen the focus of our mental lenses, and question more.

The Art of Asking the Right Questions

Unexamined information can affect us badly. We all encounter enough situations regularly in which information is dressed up to look legitimate, often with the help of numbers and statistics. But numbers can lie. Statistics can be twisted. I am not trying to cause paranoia; rather, I am arguing for a more alert mindset, one in which we have learnt when to ask which questions.

To help us interrogate information, we can follow a standard process, starting with these basic questions: Who is this information coming from? Why – and particularly why *now*? What's in it for them? What are we not being told? These questions don't require maths skills but they can give us a solid starting point of evidence for probing the information further. Knowing if the data then needs further examination comes down to how well versed we are in understanding what we can trust. We start learning how when we know how to avoid common pitfalls.

PART FOUR

Learning to Live with Uncertainty:
Risk, Game Theory and Imperfect Information

On Playing Games

One of my ultimate favourite things to do whenever I am stateside is to jump into the passenger seat next to Grandpa Bob (GPB) in his red Mini Cooper, cue the tunes, turn up the volume and then zoom down the Garden State Parkway to Atlantic City. The 90-minute drive is our time to catch up on 'what's been going on'. Occasionally, a song will remind him of the past and he will tell me stories from his youth. Like when in November 1967 the seventeen-year-old Bob, member of the concert committee at his high school, Union Catholic in Scotch Plains (New Jersey), helped stage a fundraiser and got The Who to come and play. Another time they managed to get Eric Clapton and his then band Cream to perform (after deciding against Jimi Hendrix because he was seen as 'a bit naughty'). I would love to have been there. So as designated passenger seat DJ, I take my job extremely seriously and as we pull into the car park at the casino I will never fail to play our battle anthem. We sing it at the tops of our voices while moshing to it and thumping the rhythm out on the dashboard. The New Zealand All Blacks have the haka; Grandpa Bob and I have Led Zeppelin's 'Immigrant Song'. That's how we get ready for the felted battlefields. Because, now, here at the casino, we are warriors.

Of course, we actually look nothing like warriors. Put GPB in a red and white costume and he'd totally pass for Santa Claus. The fact that I still get IDed at the door has me chuckle in disbelief every single time, but if I'm honest it's actually a wonderful pre-game ego boost that I will miss terribly when it no longer happens. So, basically it's Santa Claus and Babyface who enter the poker room.

As well as looking pretty different, we also differ quite a bit as players. I consider myself a tight-aggressive player, whereas GPB is a super-tight player. What does that mean? He will never risk all his money unless he knows he is definitely winning. He rarely bluffs – and when he does he will also not risk everything and tends to fold when he gets pushback from another player. There is absolutely nothing wrong with this type of play at all. And let's be clear, GPB plays for fun. He is not incentivised to implement complex strategies that could put his bankroll at risk. It just means he is limited to playing a certain range of hands.

Earlier in the book you heard how poker players assess their hand strength on the basis of a number of variables and predominantly use 'thinking in ranges' to help guide their decision-making. As a reminder, these ranges are mathematically calculated precise instructions for optimal play, and poker players use them in two ways. Firstly to guide them as to what to play, when and how. And secondly to help determine the range of hands their opponents may be holding. If we can place a player down within a certain range, then we can continue to define the win-rate probability of a given hand against their holding, if we just dealt out the cards to showdown (all the cards on the board). For example, if GPB was holding a pair of Jacks and we hold a pair of Tens then GPB will win 81% of the time. However, if we had Ace-King instead, two higher (over) cards to his Jacks, then GBP's win rate falls to 56%. You can see why a pair against two over cards is often called a coin-flip or a race. We don't need to know the exact maths behind it; so long as we know what these probabilities are, they can help us make the right decisions along the way.

Probability

Every single aspect of our lives has a quantity or a quality expressed by a number. From the moment we wake up, our days are ruled and guided by numbers: the time at which we have to leave the house to make it to the right number bus we jump on to travel the number of stops we take to work, and the number of cups of coffee we drink before lunch. Imagining our world today without numbers is hard if not impossible. Many of our most important decisions are made based on the information numbers give us. Moreover, we also base our assumptions on them. Whether an asteroid is about to hit Earth or whether we may be hit by a bus on the way to work, we use thinking in probabilities to assess, validate or affirm assumptions and risks.

Indeed, there was a time when humans made decisions solely on the basis of degrees of belief. That changed in the middle of the seventeenth century, when the theory of probability was established for the first time by three French mathematicians – Blaise Pascal, Pierre de Fermat and the Chevalier de Méré.

When people explain probability they often use the standard example of flipping a coin. What would you consider the probability of getting heads when flipping a coin? There are two possibilities: you could get heads or you could get tails. So that would be 1/2 or 50%. Easy. It is still 50% for each flip even if you flip it an infinite number of times. When rolling a die with six equal sides the probability calculations would look like this: you could get a 1, 2, 3, 4, 5 or 6 – they are all equally likely. So the probability of rolling a 3 is 1/6 or 17%. What is the probability of rolling a 2 or a 4? Well now you have two possibilities . . . so that would be 2/6 . . . 33%. The probability of getting an even number? Three numbers on the die are even. So that makes three possible numbers out of the six that could be even, meaning 3/6 = 50%.

At the tables, poker players use probability calculations all the time when deciding whether to call, bet, raise or fold. The rule of thumb is calculated via the rule of four and two. Here is how it works: the flop (first three cards on the board) show two hearts and one spade. You are holding hearts, with the Ace of hearts giving you the nut flush draw. You only need one more heart to come down for you to make a flush and win. To calculate your odds you take the number of hearts left in the deck and then multiply it by four. Because each suit has thirteen cards, you know there are only nine hearts left in the deck – two are on the board and two are in your hand. Therefore, nine x four = 36. Giving you a 36% chance of hitting a flush. Your odds increase if you add the remaining Aces to your calculation. Say you don't make the flush but you could still win if one of the three remaining Aces appears on the board. So you can add those to the cards that could give you the winning hand. Nine hearts + three Aces = twelve cards; multiply this number by four and suddenly your odds of winning jump to 48%.

Probability is a measurement of the likelihood of something happening. To illustrate, here is another example. Take a bag filled with multicoloured stones: 30 yellow, 20 blue, 20 pink and 10 white. There are 80 stones, so 80 possible outcomes.

So if there are 30 yellows out of a total number of 80, there is a 37.5% likelihood that you get a yellow stone.

Or let's say you're playing a game and you have 5 yellow stones, 4 green and 2 red in the bag: 11 stones in all. What is the probability that you will pull out a green or a red stone?

You have a total of 11 possibilities (5Y+4G+2R). Six of the eleven are red or green, meaning that you have a greater than 54% chance of pulling a red or green stone .

If you're now wondering why you're looking at maths calculations, especially after I told you earlier that you don't need to be a maths guru, let me explain.

Let's get back to our coin flip from earlier: imagine you're flipping the coin 50 times and it falls on heads every single time. So now what's the probability that it comes up heads on the 51st toss? The correct answer is 50%, because we are assuming it's a fair coin and a fair coin always has an equal 50/50 probability of coming up heads. That's how we define 'fair'.

The examples above illustrate mathematical concepts that are used to establish probabilities, which in turn represent degrees of belief. Having a basic understanding of how these numbers are put together can tune our thinking and sensitivities to things that may seem unlikely. Most of us don't have it, but I believe it should be an essential part of our base thinking. It's only when we come across something that defies all our assumptions and beliefs about the world that our bullshit antennae can go up. As it did for one casino director.

It was spring 1968, and Signor Ladera, the managing director of the Sanremo casino in Italy, was trying hard not to panic. On his desk in front of him, neatly aligned and stacked up in equal wads was the largest sum he had ever had to take out of the vault: $1 million. It would take weeks to recover from this hit, and the casino certainly couldn't sustain another payout like this one, but he knew there was little he could do to prevent it.

The reason for it was sitting across from him on the other side of the money mountain: a tall, slim man in a dark suit with hundreds of tiny little crinkles in it that had gradually etched themselves into the fabric like fissures in the ground. If the suit hadn't already been a giveaway of the long hours of sitting at the tables, then his eyes were. Flushed red behind thick, dark-rimmed glasses, they were now looking straight at Ladera, who took a deep breath and said: 'We are going to have some reorganisation. Please do not return for two weeks.' Ladera could only ask him. Explicitly banning the man from coming back to the casino, let alone reducing its maximum permissible stake would be bad publicity. Any which way Ladera looked at his predicament, he knew there wasn't much he could do. If he tried to change the rules for a consistently winning customer to protect the casino from haemorrhaging money, it would give the impression to other gamblers that the Sanremo casino was banning winning customers, and that it was only happy while its customers lost. But the man sitting in his office wasn't an ordinary gambler, nor was he just lucky.

Richard Jarecki had figured out a way to win consistently at roulette. But just how did this professor and lecturer in forensic medicine at the University of Heidelberg in Germany manage it?

At the time, Jarecki told everyone that it was a computer he was using to crack roulette. In reality all he was doing was painstakingly observing each table for thousands of spins until he figured out what the table's mechanical bias was. He had realised that minor manufacturing defects and ageing can lead some wheels to favour certain numbers. In 2018 his late wife revealed to a journalist at the *San Francisco Chronicle* that they 'would record the results of every turn of a given roulette wheel to discover its biases, or tendency to land on some numbers more frequently than others, usually because of a minute mechanical defect caused by shoddy manufacturing or wear and tear.'

This was no longer a game of chance. Jarecki had turned it into a game of probability in which the element of risk was reduced enough for him to bet on a mathematical basis that turned him not just into a winning player but also a '... menace to every casino in Europe,' as Ladera said in an interview in 1969. Sussing out the tables' biases gave him enough of an edge to make millions upon millions in the process.

Wheels with imperfections that can lead to biased results are pretty much a thing of the past. Today, imbalanced wheels are rare because casinos have upped their game. Their in-house anti-bias roulette-wheel maintenance teams ensure that all their wheels are balanced.

One could argue that Jarecki deserved to win. To gain a small edge, he put in hours and hours to study his opponents – in this case the roulette tables. Was it skill? Jarecki, who died in 2018, would argue that it was. He is said to have treated gambling as a profession rather than an addiction. Does it make roulette a game of skill? Hardly. With odds of 2.7% for hitting a specific single number on a roulette wheel with the numbers 0 to 36, that argument is difficult to sustain.

Games of chance must be distinguished from games of skill. When you play roulette, dice or slot machines you are handing over your money to fate and you have no direct power to influence the outcome. In games where skill can determine your winnings or losses, choice is a defining factor. In games of chance, probability and odds come into play – and the odds and probability in these games don't tend to be in your favour.

The point is, if our assumptions that are based on mathematically sound probabilities are at odds with the evidence before us, then it would serve us well to interrogate such evidence. Probabilities put clear meaning behind words such as 'likely', 'unlikely' or 'sometimes'. They do so via numbers.

But numbers don't speak for themselves. They require our active thinking. Why? Because to assess what we're being presented with, we need to use deductive reasoning. It's the key to making logical inferences from the information given, and then reaching the logical, correct conclusion.

Even if you've never played a hand of poker, you can obtain a ton of information just by observing how many hands your opponents play, because in poker a percentage number can reflect your aggression – or lack thereof. This is referred to as VPIP and stands for 'voluntarily put in pot', a measure of how often players put money into the middle, given the opportunity. In addition to a player's VPIP we can also see what happens when another player applies pressure, or how a player copes as the strength of a hand changes with the cards on the board. We can start understanding a player's thinking. And, once you know how a player thinks, you have an edge over him and can use it to exploit his play. Unwieldy though it might sound, poker is a game about thinking about what the other player is thinking. When you know what the other players' tendencies are, and how they would act in certain positions with certain cards, then you have the added advantage of information.

When GPB and I walk into a poker room, it now goes without saying that we do not sit at the same table. We know too much about each other's style of play and we want to buy our post-poker pizza with other people's money, not each other's.

Real life is full of games. In fact, any interaction between two or more people in which each person's reward, payoff or situation is affected by others' decisions, is what we call a game. Easy, right? If you can predict how people will make decisions when they have a choice to make, we call it game theory. Originally, game theory started out as a look at how people behave when they are playing games. Now it is used to analyse not just how people play, but how they negotiate and interact with each other.

Solomon's Wisdom

Today, a simple DNA test can determine the parents of a child, but those methods weren't available some three thousand years ago during King Solomon's reign, when a case was brought before him in which two women both claimed to be the mother of a baby boy. After some thought, Solomon, who was known for his wisdom and good judgement, proposed a solution: to cut the baby in two and give each mother one half. The true mother screamed in horror and asked Solomon not to harm the child, but to give it to the false mother instead. Solomon, who had thought about the incentives the two women faced, structured a game that revealed the women's identities through their actions. It's an early example of applied game theory.

Game theory makes predictions about others' behaviour, on the assumption that they behave rationally. In this case, Solomon predicted that the true mother would not want to see any harm come to her baby, even if it meant she had to give it up.

Game Theory

You don't have to be a cerebral mathematician to apply game theory. Consciously or unconsciously, we all use it in real life most of the time. You could say that nearly everything you do that involves other people can be viewed as a sort of game theory approach. Perhaps you have found yourself in a fledgling relationship, and are deciding whether – or not – to say 'I love you'. You weigh up the possible outcomes, and how you may feel if you don't hear it back. It's a big deal. So you spend time agonising over possible scenarios. And by agonising, I mean you're really working out all the possible outcomes. You get to a win-win when you say 'I love you' and your partner says it back to you. But if one of you doesn't say it back, it's a blow that is hard to overcome. Rejection is the feeling that will linger and perhaps even end the relationship. It is perhaps why the standard, dominant attitude at the beginning of a relationship is to just not say anything about being in love.

That's game theory: working out all the possible outcomes and then making the best decision with incomplete information. Imagine this: I give you and a stranger an envelope. I also give you each a dollar bill. Before I turn around and close my eyes so that I can't see what you will do, I give you two choices: you can put the dollar in your pocket or you can put it in the envelope. Then, once you've done so, I will turn around and you will hand me the envelopes. I tell them I will open one envelope at a time: if there is a dollar in the first one, I will add another to it, so making it two dollars. If the envelope has no money in it, I won't add a dollar. Then I say I will switch the envelopes, giving you the one the stranger had, and vice versa, either with money or not. Looking at this, it's easy to see that if you and the stranger don't care about each other, the smarter thing to do would be to put the dollar in your pocket. If both of you are selfish you will each get one dollar, but you would double your money if you each cooperated and put the dollar in the envelope. The scenario is a variation of the standard prisoner's dilemma in which two bank robbers are held and interrogated separately with the aim of getting one or the other to confess and give the other up. Each is told that the first one to tell on the other will receive a reduced penalty. However, if both keep their mouths shut, there's a chance they'll both go free. In both examples we see people acting in a manner that's best for themselves, which is why some game theorists argue that this may not promote the social good. The argument is that people and organisations are often driven by self-interest first.

When we apply game theory, we start to think about how people are likely to behave, what outcomes to expect and how we can use this knowledge to get the outcome *we* want.

GTO

In 1928, the mathematician John von Neumann proved that all zero-sum games have optimal strategies. As does the zero-sum game of poker. In fact, there are poker players who have used computers to study the best mathematical outcomes for any two-card holding in any particular position, giving them the optimal move and generated Nash equilibrium solutions (see below) for any particular position on the table. It's called Game Theory Optimal, or GTO for short, and is why you will see some good players go all in with two low-ranking cards when the maths predict this move will work out in their favour.

GTO is really the theory behind poker. It means all possible scenarios have corresponding perfect play, regardless of what the other player is holding. It is based on two considerations: on what you are holding and on the assumption that the other player, too, is playing according to the theory. It really only makes sense if you are both playing GTO. Mind you, when you have evidence that the other player is deviating from perfect play, because of a tendency, weakness or tell that you picked up on, then you can also deviate and exploit the play. So GTO is a sort of baseline poker play, and a player should only move away from it to exploit the other player's weakness. It creates a foundation from which you can deviate as you play a range of people with varying tendencies, but the downside to it is that when all players follow the optimal strategy, no one will have an edge over the others, because their play is indifferent to their opponents' actions. In theory, a perfectly played game will have no winners. If you are to maximise your winnings, you're actually going to have to deviate from GTO to exploit the weaknesses and mistakes of your opponent. It's far more profitable than playing in a perfectly balanced, GTO way. The flip side of that, of course, is that the moment you deviate from GTO, you yourself are unbalanced and are no longer playing perfectly. However, it's okay to do so because you are deviating with purpose: to punish your opponents' mistakes and get the maximum value out of the play. In practice, no one ever plays perfectly. We are humans and we do not make decisions in a vacuum.

A Beautiful Mind

GTO has at its heart the Nash equilibrium, named after Nobel Prize-winner John Nash who took Von Neumann's Minimax theorem in two-player games and extended it to multi-player games. Each player has to think about the other player's choice and figure out what their own choice should be in light of that. A Nash equilibrium is reached when each player adopts a strategy that is best in their own interest, in response to the other player's strategy. In other words, everyone has a strategy and they're in equilibrium if nobody can do better by changing what they're doing. And yes, ultimately, Nash equilibrium is thinking about thinking!

Take the example of rock paper scissors. The rules are simple: upon a signal, both players will choose either rock (fist), paper (open hand, face down with fingers together) or scissors (index and middle finger extended in V-shape representing an open pair of scissors). Rock blunts scissors, scissors cut paper and paper wraps around rock.

The optimal play is to adopt a strategy at random. Why random? When you randomise your choices, you become unpredictable. Whatever their strategy, the only thing your opponent can go on is the one in three chance of beating you. The result is that when you play each option, exactly one-third of the time, you become unexploitable, no matter what your opponent does. This is optimal because all three choices have some other single choice that always beats them. If you were to deviate from this and, say, slightly favour rock, and your opponent spots this rock-shaped bias, then you'd be opening yourself up for defeat.

The author of *The Mathematics of Poker* Jerrod Ankenman points out to me that while RPS makes clear how GTO strategies make the opponent indifferent between choices, the game is too simple for GTO to win without exploiting.

Why Game Theory Isn't Enough

So why not apply game theory to everything and forget about all the other skills in the book? Because there is a small but significant snag with pure game theory. It assumes that all decisions are based on reason and logic rather than emotion or feeling. In economics, it means considering all the information, evaluating the costs and benefits, and taking time to make a decision that promises greatest personal gain. That's in theory. In practice, it's not enough. Because of course, people don't always act like that. Even the most rational people can forgo the logical path and give in to emotional benefits over practical ones. So, understanding how the other person thinks isn't just about knowing what they should be thinking, but also understanding how they are emotionally triggered and what is or isn't important to them. It requires that we take into account everything we know about a person and their tendencies, and take this into account when we think about their likely choices – while at the same time recognising that we ourselves may not always act rationally. So on top of everything else we have to factor in our own weaknesses and the vulnerabilities that can influence our otherwise logical thought processes. Ankenman tells me that you are still working on the O (Optimal) in GTO when you are adjusting your strategies to directly respond to irrational and illogical actions. This may sound like an exhausting process, but to win we need to be able to adjust. The famous ancient Chinese military strategist Sun Tzu hammered this one home in *The Art of War* some 2,400 years ago:

> If you know the enemy and know yourself, you need not fear the result of a hundred battles. If you know yourself but not the enemy, for every victory gained you will also suffer a defeat. If you know neither the enemy nor yourself, you will succumb in every battle.

Imperfect Information

Looking for information is what we do every single day. How

effective we are at obtaining the information depends not just on access to information, experts and time constraints, but above all on our ability to ask the right questions. Let's use the example of polling as a method to predict behaviour. There can be pitfalls here, too, because more data doesn't necessarily equate to better data. It comes down to the quality of the data as well, and that in turn depends on a number of variables; at the very least a measure of how many people were polled, and also who and where. And that's just the minimum requirement. Quality polling should also be clear on what exactly was asked and when. The following example from the history books illustrates this beautifully.

The year was 1936. For two decades, since 1916, the *Literary Digest* had been conducting polls on American presidential candidates with great accuracy, having predicted the winners in 1920, 1924, 1928 and 1932. The *Digest*'s subscription base meant it had an unrivalled reach to the millions it asked about their voting intentions in so-called 'straw polls' – a term that apparently gets its name from people throwing straw balls up in the air to see which way the wind blew. The first such poll was a pre-election presidential vote on 24 July 1824 in Pennsylvania.

In 1932, the *Digest* had 20 million subscribers. At the time no other publication could come near the scale of the straw polls it could run. Several months before an election, the *Digest* would send out 'ballots' to its subscription base to poll on how the nation was going to vote – but the flaw in this was two-fold. Not only were the ballots sent out months before the election, they were also sent out to a specific demographic that by its nature excluded a significant voting base – the poor and working class.

At the time, straw polls were conducted not just by the *Digest* but by a number of newspapers, which sent out swarms of reporters in person to get as many 'votes' as quickly as possible. 'Ballots' would be passed out in communal hotspots and gathering points, with ballot boxes installed to collect the votes. Perhaps the crudest method was when newspapers printed coupons in the paper for readers to fill in and send back – an earlier version of the ubiquitous internet polls run by media outlets. These were votes with no indication of demographics, and as you can imagine, the ballots returned by the subscribers of the *Washington Post* were different from those returned by readers of *The New York Times*.

The turning point came in the autumn of 1935 via a new syndicated column called 'AmericaSpeaks!' in the *Washington Post*, which promised to report what the public thought about the issues of the day through nationwide public opinion polls. It was written by a 34-year-old professor of journalism cum advertising executive who had risen to stardom after throwing the entire advertising industry on its head a few years earlier by creating readership profiles and spearheading the tailoring of ads through effective market research. As a result, text-heavy ads were replaced by ones that used a picture or illustration with just a caption. But he didn't stop there. Next, he took on the political scene. Soon the entire nation would know his name: George Horace Gallup.

Gallup was eager to learn and report on 'the will of the people'. He developed what is now referred to as Gallup methodology, involving face-to-face interviews. With his method, Gallup was able to provide unprecedented detail about mass opinion and behaviour.

The *Literary Digest* was at that point practically synonymous with polling. For the 1936 presidential election it polled a whopping 10 million individuals – not just its subscriber base, but also lists of people who owned cars or telephones. Of those, 2.7 million replied. From this, the magazine then predicted that Franklin D. Roosevelt's opponent, Governor Landon of Kansas, would win overwhelmingly. Gallup, on the other hand, polled a mere 50,000 people (less than 2% of the *Digest*'s replies). He knew that a huge sample size did not guarantee accuracy. Instead he canvassed groups of people who were representative of the entire electorate and predicted Roosevelt would get 56% of the vote. Roosevelt went on to get 60%, and Landon's tally of eight Electoral College votes is still equal lowest in US history.

Gallup's method threw a metaphorical hand grenade into the longstanding methods of the *Digest*, which until then had been the go-to place for polling numbers for newspaper editors, politicians and general public. The *Literary Digest* folded within eighteen months of the election, but Gallup's company is still going strong today.

Polling as a method is an imprecise practice. While it may give some indication of an outcome, there are many fluctuating variables that will yield differing results. Non-voters, undecideds, and the sample polled contribute to these imperfect results, but a variable that turned out to have a significant influence was until fairly recently dismissed: dishonesty. The trouble is, people lie. Or as Seth Stephens-Davidowitz, and American data scientist put it in the title of his 2017 bestselling book, *Everybody Lies*.

Stephens-Davidowitz is a digital sleuth who went where no one had gone before: he followed the trails people left as they searched for information online. 'People looking for information is information in itself,' he says. He spent four years following these traces of truth, analysing Google data. The young researcher started studying people's searches online, tracking when and where they were searching for information, quotes, people, things and medical information. He argued that people often use Google to confide in it: 'Is my penis too small?' 'My husband likes to breastfeed.' 'I hate my boss.' He found that people withhold socially unacceptable views from, say, pollsters, friends and family, but are more honest with Google. Not everyone believed this to be a viable thesis, so much so that his study 'The cost of racial animus on a black candidate: Evidence using Google search data' was rejected by many peer reviewers who simply didn't believe that that many Americans could be racist. Five scientific journals rejected his study because it did not fit with what people were self-reporting. In addition, Google searches seemed such an against-the-grain data set to use as a basis for the scientific method. (The study was eventually accepted in 2014.)

Then something happened that no one believed would be possible. Against virtually all predictions and polls, Donald Trump was elected President of the United States of America. Stephens-Davidowitz acknowledges that more election cycles are needed to determine whether Google data is indeed a dependable tool for predicting an election. What it *can* do is reveal undisclosed behavioural and social patterns by broad swathes of the nation that can be significant to an election, especially when it comes to race, hatred and bigotry. Many pundits disregarded the possibility of a Trump presidency. Including, America's most famous statistician, Nate Silver. So much so that an article on Silver's FiveThirtyEight website ridiculed the idea of Trump becoming the Republican nominee. When Trump then did snag the nomination Silver still only had him at around 28.5% chance of being elected to become president (to be fair he gave Trump a bigger chance of winning than almost any other media source). After the election Silver went back to the data sets to see what he had missed, looking at where Trump performed best (the Northeast, the industrial Midwest and the South) and where he didn't do so well (the West). What he was looking at was an odd map where the one single factor for Trump was what Stephens-Davidowitz had been ridiculed for pointing out four years earlier: areas that supported Trump in the largest numbers were those that made the most Google searches for a horrible racial slur, one I refuse to add to this book. Trump's election and his subsequent hate-fuelled presidency have given voice to those who had been harbouring their racism and hatred towards immigrants in 'secret' for so long.

I got the chance to speak with Stephens-Davidowitz in early

2022 and to ask him if, since the publication of his research and book, he had observed any changes in polling methods, and if his work had been able to influence how data was being analysed. Speaking from his apartment in Brooklyn via Zoom, he told me that people are now looking at Google searches as alternative indicators for some of these questions, particularly in the corporate world. Here, companies tell him all the time that they are no longer doing focus groups or surveys. They feel these don't offer any value. They choose to look at the searches or some real-time data that isn't affected by social desirability bias. Not so in politics. 'In political polling, I'd say there's basically been no change,' he told me. I was surprised. Why did he think that people haven't used the knowledge that he brought to the table? One problem, he believed, is that each of these elections were so different. Candidates could influence the search patterns, especially ones who were so totally unlike every candidate who had come before – like Donald Trump. The search patterns around Trump were different from the search patterns around every candidate we had previously seen, and a lot of the patterns that had worked in the past didn't work with Trump. Where there were still clear usages for polling, he told me, is around searches to understand the issues people really care about. When people were searching 'how to vote, where to vote', it really did give us information about who would actually show up. He gave me an example closer to home: the number one Google search in the UK after the Brexit vote was 'What is the EU?'

If polls can be this misleading, you're probably now wondering why they're still conducted. In fact, high-quality polls can still be useful. These polls use a combination of methods such as live interviews, with both landline and mobile phone recruits, and online surveys. All the same, polling is imprecise and there will always be margins of error – margins that can be hugely significant. In the 2016 US presidential election, Hillary Clinton was polled to be ahead by 3.3%; she went on to win the popular vote by 2.1%, but due to the Electoral College system in the US, she still lost.

One way of assessing the accuracy of a poll is to look for similar polls conducted around the same time and see if the results are the same. If they are not, then it is key to look at whether a) the same kind of people were polled, b) the interviewing technique was the same and most importantly c) whether the same wording was used to phrase the question. All three can influence the result of a poll, especially the phrasing.

In 2015, NatCen Social Research, which styles itself as Britain's leading independent social research agency, conducted a telephone poll in which it asked whether people supported giving sixteen- and seventeen-year-olds the right to vote in the referendum on Britain's membership of the EU. 52% voted yes, 41% no. The remainder neither agreed nor disagreed. The poll also asked people whether they supported or opposed reducing the voting age from eighteen to sixteen in the referendum on Britain's membership of the EU. 56% were against reducing the age and only 37% were in favour: two drastically different results for what in essence was the same question. So the next time you read about a poll result, try considering whether a question was framed in a way that could have skewed the results in a particular direction.

Stephens-Davidowitz also recommends investigating the organisation that conducted the poll to see if it is a reliable company (he recommends Pew Research or Gallup). Then he suggests we consider whether the topic is sensitive enough that people may be underreporting socially undesirable attitudes and behaviours, and overreporting more desirable ones: 'Consider if people could be lying, or is it something where you think people will be honest?' he cautions.

Another useful tip is to look at the size of the sample. The rule of thumb is that the more people that have been surveyed, the better. Generally, there is a +/- 3% margin of error on surveys of 1,000 people. This number shrinks to 1% when you increase the sample pool to 9,000.

Even if numbers aren't your thing, you can still apply statistical thinking to a poll and it doesn't require any knowledge of numbers whatsoever. You simply need to find out what question was asked, then look at who answered it.

Remember, too, when considering who was polled, that opinion polls use only a subset of a population to find out what it thinks about a specific issue. The result is then taken to be representative of the rest of the population. So, for it to be accurate, the sample is key – as we saw with the ill-fated *Literary Digest*.

Non-Rational Actors

You may think that given the chance (and the information), you will absolutely act reasonably and be rational. Maybe, but what is also true is that we *aren't* always able to act reasonably and rationally – it's one of the things that make us human. One of the most influential psychologists of our time came to this realisation at just eight years old. It would be a defining memory that would later inform his life's work and eventually assist in winning him a Nobel Prize.

Daniel Kahneman isn't quite sure about the exact year, but he recalls that sometime in late 1941 or early 1942 he was late getting home in German-occupied Paris. He had forgotten the time while playing with his friend, and that was a problem. His curfew had passed, and Jews were not allowed outside past 6 p.m. To avoid trouble he turned his sweater inside out, trying to hide the Star of David which all Jews were required to wear and started hustling towards home. The last person he wanted to be stopped by was a German soldier and one was walking straight towards him. From his uniform he knew this soldier belonged to the greatly feared SS. Frightened, Daniel picked up his pace, but the soldier called him over. What happened next was totally unexpected: the soldier picked Daniel up and hugged him. Then he put him back down, pulled out his wallet, showed him a picture of a boy and then gave him some money. Sixty years later, Kahneman recounts this moment: 'I went home more certain than ever that my mother was right: people were endlessly complicated and interesting.' He proved this over and over with the body of work he compiled (most of it with his long-time friend and colleague Amos Tversky). The brilliant duo produced some of the most cited works on behavioural economics and their impact on life and our understanding of human behaviour cannot be overstated.

With prospect theory, Kahneman and Tversky showed that people don't always act rationally when managing risk and uncertainty. In risky situations, the way we make decisions about winning and losing varies significantly. We value what we could win or lose in different ways. Rationality can fly out of the window. Typically, we tend to be guided by the emotional impact of losing time, money, effort, goods, and so on, and react far more strongly to the prospect of loss than to the prospect of gain. Whether we become risk-seeking or risk averse depends on how much we value the potential loss.

This is a cognitive bias, or error in thinking, that researchers refer to as 'framing effect', where choices and decisions differ when an outcome is presented as a loss or a gain. The framing effect elicits systemically different choices and can be observed in all contexts of life, whether in politics, finance or medicine.

Irrational Behaviour

In 1979, Kahneman and Tversky first published the idea that people tend to be risk averse. By 2010, their paper on the subject had become the most cited in all economics. Their work would motivate other behavioural economists to investigate how people made decisions based on how problems were presented, and people's attitude to risk. Consider the following problem:

A: could you live on 75% of your current income?
B: could you give up 25% of your income?

The answer should be the same.

Let's try another example – and this one feels weird to me as I'm writing after the 2020 pandemic struck, because (and I'm not making this up) Kahneman and Tversky called this thought experiment 'the Asian disease' problem. Before I dive into that I'd like to highlight that Kahneman addressed the naming of this study in his book *Thinking, Fast and Slow*, as since its publication some people have called the label 'Asian' unnecessary and pejorative. He writes: 'We probably wouldn't use it today, but the example was written in the 1970s when sensitivity to group labels was less developed than it is today. The word was added to make the example more concrete, reminding respondents of the Asian flu epidemic in 1957.'

For it, they asked participants to imagine an outbreak of a deadly disease in a community, which was expected to kill 600 people. There were two options available to combat the outbreak and save lives, but neither option could save everyone. Programme A was described as certain to save 200 people. Programme B gave a 1/3 probability that everyone could be saved and a 2/3 probability that all lives would be lost. The question was, which would you choose? Hold that thought.

Then people were asked to think about the same problem, but posed differently. Programme C was described as meaning 400 of the 600 people would die. While programme D posited a 1/3 probability of saving all 600 and a 2/3 probability that all 600 people would die (in essence, exactly like Programme B). Which would you choose now? Hang on. Look back at Programme A and B and now compare those with C and D. Notice something? They are indistinguishable from one another in real terms. One would expect that they would elicit the same responses, right? Wrong.

In the study results, 72% of the participants chose Programme A over Programme B . But even though C had the same outcome as A, and D the same outcome as B, 78% chose D over Programme C: the explicit mention of 400 deaths was too much to handle. How could two identical problems elicit drastically different outcomes? It came down to how the problem was framed. When phrased positively in terms of survivors, participants preferred the certain option (Programme A was framed as a gain). But when deaths were mentioned and the question was posed negatively in term of lives lost (as in Programme C), the risky option was preferred. The answer to a question should be the same regardless of how it is posed, but what Kahneman and Tversky showed is that it's not clear cut, because the outcomes depend on how the questions are asked and ultimately on how we feel about gains and losses. Further, even if we aren't risk averse we are definitely loss averse, which suggests that our decision-making isn't so much guided by uncertainty but rather by the fact that we hate losing. Loss aversion, it turns out, is a powerful driving force. On the flip side, when all the options are bad we tend to be more risk-seeking. But we revert straight back to being more risk averse as the stakes rise, and I am not just talking about poker here.

Risk

If you think risk management is a domain solely reserved for bankers and financiers, you are mistaken. You manage risk many times a day, every single day.

The word 'risk' has its roots in Latin (*resicum*) and is derived from the Italian word *risichiare*, which means 'to dare'. Risk has little in common with uncertainty. Taking a risk is a decision we make after we've reviewed the information in front of us. The prerequisite for taking any informed risk is to ask questions. What information is relevant? How confident are we about the outcome, and how do we manage dealing with the risk? The quality of your questions will help determine more accurately the level of risk and whether it is worth taking.

When we take a risk, what we're essentially doing is gambling. Ideally, it means we have made a decision where we do not know for certain what the outcome will be, but we do know future states of all possible scenarios, which will have been calculated using numbers. In short, understanding a risk means being aware of the numbers and the consequent outcomes involved. If you're faced with a risk and not looking for numbers or using them in your decision-making process, you're appealing either to some sort of higher power or to your gut feeling. And our intuition is a poor basis for decisions like this.

Multiple studies have shown people often fear things that are actually pretty unlikely to kill or hurt them. Take the fear of sharks. In 2015, the market research company Ipsos MORI polled over 1,000 adults in America. It found that over half of them were terrified of sharks, and nearly 40% of those were too afraid to swim in the ocean because of them. How justified is this fear? There is a 1 in 4,332,817 chance of dying from a shark attack, according to data from 2021 provided by the International Shark Attack File of the University of Florida's Museum of Natural History. You're more likely to die of heart disease (a 1 in 5 chance), cancer (1 in 7) or in a car crash (1 in 84) than be gorged on by a shark. Apples and oranges, I hear you say? Then if you want to know what animal is most likely to kill you, the sharp-toothed predator isn't the deadliest animal in the world. That's an insect: the mosquito.

Mosquitoes can carry and spread a long list of human diseases, killing nearly 3 million of us humans every year. In 2020, malaria alone caused an estimated 619,000 deaths. The WHO reports that the worldwide incidence of dengue, also carried by mosquitoes, has risen 30-fold in the past 30 years, and more countries are reporting their first outbreaks of the disease. More than half of the world's population lives in areas where mosquitoes are present, and there are several different types of mosquitoes, some with the ability to carry many different diseases.

And if humans aren't afraid of animals, they fear that 'Frankenfoods' will eat them from the inside out. A significant number of people believe genetically modified (GM) foods to be unnatural and the product of evil. Here, too, fringe studies that were later challenged and then withdrawn managed to stoke enough fear to significantly affect popular perception, so much so that in 2016 the UK's Royal Society felt compelled to put out a report to help clarify the science and debunk false beliefs about GM foods.

The report was clear that GM foods are safe to eat. There is no evidence that a new crop variety produced with GM techniques is any more likely to have unforeseen effects than food resulting from conventional cross-breeding. Furthermore, since the first widespread commercialisation of GM produce 20 years ago, there has been no evidence of ill effects linked to the consumption of any approved GM crop. The trouble is, once fear has taken hold, even facts have a hard time reversing beliefs.

One of the biggest fears people have is that of other people. In 2016, in an annual survey, Chapman University in California asked over 1,500 Americans what they feared the most. 41% of those surveyed feared a terrorist attack. Yet per year, the number of Americans who are killed by terrorist attack is vastly dwarfed by the number who die from gun violence. According to data from the US Centers for Disease Control, in 2021 the total number of deaths from gun-related injuries in the United States stood at 48,830 people. In comparison, the data published by the Global Terrorism Database for 2019 showed that 51 people died from terror attacks in America. These figures highlight a prevalent misperception of reality, one that appears to distort people's opinions and behaviour. In the US, President Donald Trump successfully exploited these misperceptions about the danger of foreign attacks. By creating false narratives he rallied his base to support him without question. Sadly, false and unsupported beliefs manage to take hold of society in every corner of the world, and they can have significant consequences.

In the UK, for example, a study a few weeks before the Brexit vote took place in 2016, highlighted how misperception fuelled the anti-immigrant narrative that was heavily pushed by the Leave campaign. People polled in the UK wildly overshot in their estimation of how many EU-born residents were in the country. On average they thought EU citizens made up 15% of the UK population (at the time that would have been around 10.5 million people), when official estimates put it at 5% (around 3.5 million). The Brexit debate carried a number of false narratives, including the cost of being an EU member state and the payments the UK made to and received from the EU. One of the false claims the Leave campaign used to fuel the public's misperception was that an extra £350 million a week would be available for the National Health Service if the UK left the EU. This statement turned out not to be true.

Why do people often hold erroneous beliefs, and why is it sometimes so difficult to convince them of their falsity? It's partly a matter of perception. One reason these falsehoods are successful in infiltrating society is that when people perceive (rather than know) something to be true, they hold on to this perception and consider themselves to be well informed. There is a lot of feeling and fearing, rather than active thinking going on.

Factfulness

People will frequently voice opinions and make assertions based on what they believe, or what they feel the truth to be, rather than on the basis of established fact. And if you were one of the thousands of people lucky enough to hear Hans Rosling speak in person, you will be well aware of this. Swedish medical doctor Rosling, who died in 2017, used data compellingly to educate audiences about the state of the world and debunk many false assumptions and beliefs, often showing that things aren't as bad as people are predisposed to assume.

Take notions about world health and wealth. It used to be true that Western countries were richer and healthier than the rest of the world. But Asian giants such as India, China, Bangladesh and Pakistan are catching up. The picture started to change after the Second World War and with the independence of some former British colonies. At first the progress was gradual, but in the past 20 years, life expectancy and wealth per capita show a closing of the gap and a world converging. Fifty years ago life expectancy in more than half of the world was below 60 years. Today, with the latest data available from 2019, only six countries are below that age. Since the Second World War, countries like India and Bang-ladesh have catapulted their life expectancy rates by more than 20 years. Today, people live on average to about 70 years in India, and about 74 years in Bangladesh. These numbers put them much closer to the average life expectancy in Western countries like the UK and USA, of 81 and 79 years respectively.

In 2015, Rosling (then Professor of International Health at the Karolinska Institute, Stockholm) was invited to give a lecture at the World Economic Forum in Davos. Each person in the packed room had been given a clicker for audience participation. Rosling asked his audience to estimate the global vaccination rate of one-year-olds. This was a question he had asked at over 100 lectures addressed to more than 12,500 people – and it was one where previous audiences had given the wrong answer most often. The highly educated and supposedly knowledgeable audience at

Davos did no better. Given the option of choosing between a vaccination rate of 20, 50 or 80%, only 23% estimated correctly that eight out of ten children globally were receiving life-saving vaccines. The audience knew more about money than health, Rosling joked (it was the World Economic Forum, after all). But misperceptions are no joke. When we make statements that are based on instinct and ideas rather than facts, we're not only likely to be wrong, but we're also spreading misrepresentations of reality.

Rosling never proclaimed that everything in the world was fine. Yet his unwavering efforts to show how misperceptions and generalisations run counter to the actual positive numbers and progress made meant he was often labelled an optimist. The term angered him. He preferred to think of himself as a 'possibilist' – a word he made up to describe someone who neither hopes without reason, nor fears without reason, but who constantly resists the overdramatic world view. The reality is that we do tend to remember and hold on to bad news. Good news doesn't sell, and we're more willing to notice and remember the bad and negative than the good and the positive. We also tend to believe unlikely stories if they fit our beliefs and preconceptions. This leads us to jump to conclusions and assumptions that are not based on evidence, and to systematically underestimate the progress in the world.

Of course, the counterargument is that we have to rely on the experience and knowledge of others: we cannot go out and gather first-hand knowledge about everything, everywhere, in every culture and society. That would be impossible. The good news is that a fact-based world view doesn't require this. There are many tools out there to help, one of which was provided by Rosling. He called it the Gapminder Foundation.

Set up in 2005, the foundation aims to expose views that are inconsistent with the evidence and overcome the walls of misconception. Rosling died in 2017 of cancer, but his son Ola and daughter-in-law Anna continue to run the foundation and pursue its mission. Rosling also left the world *Factfulness*, a book published posthumously in which he teaches a method that is easy to adapt: find the data and learn how to interpret it. Sounds easy enough. There is just one problem: most of us can't even make it to the starting line, because we aren't even trying. Partly because we don't care enough about numbers.

Science Literacy

If a 2013 poll by Ipsos MORI is anything to go by, statisticians have an uphill battle to convince society that an understanding of numbers is vital. Nearly 50% of 1,034 British adults aged 16–75 said that their own experiences or those of their family and friends were more important than statistics in helping them keep track of how the government is doing. Only 9% said that statistics were more important than their own experiences. Most people don't feel particularly embarrassed about their lack of data literacy; they value reading or writing more. As part of the 2013 poll, 516 British adults were asked what would make them most proud of their child. More than half chose 'If they were very good at reading and writing'. Just 13% opted for 'If they were very good at numbers'.

Learning how to read numbers is a basic tool we need to help us understand our world today, especially as we are bombarded by numerical data (statistics) on a daily basis. Statistics is a discipline that collects data on a question asked, analyses it and then presents it in charts or lists. A basic understanding of numbers is obviously key to understanding statistics, but that shouldn't obscure the fact that statistical thinking is just another form of critical thinking: you have to be able to ask the right questions. In practice, it's about interrogating data and deciding which bits are relevant to our decision-making.

So much of our environment today is influenced or even deter-mined by data that it is no longer viable to be data illiterate. And it's certainly no longer viable to not teach our children how to read, write and interpret data in context. At the very minimum, it's our responsibility to guide future generations how to identify problems and frame questions, how to access and understand data and then how to use that information as part of their deci-sion-making. Our individual success and that of our collective humanity would benefit from purposefully enhancing this skill.

In January 2019, the WHO named the anti-vaxxer movement as one of its top ten global health threats. Yes, that's a year before the Covid-19 pandemic hit. The alarm was caused by the resur-gence of yet another highly infectious disease that had been nearly eliminated all over the world: measles. And the resurgence was caused by a lie.

In 1998, Andrew Wakefield, a British researcher, published a paper in the medical journal *The Lancet* claiming that the MMR vaccines caused autism. Several research groups tried to rep-licate the findings without success. They concluded that none of the study's findings had any merit. Wakefield was given the opportunity to replicate his findings but he repeatedly refused to prove the results of his study. In 2004, *The Lancet* admitted that it should not have published the paper and in 2010, a whole twelve years after its publication, the paper was finally retracted. A few months after that, Wakefield was struck off the medical regis-ter. Then in 2011, the ultimate proof that Wakefield's study was fraudulent appeared in the form of a paper in the *British Medical Journal*. It came to light that he had not only altered numbers and facts to establish a false narrative, but he had also pocketed the handsome sum of over £400,000 in exchange for it. The money came from British trial lawyers who were attempting to prove that the vaccine was dangerous. The fact that the payments began two years before *The Lancet* published Wakefield's paper constituted yet more evidence. But this all came many years too late. MMR vaccination rates in the UK had fallen from 95% in 1996 to 80% in 2004. They are now back up to 94% (for the first of the two MMR shots), but this is still below the 95% target which is essential to achieve herd immunity. The ripple effect from Wakefield's study can still be seen. People are once again dying in their tens of thousands from a disease we had nearly wiped from the planet. In 2018 140,000 people died from measles: and around 97% of those deaths were entirely preventable.

Even though scientists have managed to find vaccines to reduce the deadliness of Covid-19 virus, there is still no solution to people's reluctance to get jabbed. It is doubtful there ever will be. For one, scientific knowledge is rarely completely clear-cut.

Very few scientific ideas or theories are completely, 100% irrefutable. There is always some level of uncertainty (yes, even with climate change). Where the conspiracy theorist lives is in that uncertainty. And if you are a flat-earther or a climate-change denier, that's where you live too. The other reason people live in uncertainty is when they have some kind of emotional attachment to the counterpoint. And in this space is where opportunists, lobbyists, politicians, marketers and others will try to enter and exploit others for their own gain, by sowing fear, uncertainty and doubt (FUD).

The first use of FUD as a marketing method is attributed to the computing giant IBM, where the sales force would use it as a technique to direct potential customers towards the company's own products. The team would portray IBM as the low-risk alternative by highlighting all the things that could go wrong if customers were to choose a cheaper competitor.

FUD sells not just products, but news, too. That's why newspapers prefer to run stories that evoke fear and uncertainty rather than happy, positive news. And stories become especially newsworthy if they can cast doubt on particularly longstanding ways of life and long-accepted science.

How do we counteract this? A study published in the journal *Nature Human Behaviour* in June 2019 did find that using facts was an effective strategy for countering science misinformation. Not everyone is convinced. Angela Saini, the multiple-award-winning journalist and writer, and a member of the UK Royal Society for the Arts Disinformation Advisory Group, initially agreed with this study. But today, she tells me, she no longer believes it to be correct: 'I used to think it was that we just need better fact-checking. We just need better experts out there. If we're putting information out there and we clean up the internet, then surely that'll be enough. And actually, I don't think that anymore.' In two of her books, Saini compellingly debunks longheld beliefs on race (*Superior*) and women (*Inferior*). Her research found that, contrary to common perception, conspiracy theorists and people who believe in pseudoscience are not ignorant and uneducated. A large proportion of anti-vaxxers, if not the majority, are well-educated, middle-class mothers. By comparison, working-class mothers tend to vaccinate. And in the developing world, where the levels of education are lower, vaccination rates are high. Saini believes that this shows it is not about access to the facts. Rather, it's a deliberate choice: people are choosing one narrative over another. They are being led by emotion. For some, a story online about a mother whose child had a vaccine injury can be enough to make them doubt the science and think that vaccines aren't safe. Now, it's true that a tiny proportion of people have vaccine injuries and allergies. But look at the numbers: at most, 0.0006% of people who receive the tetanus vaccine have a life-threatening allergic reaction. By contrast, tetanus has been fatal in 11% of reported cases. Yet this relatively tiny number of personal anecdotes and vaccine injury stories can have a huge impact on how parents feel.

Data and risk literacy can help you avoid being ensnared in manipulative FUD narratives. The good news is that you don't have to be a maths genius to become data- and risk-savvy. Just understanding the difference between uncertainty and risk can help. Risk is calculated knowledge of the future states of the world, of the probabilities that an event will occur and its possible consequences. Uncertainty, on the other hand, is when we cannot know the future possible states, probabilities and consequences of something. Both risk and uncertainty are our constant companions, and both are significant components in our decision-making processes.

Uncertainty: Learning to Live With It

Life would be stupendously dull and boring if uncertainty wasn't part of it. It would be devoid of joy, excitement, and pleasure. The impulse that drives us toward our goals, directs our desires and stirs our needs is uncertainty. Here is why. Remove uncertainty and you would land in a monotonous world in which the thrill of exploration and crossing new frontiers vanishes. The question about uncertainty in life is this: Would we still *want* to live it without uncertainty? Would we still love living if everything were guaranteed to us; if day in, day out, we never had to worry about anything? Would we still feel the same about achievements and success? Think about how you feel when you accomplish something. Think about why you feel that way. The chances are you're feeling what you're feeling because in life, success isn't just handed to you, let alone guaranteed.

Yet we have been conditioned to worry about uncertainty. Wherever there is worry, fear isn't too far behind. The problem is that once a powerful emotion such as fear has taken control of our mind, it bulldozes the rational part of our brain. When we are afraid, critical thinking is impossible.

Scientists have been able to show that fear activates the brain – in particular the amygdala, which in humans is involved in the recognition, expression and experience of fear (but it also kicks in when you hear your favourite music, or when you're sexually aroused). Yet while all fears activate the brain, not all are the same or have the same effect.

There are two distinct types of fears. There are fears that are naturally encoded in the brain (innate) like our fear of sudden loud sounds or our fear of falling. Those are induced without any prior experience. Then there are those that have been learnt through trial and error, which we can best see in toddlers' learning (touching a hot plate can hurt, for example). Through learning, things become less scary and we fear less. But we must learn to fear the right things so that our decisions and choices are more accurate and in line with actual facts. One way of doing this is to pit our fears against the associated risks. If we are able to assess and understand the consequences of the risks involved, it can help us manage our emotional bias and lead us to better judgements and better decisions.

Learning About Risk

Risk and risk assessment are integral to the game of poker. Perhaps it is here that we can find the strongest parallels with life. Again, though, this isn't a book about teaching you how to play poker. It's about the fundamentals that underpin it. Part of those being the ability to see and assess risk and the understanding of how to deal with uncertainty. On some level, poker players are a bit like scientists.

Uncertainty drives science and scientists, who find pleasure in the unknown and learn to cultivate doubt. Carl Sagan put this most beautifully: 'Science is not just about knowing things, but knowing what you don't know and what you can't know.' The recent pandemic showed exactly how most of the rest of us deal with great scientific uncertainty: badly. What happened there is what generally happens (and will continue to happen) when members of the public aren't sufficiently helped to understand and assess scientific uncertainty. That's when public scepticism grows, bringing with it a great deal of poor decision-making and misjudgements about scientific issues that then have real societal consequences.

Non-scientific narratives muddied the evidential waters during the pandemic, making the already dire global crisis even more challenging, leading to misperceptions of risk – and from there to an inaccurate assessment of actual danger to life. In late 2019 to early 2020, when the coronavirus had not yet taken hold in the UK, a theory was circulating that the virus was much like the flu, 'just a little more intense'. While in most cases the virus is relatively mild and patients recover without special treatment, when you pit ordinary flu against Covid-19, the numbers aren't even in the same league – neither infection nor death rate.

A person who gets the flu will, on average, infect 1.4 people. If those 1.4 people then spread it to other people at the same rate, and this repeats ten times, around 29 people will catch the flu. Thanks to vaccines and natural immunity, the mortality rate for the flu is as low as 0.3%. Before vaccines became available to stem the infection, according to the WHO the death rate from Covid-19 was over ten times that: 3.4%.

Someone with coronavirus will infect about three people. If each of those three pass it to another three, and you multiply this by ten, the first person in that chain becomes responsible for infecting 59,000 people. As we now know, not a corner in the world was safe. The sheer numbers brought the world to its knees and ushered in a global lockdown.

Why am I giving you yet more numbers? The virus showed what happens when we misjudge risk and why numbers do matter. During the crisis, every digit and every prediction was reported and analysed on a daily basis, worldwide. We were fixated on numbers, because they projected how many of us would live or die. At the start, however, few saw the scale of the problem heading our way and took it seriously. Some of the biggest nations underestimated the threat and were slow to respond to the WHO's urgent call for immediate action. It meant the virus spread at an unprecedented speed, creating a stratospheric rise in infections and deaths.

When an increasing number of people collectively make emotion-led decisions, disregarding numbers and misjudging risk, there are consequences for all of us.

At the same time, there are further variables that influence our individual decision-making – and these can be very personal. The path that has led each and every one of us to arrive at a decision varies greatly. Give two people the same decision to make and they may make opposing choices, because our thinking and belief systems have been shaped by our personal understanding of the world as well as by our own unique experiences. What also matters, and perhaps is even more relevant at times, is how our tendency towards some decisions is influenced by the position we hold within society. In short, where we start out demographically heavily affects how society rewards us. This is true across the animal world, too, where rank plays a significant role when it comes to an animal's health, survival and wellbeing over time. Take chimpanzees, a particularly hierarchical primate society. Chimps born to lower-status females are constantly exposed to aggression from higher-ranked chimps, who will seek to establish dominance or to protect their resources. In cases of conflict, lower-ranked chimps have a much smaller chance of being supported by the group. In the human world, the picture is much the same. We have heard already how women are treated differently when it comes to risk-taking. It's no secret that gender discrimination is the reason why women receive lower pay and lack of opportunity. How society treats people of different ethnicity, race, gender, sexual orientation and socioeconomic status is something that individuals keep in mind when they are making a decision, even if they're not consciously doing so. Inequality of opportunity is pervasive in society. Whether it involves employment, education, healthcare, housing or criminal justice, society doesn't treat everyone the same. Decision-making can differ psychologically and materially from person to person, so with our place in society in mind, what we individually value in life and what we consider worth taking a risk for can vary a lot.

Risks Worth Taking?

The setup of the gameshow *Deal or No Deal* almost feels like it was designed as an economics experiment rather than an entertainment show. Developed by a Dutch production company, Endemol, it was first aired in the Netherlands in December 2002. Six years later it was a global sensation and versions of the game have run in some 40 countries, including the UK, Germany and the US. Why does it make for such gripping viewing? Because contestants can win life-changing amounts in prize money.

The game centres around 26 briefcases, each holding varying values of hidden prize money ranging from just about enough to pay for a cup of coffee to an enormous amount that could pay for an entire café. The overall goal is to eliminate the briefcases containing the lowest prize monies and be left with the highest amount. It begins with the contestant picking a briefcase containing an unknown sum, and the choosing and opening of cases continues with the contestant picking a further six of the remaining 25 unopened briefcases. Those six are then opened to reveal the prizes no longer available to the contestants. Then it's decision time. The contestant is asked to accept a 'bank offer' and walk away with a guaranteed amount of cash, or to play on. The question is simple: 'Deal or no deal?' If the contestants respond,

'No deal,' they have to open five more briefcases, which is then followed by a new bank offer. As the game proceeds, more cases are picked then opened, giving them a better idea of what money could potentially be in the remaining briefcases. The sums offered by the banker depend on the value of the unopened briefcases, and are usually smaller than the average of the remaining prizes. An ideal scenario would be one in which the minimum sum in the remaining briefcases is an acceptable amount of money to take home. Let's say you're left with three briefcases: $5,000, $10,000 and $75,000. You are guaranteed at least $5,000 no matter what and you are happy with that, even if you turn down offers from the banker. But it doesn't always work out that way. Particularly when the sums remaining leave the contestant with a risk of walking away with next to nothing.

On the US version of the show, one contestant ended up doing just that. In December 2018, with only one case remaining apart from his own, he had a chance of walking away with a whopping $333,000, the amount the banker offered him. He had to decide between accepting the sure money from the banker, or taking the 50/50 chance of either winning $750,000 (the only higher prize, $1 million, had been eliminated) or $5. He took his chance and ended up with a fiver. What happened? Why would one take the risk of losing hundreds of thousands of dollars of guaranteed cash? People are forever complex, and they don't always act rationally. Real-life choices rarely adhere to an expected path, because as we have found out in this book, people aren't simple, calculating machines. That's why analysing the behaviours of contestants in gameshows with a 'risk and reward' element has always been popular among researchers – and *Deal or No Deal* provides a perfect study field. The gameshow offers a key aspect of the decision-making process that can't be replicated in the lab or classroom: life-changing prize money. Germany had a top prize of €250,000. In the US the maximum prize payout was $1 million.

In 2007, the Dutch edition was sponsored by the national lottery and had a potential top prize of €5 million up for grabs.

Risk in Gaming

The data sets from the Dutch, German and US versions of the shows which used the basic model of the game was analysed by a group of researchers, who focused solely on decision-making patterns ignoring the contestant's gender, age and education. They did this partly because, during the game, the contestants were free to consult with friends and family, which means their decisions were no longer down purely to their individual traits but were often, in effect, taken by a couple or a group of people. The researchers suggested this made the significance of the individual contestant's age, gender or education very low to the point of being virtually irrelevant. So what they found, in short, was that the contestants' decisions all depended on their reference points and what had happened before the point at which a decision needed to be made. In fact, the decision-making behaviour seemed very much path-dependent. The data showed that contestants' propensity to risk aversion was especially reduced after earlier expectations had been shattered by unfavourable outcomes, or surpassed by favourable outcomes; in other words, the way they'd fared in the game thus far (the prior outcomes) influenced their critical decision-making. Contestants were less risk averse when they had been lucky and had eliminated low-value briefcases. But they were also less risk averse when they'd had a bad run of picking the wrong briefcases. In fact, people were more likely and willing to gamble when they had not accepted their losses.

I see this type of decision-making behaviour all too often at the tables. In poker we call it 'tilt'. Players are on tilt when their decisions start to be guided by negative emotions, particularly after a losing streak, or when they've just had a big loss. Or both. This tends to be exacerbated even further when they've played by the book and made the best possible decisions according to GTO, but luck has gone against them. Those players who aren't able to handle their bad run start veering from the ideal play. They make bad decisions and end up on tilt. They start playing hands they shouldn't be playing, bluffing more and calling more hands when they should be folding. Good poker players know when they are on tilt and mostly manage their thinking and behaviour accordingly. It takes discipline to make sound decisions at the poker table. The game will test your endurance, it will push you to your emotional limits and it will be ruthlessly unfair – just like life can be. What you need to know is that you're in control. Yes, you are. When it comes to adversity, it's up to you how you respond. You have the freedom and power to decide who you want to be – at the table and in real life.

Life is a game – whether you are making decisions, influencing others, or just trying to tease out information. But these interactions don't need to end up with winners or losers. In fact, let's try – as individuals and as a society – to move away from zero-sum thinking.

The Making of Zero-Sum Mindsets . . .

We are often led to believe that life consists solely of winners and losers; that we live in a world in which resources, power and status are limited, where any gain by one person (or group) always means a loss for another. The issue with a zero-sum world view is that it tends to promote a win-lose mentality, and this fuels conflict.

Life's games, no matter how competitive they may seem to us, are usually not zero-sum ones. The world is actually full of non-zero-sum scenarios where one player's gain is not necessarily the other's loss. Both win-win and lose-lose situations can be observed pretty much everywhere, from the marketplace, to government, to countries at war or even kids in the playground. Any trade is a non-zero-sum game – you exchange money or a service in exchange for a service or money. It's how we think about these interactions that's important, as they can affect how we make decisions, how we feel about our lives and our own perceived happiness. Once more, gaining an understanding of *why* we think what we think will help us.

In 2023, a team of researchers from Harvard, the University of British Columbia and the London School of Economics sought to measure the extent to which people's mindset can be described as 'zero sum' and whether this correlates with some of the policy and political views we see. And if it does, then why. Nearly 15,000 individuals living in the United States responded to the researchers' surveys, which covered questions about people's ancestors – their parents, grandparents and great-grandparents. Their aim was to begin to understand the historical determinants, meaning the deep-rooted experiences, that shape people's psychological traits.

Some parts of the survey included the presentation of statements about income such as: 'In the United States, there are many different income classes. If one group becomes wealthier, it is usually the case that this comes at the expense of other groups.' Participants were asked to indicate to what extent they agreed with these statements.

The researchers found zero-sum mindsets aligned with policy views that supported affirmative action, redistribution, or other policies that helped level the playing field to make things better (essentially to help the losers of zero-sum games). On average, the more liberal people are, the more zero-sum their view of the world. This sounded counterintuitive and confusing to me. Perhaps it was because when we think of zero-sum, what comes to mind first are the narratives that fuel an 'Us vs Them' rhetoric, and those tend to come from conservative individuals or groups. To help me understand, I got in touch with Sandra Sequeira, a professor at the London School of Economics. The emphasis is on 'average', she tells me, and goes on to further explain that zero-sum views aren't monolithic nor confined to a specific party. They cut across both left and right. And one of the team's most surprising findings was that this gradient of zero-sum thinking exists within both Republicans and Democrats. 'This variation within party is really interesting,' says Sequeira, and this cross-party zero-sum thinking can explain a lot about the recent political puzzles in the US. Democrats who voted for Trump were also more zero-sum thinking, as were Democrats who showed more empathy for the 6 January Capitol rioters, or who reported that there was some truth in conspiracy theories like QAnon. Republicans who favoured more redistribution also had a more zero-sum view of the world.

Sequeira agrees when I talk about the connection between being zero-sum and preferring more redistribution. 'This is likely to be driven by a combination of people who would benefit from redistribution and people who derive value and utility from thinking that they are benefiting those who are worse off. This coalition then translates into the Democrats being more zero-sum on average.'

Separately, respondents were also more likely to view the world as less zero-sum if they had seen themselves, their parents, or their grandparents experience more upward mobility.

One of the primary sources of this upward mobility is immigration. The analysis showed that individuals also tended to be less zero-sum if they, their parents, or their grandparents had immigrated to the United States. Immigrants typically made a better life for themselves in the United States and experienced better living conditions than in the country they had left, and so if a respondent was born outside the US, then they tended to have a less zero-sum view of the world.

Researchers saw the opposite when it came to race and slavery. African Americans and black individuals thought in more zero-sum terms. Respondents who had ancestors who had been enslaved, or lived in a location with more enslavement, including non-black individuals whose ancestors were among enslaved indigenous populations, or those who had migrated to the US as indentured labourers, reported more zero-sum world views.

Age also plays a role. Specifically, *when* you were born can affect how you see the world. How come? Economic growth, or the lack of it, has quite a bit to do with it.

The US had seen a sort of golden age of economic growth in the two or three decades before the 1970s, and the common perception was that anyone could achieve economic success so long as they worked hard enough. The 'American Dream' was at its peak. As an example, between 1960 and 1970, pre-tax income for the bottom half of the US population grew by 53%. Looking at it this way, 50- to 80-year-old respondents had experienced periods of affluence, whereas those born more recently find themselves in a world of economic stagnation. Nathan Nunn, another of the study's investigators, explains that this is why older respondents have a less zero-sum view of the world. He says it helps explain why they tend to believe that if people are poor, they just aren't working hard enough and why younger people, who tend to be more zero-sum, are more supportive of social welfare programmes than older people.

Does this hold true outside the US? Yes, according to the World Value Survey of 200,000 respondents from across 72 countries, which shows the same patterns. The greater the economic growth in your country in the first 20 years of your life, the less zero-sum you tend to be. Going beyond the US, zero-sum thinking tends to be correlated with more liberal thinking and people who tend to be more in favour of wealth redistribution, tilting access to recourses towards disadvantaged groups, and redistribution policies such as taxation and universal healthcare.

This gives us some understanding about how our thinking is influenced by our background, upbringing and economic experiences; in other words, our history plays an important role in how we are predisposed to seeing and thinking about the world. These predispositions can be triggered by interactions and cues from whatever our current environment might be, but let's not allow others to manipulate us to think about an issue in a certain way without understanding their motivations, because it can have dire consequences for us as a society overall.

In each generation, one way or another historians have witnessed the most polarised times in which democracy was at risk. The year 2020 certainly made a run for the top spot for democracy-under-siege. There are and were, of course, a multitude of reasons why in this particular year previously unshakable democracies were in real peril. In both the US and UK the very foundations of democracy were shaken by polarising speech and ideologies that tapped into zero-sum thinking: dividing the world into winners and losers, where one person's gain is presented as another person's loss. It is a strategy straight out of the politics handbook that is often accompanied by misinformation and untruths. And plenty of us fall for it.

Researchers at Columbia University in New York examined this relationship between political ideology and zero-sum thinking, when one party's gain could only be obtained at the expense of the other party's losses. Data from three thousand two hundred and twenty-three participants across six studies made clear that, especially in US politics, zero-sum thinking was prevalent. It may seem obvious now, but the signs of strong zero-sum thinking were there for years. In 2011, a study showed that white Americans increasingly felt that there was 'anti-white' bias, and that the

decrease in anti-black prejudice was offset by anti-white prejudice. The study's principal researcher, Michael Norton, told NPR
(National Public Radio) in a subsequent interview: '[. . .] white
people believe that racism against blacks has decreased; they also
believe that racism against whites has increased. They really see
it as kind of a fixed pie of resources, a zero-sum game. One job
for a black person equals one job that a white person didn't get.'
In 2016, Trump won the US presidency precisely by tapping into
this ideology, and he continued to push it when he was in the
Oval Office. In April 2020, he went ahead with an executive order
that was described as an 'immigration ban'. He claimed it would
help put American workers back to work. The narrative about
immigrants taking away jobs, homes and healthcare is fallacious,
yet framing the narrative and talking about the issue in this way
was enough to nudge others into a zero-sum mentality – even
though studies showed the opposite to be true. In the long run,
American counties with historically higher immigration also had
higher income, less poverty, less unemployment and higher rates
of urbanisation.

Sure, there are aspects of the world that are zero-sum. If I apply
for a job, but someone else gets it, that's a zero-sum outcome for
me. But the point is this: when we see the world as zero-sum,
where one side always loses and one always wins, we are unlikely
to entertain any attempts to come together to collaborate and
compromise.

All this leads us back to the idea of taking winning off the table.
Our focus (and this is another, final lesson from the poker table)
should be process-orientated, not results-orientated.

When we focus on doing all the things we are supposed to
do right, then we will actually maximise our chances of success.
In poker, this means always knowing the GTO, and playing as
close as possible to that, while absorbing as much information
as we can and acting accordingly. In life it comes down to how

well we gather data, then challenge the sources and the information. This includes learning to interpret the stories of others astutely – appreciating the power of narrative, and how it can be exploited. And finally, it also comes down to our ability to seek and find alternative voices and perspectives, which will help us further examine what we are being told. The point is that we can control the way we interrogate information in order to get the truth. And when we use all the tools available to us, and we apply our best critical thinking, we can maximise the chances of a good outcome. It won't be guaranteed, but that's okay.

We know that we can't make good decisions consistently unless we have the right information. We also know we cannot know everything all of the time all at once, let alone act or think perfectly. And we don't all value the same things. Our personal values drive our day to day, but we have to put those in a hierarchy and decide in what order they come, what we need to prioritise. So, every day we make trade-offs to get the things we want and value. And that's okay too, so long as we are honest with ourselves and understand our own limitations. My writing takes priority over my poker-playing. And I know that the limited time I devote to studying and playing poker is unlikely to ever place me amongst the top poker players of the world. I am okay with that.

Whatever your values or your goals, I hope that this book inspires you to ask more questions and – because you have learnt how to look for information and detect when something is amiss – that it has left you feeling empowered to demand the facts and figures that you need.

A Tribute

This book would not exist were it not for the one person who knew I was a writer way before I even thought I could be one. Not only did he encourage me to make the leap, but when I hesitated, he pushed aside all my fears and told me: 'Know that no matter what happens, I got you!' Jeff, meeting you outside in the snow at Terminal 2 at Heathrow remains the luckiest day of my life. Ever since then you have made me believe that nothing is out of my reach – and with you by my side there is absolutely nothing I fear. My love for you transcends life itself.

A key moment in the journey towards this book was a chance encounter at a London restaurant, where sitting at the table next to me was the then editor of the *Independent*, Amol Rajan. I was a total stranger to him, yet he showed me great kindness and shared valuable advice. Dear Amol, we have not met again since, and you might not even remember me, but if you happen to read this, please know that you helped that young science writer more than you can imagine. Acting upon the advice you gave me then, I landed several commissions that supercharged my writing career. I will forever be grateful to you.

I am eternally thankful to my friend the novelist Katherine

Taylor, who when publishers showed an interest in my writing, introduced me to my agent, Elizabeth Sheinkman at Peters Fraser + Dunlop. If there is a rainmaker, it must be you, Elizabeth. Deals aside, you have become a source of strength and sound guidance. I am most grateful to you for getting me a deal with my dream publisher. I remember leaving my first meeting with Rebecca Gray at Profile Books full of excitement. She had told me not to worry about timing, but to 'just get the science right'. Rebecca, I couldn't have wished for a better publisher. Even when I kept missing the deadlines you responded with unwavering faith and rock-solid support. Thank you for believing in me. Thank you also for picking Shan Vahidy to edit; I loved working with such a great thinker. Shan, my heartfelt gratitude for the passion you have shown for this book. You saw what I couldn't or didn't, and thank you for pushing me to use my voice more and for continually challenging me to dig deeper and be more precise.

Helping me with accuracy was Peter Wrobel. How do I even thank you for meticulously combing through the data and the facts?! There are not enough words of gratitude in the dictionary for how thankful I am to you and for our friendship. I cherish and love you. I will forever be indebted to the magnificent Angela Saini for introducing us to each other. Angela, I could fill pages on how much your friendship means to me. Thank you for being such a loving friend and holding my hand throughout the writing of this book.

Yes, there were plenty of moments when I felt unsure, but it was during these that my challenge network would come to the rescue: friends who told me what I needed to hear, not what I wanted to hear. I have always loved Mun-Keat Looi's direct and clear feedback, which over time has exponentially improved my writing. If you are ever lucky enough to work with this amazing editor, you are in for a treat. Thanks, MK, for reading so many drafts of this book and for not holding back on your thoughts. I appreciate you and our friendship with all my heart.

The fiercest challengers were my friends at my writers' group Neuwrite. Thank you for the unbridled feedback Roma Agrawal, Güneş Taylor, Subhadra Das, Gina Rippon, Hana Ayoob, Emma Bryce, Liam Drew, Paula Rowinska and Simon Makin.

My friend, the immeasurably creative and brilliant writer, Monica Meira Vaughan and I share a passion and curiosity about the world that makes me feel alive and excited whenever I am with her. Moni, thank you for introducing me to poker. You opened a door to a new world full of adventure for me, adding yet another colourful dimension to my life. I love you.

I came away in awe from interviewing author, US Women's Chess Champion and poker pro Jennifer Shahade – a cerebral and fearless human, who above all regularly steps up for others, including complete strangers. This is what she did for me and how we became friends. Jen, you make me believe I have an unfair share of luck in my life. Thank you also for introducing me to the effervescent Irish poker pro David Lappin. You told me not to be sentimental about this but pal, I can't help it: I will never be able to thank you enough for the hours you spent reading to help me make sure the poker content was accurate. *Go raibh maith agat*, David, from the bottom of my heart.

Getting it right in poker is hard, but it is made easier when you know where to get help from. I want to thank Dara O'Kearney for writing some of the best poker study books there are. My profound gratitude goes to Fedor Holz. You are a natural at teaching, and I feel incredibly lucky to have benefited from your mentoring. Thank you for selecting me as part of the group who entered the Grindhouse in the Austrian Alps. I left transformed, laden with knowledge and skill. Perhaps the best takeaway has been my fellow Grindhouse pals Grzegorz Kozieja, Samuel Mullur, Fabian Niederreiter, Tobias Eichenseher, Charlie Chiu, Bhushan Sohani, and Siegfried Kapeller. You guys keep inspiring me to study hard. I love learning from you, but I love playing poker with you the most.

Finally, thank you for making time to read. I hope you enjoyed *The Truth Detective*.

References and Further Reading

Anand, Viswanathan & Susan Ninan (2019) *Mind Master*, Hachette India

Baggini, Julian (2018) *A Short History of Truth*, Quercus

Bernstein, Peter L. (1998) *Against the Gods*, Wiley

Blackburn, Simon (2001) *Think*, Oxford University Press

Blastland, Michael & David J. Spiegelhalter (2014) *The Norm Chronicles*, Profile Books

Burnett, Dean (2017) *The Idiot Brain*, Guardian Faber Publishing

Byrne, Emma (2018) *Swear!ng Is G*od f*r You*, Profile Books

Chalmers, David J. & Tim Peacock (2022) *Reality+*, Allen Lane

Chamine, Shirzad (2012) *Positive Intelligence*, Greenleaf Book Group Press

Cheng, Eugenia (2018) *The Art of Logic*, Profile Books

Chivers, Tom & David Chivers (2021) *How to Read Numbers*, W&N

Cialdini, Robert B. (2006) *Influence*, Collins

Dixit, Avinash K. & Barry J. Nalebuff (1993) *Thinking Strategically*, Norton

Dixit, Avinash K. & Barry J. Nalebuff (2010) *The Art of Strategy*, Norton

Duffy, Bobby (2018) *The Perils of Perception*, Atlantic Books

Eberhardt, Jennifer L. (2019) *Biased*, William Heinemann

Ellenberg, Jordan (2015) *How Not to Be Wrong*, Penguin Books

Fisher, Roger & Daniel Shapiro (2007) *Building Agreement*, Random House Business

Gigerenzer, Gerd (2015) *Risk Savvy*, Penguin Books

Goodwin, Paul (2020) *Something Doesn't Add Up*, Profile Books

Henrich, Joseph (2020) *The Weirdest People in the World*, Allen Lane

Huff, Darrell (1991) *How to Lie with Statistics*, Penguin Books

Kahneman, Daniel (2011) *Thinking, Fast and Slow*, FSG

Kahneman, Daniel, Olivier Sibony & Cass R. Sunstein (2021) *Noise*, William Collins

Kucharski, Adam (2017) *The Perfect Bet*, Profile Books

Kuhn, Gustav (2019) *Experiencing the Impossible*, MIT Press

Levine, Timothy R. (2020) *Duped*, University of Alabama Press

Lewis, Michael (1990) *Liar's Poker*, Penguin Books

Lewis, Michael (2017) *The Undoing Project*, Penguin Books

Matsumoto, David Ricky & Linda P. Juang (2017) *Culture and Psychology*, Cengage Learning

Meadows, Donella H. & Diana Wright (2008) *Thinking in Systems*, Chelsea Green Pub

Navarro, Joe (2018) *The Dictionary of Body Language*, William Morrow

O'Brien, James (2018) *How to Be Right*, WH Allen

O'Connor, Cailin & James Owen Weatherall (2019) *The Misinformation Age*, Yale University Press

Orlin, Ben (2018) *Math with Bad Drawings*, Black Dog & Leventhal

Pearl, Judea, Madelyn Glymour & Nicholas P. Jewell (2016) *Causal Inference in Statistics*, Wiley

Pennebaker, James W. (2013) *The Secret Life of Pronouns*, Bloomsbury

Raeburn, Paul & Kevin Zollman (2017) *The Game Theorist's Guide to Parenting*, Scientific American/FSG

Raz, Amir & Sheida Rabipour (2019) *How (Not) to Train the Brain*, Oxford University Press

Rippon, Gina (2019) *The Gendered Brain*, The Bodley Head

Rosling, Hans, Ola Rosling & Anna Rosling Rönnlund (2018) *Factfulness*, Sceptre

Rowntree, Derek (2018) *Statistics without Tears*, Penguin Books

Sagan, Carl (2008) *The Demon-Haunted World*, Paw Prints

Saini, Angela (2019) *Inferior*, 4th Estate

Saini, Angela (2019) *Superior*, 4th Estate

Sapolsky, Robert M. (2018) *Behave*, Vintage

Shariatmadari, David (2019) *Don't Believe a Word*, W&N

Silver, Nate (2013) *The Signal and the Noise*, Penguin Books

Stephens-Davidowitz, Seth (2018) *Everybody Lies*, Bloomsbury

Stone, Douglas, Bruce Patton & Sheila Heen (2011) *Difficult Conversations*, Portfolio Penguin

Sun Tzu, Ralph D. Sawyer & Mei-Chün Sawyer (1994) *The Art of War*, Barnes & Noble

Swaab, Dick (2016) *We Are Our Brains*, Penguin Books

Syed, Matthew (2016) *Black Box Thinking*, John Murray

Thaler, Richard H. (2016) *Misbehaving*, Allen Lane

Thaler, Richard H. & Cass R. Sunstein (2021) *Nudge*, Yale University Press

Thouless, Robert H. & C. R. Thouless (2011) *Straight & Crooked Thinking*, Hodder Education

Todorov, Alexander (2017) *Face Value*, Princeton University Press

Voss, Christopher A. & Tahl Raz (2017) *Never Split the Difference*, Random House Business

Notes

Introduction

Pokernews (2017) 2017 PokerStars Festival London, www.pokernews.com/tours/pokerstars-festival/2017-pokerstars-festival-london/main-event/chips.153566.htm

Part One

Aronson, J. K., et al. (2019) Key concepts for making informed choices, *Nature*, doi.org/10.1038/d41586-019-02407-9

Aspen Institute (2017) Facing History and Ourselves and Allstate Create the New Town Hall to Encourage Civil Discourse in Divided Country, 6 Jun

Bach, D. R. & Dolan, R. J. (2012) Knowing how much you don't know: a neural organization of uncertainty estimates, *Nature Reviews Neuroscience*, doi.org/10.1038/nrn3289

Baker, M. (2016) 1,500 scientists lift the lid on reproducibility, *Nature*, doi.org/10.1038/533452a

BBC News (2013) AP Twitter account hacked in fake 'White House blasts' post, 24 Apr

Brand, D. (1996) Carl Sagan, Cornell astronomer, dies today (Dec. 20) in Seattle, *Cornell Chronicle*, 19 Dec

Bronstein, M., et al. (2018) Belief in Fake News Is Associated with Delusionality, Dogmatism, Religious Fundamentalism, and Reduced Analytic Thinking, *SSRN*, doi.org/10.1016/j.jarmac.2018.09.005

Brotherton, R., et al. (2013) Measuring Belief in Conspiracy Theories: The Generic Conspiracist Beliefs Scale, *Front. Psychol.*, doi.org/10.3389/fpsyg.2013.00279

Browne, B. R. (1989) Going on tilt: Frequent poker players and control, *J Gambling Stud* 5, 3–21

Browne, M., et al. (2015) Going against the Herd: Psychological and Cultural Factors Underlying the 'Vaccination Confidence Gap', *PLoS ONE*, doi.org/10.1371/journal.pone.0132562

Cicali III, A. (2023) US Online Poker Closes Out The Year Strong, iGaming Breaks Records, *US Poker*, www.uspoker.com/blog/us-online-poker-closes-out-the-year-strong-igaming-numbers-break-records/40837/

Cillizza, C. (2016) A fact checker looked into 158 things Donald Trump said. 78 percent were false, *Washington Post*, 1 Jul

Council of Europe, Dealing with propaganda, misinformation and fake news, www.coe.int/en/web/campaign-free-to-speak-safe-to-learn/dealing-with-propaganda-misinformation-and-fake-news

Ennis, R. H. (1985) Critical Thinking and the Curriculum, *National Forum Baton Rouge, La.*, 65(1) www.proquest.com/openview/7383544f9d561b8d2eeb98baa33e659b/1?pq-origsite=gscholar&cbl=1820941

Evans, T. (2020) 'The Truth', Hillsborough, the betrayal of a nation and the catalyst for letting the powerful off the hook, *The Independent*, 19 Apr

Flynn, D. J., et al. (2017) The Nature and Origins of

Misperceptions, *Advances in Political Psychology*, doi.
org/10.1111/pops.12394

Frankfurt, H. G. (2005) *On Bullshit*, Princeton University Press

Frederick, S. (2005) Cognitive Reflection and Decision
Making, *Journal of Economic Perspectives*, doi.
org/10.1257/089533005775196732

Greenfield, R. (2013) Look What the Hacked AP Tweet About
White House Bombs Did to the Market, *The Atlantic*, 23 Apr

Hutchinson, S. (2014) 15 Highlights from Carl Sagan's Archive,
Mental Floss, 6 Feb

Jacobson, L. (2015) Faculty Book: Harry Frankfurt,
Princeton Alumni Weekly, paw.princeton.edu/article/
faculty-book-harry-frankfurt

James, J. L. (2015) Mobile Dating in the Digital Age
(unpublished thesis), Texas State University digital.library.
txstate.edu/handle/10877/5529

Jarry, J. (2020) The Dunning-Kruger Effect Is Probably Not
Real, *McGill Office for Science and Society*, 17 Dec

Jenik, C. (2021) A Minute on the Internet in 2021, *Statista.com*,
30 Jul

Jerrim, J., et al. (2020) Bullshitters, *IZA Institute of Labor
Economics*, www.iza.org/publications/dp/12282/bullshitters-
who-are-they-and-what-do-we-know-about-their-lives

Kemp, S. (2021) Digital 2021: Global Overview Report,
DataReportal.com, 27 Jan

Kubota, J. T., et al. (2012) The neuroscience of race, *Nature
Neuroscience*, doi.org/10.1038/nn.3136

Leonard, C. A. & Williams, R. J. (2015) Characteristics of Good
Poker Players, *Journal of Gambling Issues*, doi.org/10.4309/
jgi.2015.31.5

Leone, M. J., et al. (2017) Time to decide, *Cognition*, doi.
org/10.1016/j.cognition.2016.10.007

Loken, E. (2019) The replication crisis is good for science, *The Conversation*, 8 Apr

Marshall, C. (2018) Carl Sagan's Syllabus & Final Exam for His Course on Critical Thinking, *Open Culture*, 28 Jan

McManus, J. (2009) What Poker Can Teach Us, *The Chronicle of Higher Education*, 5 Oct

Michalski, D. (2009) Obama the poker player, *Pokerati*, 5 Dec, pokerati.com/2009/12/obama-as-a-poker-player-cover-story-in-the-national-journal/

MIT Open Courseware (2015) Poker Theory And Analytics: Basic Strategy ocw.mit.edu/courses/15-s50-poker-theory-and-analytics-Jan-iap-2015/resources/basic-strategy/

Neergard, L. & Fingerhut, H. (2020) AP-NORC poll: Half of Americans would get a COVID-19 vaccine, *AP News*, 27 May

Nuhfer, E., et al. (2017) How Random Noise and a Graphical Convention Subverted Behavioral Scientists' Explanations of Self-Assessment Data, *Numeracy*, doi.org/10.5038/1936-4660.10.1.4

OECD (2019) Creativity and Critical Thinking Skills in School, www.oecd.org/education/ceri/creativity-and-critical-thinking-skills-in-school-moving-a-shared-agenda-forward.htm

Open Science Collaboration (2015) Estimating the reproducibility of psychological science, *Science*, doi.org/10.1126/science.aac4716

Oppenheimer, D. M. (2006) Consequences of erudite vernacular utilized irrespective of necessity, *Applied Cognitive Psychology*, doi.org/10.1002/acp.1178

Orlin, B. (2013) The Swindler's Coin, *Math with Bad Drawings*, 21 Oct, mathwithbaddrawings.com/2013/10/21/the-swindlers-coin/

Parke, A., et al. (2005) Can playing poker be good for you?, *Journal of Gambling Issues*, doi.org/10.4309/jgi.2005.14.12

Pennycook, G. & Rand, D. G. (2019) Lazy, not biased, *Cognition*, doi.org/10.1016/j.cognition.2018.06.011

Pennycook, G., et al. (2015) On the reception and detection of pseudo-profound bullshit, *Judgment and Decision Making*, doi.org/10.1017/S1930297500006999

Pennycook, G., et al. (2021) Shifting attention to accuracy can reduce misinformation online, *Nature*, doi.org/ 10.1038/ s41586-021-03344-2

Popper, N. (2010) Trading firms put their money on poker experts, *Los Angeles Times*, 16 May

Reuters (2020) False claim: doctors who treated Boris Johnson say he didn't have coronavirus, 17 Apr

Sahm, M. & von Weizsäcker, R. K. (2015) Reason, Intuition, and Time, *CESifo Working Paper no. 5134*, dx.doi.org/10.2139/ ssrn.2550130

Shao, C., et al. (2018) The spread of low-credibility content by social bots, *Nature Communications*, doi.org/10.1038/ s41467-018-06930-7

UK Safer Internet Centre, Misinformation, saferinternet.org.uk/ online-issue/misinformation

Wagemans, J. H. M. (2022) How to identify an argument type?, *Science Direct*, doi.org/10.1016/j.pragma.2022.11.015

What's the Difference Between Weather and Climate? (2018) *National Centers for Environmental Information*, 23 Mar, www. ncei.noaa.gov/news/weather-vs-climate

Part Two

Adolphs, R. (2013) The Biology of Fear, *Current Biology*, doi.org/10.1016/j.cub.2012.11.055

Agarwal, P. (2020) Exposing unconscious bias, *New Scientist*, doi.org/10.1016/S0262-4079(20)31505-0

Akechi, H., et al. (2013) Attention to eye contact in the West and East, *PLoS ONE*, doi.org/10.1371/journal.pone.0059312

Amat, J. A. & Rendón, M. A. (2017) Flamingo coloration and its significance in *Flamingos: Behavior, Biology, and Relationship with Humans*, Nova Science Publishers

Anthropology.iResearchNet, Jean L. Briggs, www.anthropology. iresearchnet.com/jean-l-briggs/

Ashley, G. C. & Reiter-Palmon, R. (2012) Self-Awareness and the Evolution of Leaders, *Journal of Behavioral and Applied Management*, doi.org/ 10.1037/t29152-000

Austin, D. (2021) Men are just as emotional as women, *TODAY. com*, 2 Nov

Briggs, J. L. (2000) Emotions Have Many Faces, *Anthropologica* www.jstor.org/stable/25605984

Business Wire (2012) Women Poised to Effectively Lead in Matrix Work Environments Hay Group Research Finds

Bzdok, D. & Dunbar, R. I. M. (2020) The Neurobiology of Social Distance, *Trends in Cognitive Science*, doi.org/10.1016/j. tics.2020.05.016

DeBruine, L. M., et al. (2008) Social Perception of Facial Resemblance in Humans, *Archives of Sexual Behavior*, doi. org/10.1007/s10508-007-9266-0

Esimai, C. (2018) Great Leadership Starts With Self-Awareness, *Forbes*, 15 Feb

Fisk, S. R. (2016) Gender Stereotypes, Risk-Taking, and Gendered Mobility, in *Advances in Group Processes*, pp.179–210, dx.doi.org/10.1108/S0882-61452016000033007

Fisk, S. R. (2018) Who's on Top? Gender Differences in Risk-Taking Produce Unequal Outcomes for High-Ability Women and Men, *Social Psychology Quarterly*, doi. org/10.1177/0190272518796512

Fisk, S. R. & Overton, J. (2019) Who Wants to Lead? Anticipated Discrimination Reduces Women's Leadership Ambitions, *Social Psychology Quarterly*, doi. org/10.1177/0190272519863424

Folz, J., et al. (2022) Reading Your Emotions in My Physiology?, *Affective Science*, doi.org/10.1007/s42761-021-00083-5

Friesen, W. V. (1973) Cultural differences in facial expressions in a social situation, *Sociology*

Geffner, R. (2006) Europa, Europa: The Story of Solomon Perel, *UC Santa Barbara*, marcuse.faculty.history.ucsb.edu/ classes/33d/projects/jewishlife/JewishPerelRuth.htm, 2020

Gerdes, C., et al. (2011) Chicken or Checkin'? Rational Learning in Repeated Chess Games, *IZA Institute of Labor Economics*, www.iza.org/publications/dp/5862/chicken-or-checkin-rational-learning-in-repeated-chess-games

Harvard Business Review (2018) *Self-awareness*, Harvard Business Review Press

Hwang, H. C., et al. (2016) Linguistic cues of deception across multiple language groups in a mock crime context, *Journal of Investigative Psychology and Offender Profiling*, doi.org/10.1002/ jip.1442

Iverson, J. M. & Goldin-Meadow, S. (1998) Why people gesture when they speak, *Nature*, doi.org/10.1038/24300

Jung, N., et al. (2014) How emotions affect logical reasoning, *Front Psychol*, doi.org/10.3389/fpsyg.2014.00570

Kiyonari, T., et al. (2006) Does Trust Beget Trustworthiness?, *Social Psychology Quarterly*, doi. org/10.1177/019027250606900304

Kodera, S. (2021) Giambattista della Porta, *The Stanford Encyclopedia of Philosophy*, 14 Jul, plato.stanford.edu/entries/ della-porta/

Kosinski, M. (2017) Facial Width-to-Height Ratio Does Not Predict Self-Reported Behavioral Tendencies, *Psychological Science*, doi.org/10.1177/0956797617716929

Krenn, B. & Meier, J. (2018) Does Facial Width-to-Height Ratio Predict Aggressive Behavior in Association Football?, *Evolutionary Psychology*, doi.org/10.1177/1474704918818590

Lawson, C., et al. (2010) Looking Like a Winner, *World Politics*, dx.doi.org/10.1017/S0043887110000195

Le Cunff, A.-L. (2020) The hermeneutic circle, *Ness Labs*

LeFebvre, L. E. (2018) Swiping me off my feet, *Journal of Social and Personal Relationships*, doi.org/10.1177/0265407517706419

Levine, E., et al. (2018) Who is Trustworthy?, *Journal of Personality and Social Psychology*, dx.doi.org/10.2139/ssrn.2910069

Li, M-H, et al. (2022) Emotion, analytic thinking and susceptibility to misinformation during the COVID-19 outbreak, *Computers in Human Behavior*, doi.org/10.1016/j.chb.2022.107295

Martinez, L., et al. (2016) Contributions of facial expressions and body language to the rapid perception of dynamic emotions, *Cognition and Emotion*, doi.org/10.1080/02699931.2015.1035229

Matsumoto, D. & Hwang, H. C. (2018) Microexpressions differentiate truths from lies about future malicious intent, *Frontiers in Psychology*, doi.org/10.3389/fpsyg.2018.02545

Matsumoto, D. & Willingham, B. (2006) The Thrill of Victory and the Agony of Defeat, *Journal of Personality and Social Psychology*, doi.org/10.1037/0022-3514.91.3.568

McCarthy, A., et al. (2006) Cultural display rules drive eye gaze during thinking, *J Cross Cult Psychol*, doi.org/10.1177/0022022106292079

McLeod, C. (2020) Trust, *The Stanford Encyclopedia of Philosophy*, 10 Aug, plato.stanford.edu/entries/trust/

Navarro, J. (2014) 9 Truths Exposing a Myth About Body Language, *Psychology Today*, 6 Oct

Ono, Y., et al. (2019) Candidates' Facial Attractiveness and Electoral Success Evidence from Japan's Upper House Elections, rubenson.org/wp-content/uploads/2019/11/ono.pdf

Pascual-Ezama, D., et al. (2021) Do Not Tell Me More; You Are Honest, *Front Psychol.*, doi.org/10.3389/fpsyg.2021.693942

Peplow, M. (2004) Science secret of grand masters revealed, *Nature*, doi.org/10.1038/news040802-19

Perry, J., et al. (2021) Trust in public institutions, *United Nations Department of Economic and Social Affairs*, 20 Jul, www.un.org/development/desa/dspd/2021/07/trust-public-institutions/

Pittman, J. (2007) Speaking Truth to Power, *Markkula Center for Applied Ethics*, www.scu.edu/ethics/focus-areas/business-ethics/resources/speaking-truth-to-power-the-role-of-the-executive/

Pogrebin, R. (2008) In Madoff Scandal, Jews Feel an Acute Betrayal, *The New York Times*, 23 Dec

Ranzini, G. & Lutz, C. (2017) Love at first swipe?, *Mobile Media & Communication*, doi.org/10.1177/2050157916664559

Rippon, G., et al. (2021) How hype and hyperbole distort the neuroscience of sex differences, *PLOS Biology*, doi.org/10.1371/journal.pbio.3001253

Rose, P. & Soole, L. (2020) What influences aggression and foraging activity in social birds?, *Ethology*, doi.org/10.1111/eth.13067

Silk, J. B., et al. (2009) The benefits of social capital, *Proc Biol Sci.*, doi.org/10.1098%2Frspb.2009.0681

Slepian, M. L., et al. (2013) Quality of professional players' poker hands is perceived accurately from arm motions, *Psychological Science*, dx.doi.org/10.1177/0956797613487384

Stanley, D. A., et al. (2011) Implicit race attitudes predict trustworthiness judgments and economic trust decisions, *PNAS*, doi.org/10.1073/pnas.1014345108

Stromberg, J. (2012) Myth Busted: Looking Left or Right Doesn't Indicate If You're Lying, *Smithsonian*, 12 Jul

Tarrant, N. (2012) Giambattista Della Porta and the Roman

Inquisition, *British Journal for the History of Science*, doi. org/10.1017/S0007087412000684

The New Yorker (2020) The Future of Democracy series

Thornton, M. A. & Tamir, D. I. (2017) Mental models accurately predict emotion transitions, *PNAS*, doi.org/10.1073/ pnas.1616056114

Toegel, G. & Barsoux, J-L. (2012) Self-Awareness: A Key to Better Leadership, *MIT Sloan Management Review*, sloanreview.mit.edu/article/ self-awareness-a-key-to-better-leadership/

Toussaint, K. (2020) Feeling stressed out at the office?, *Fast Company*, 9 Jan

V-Dem (2021) Democracy Report 2021, www.v-dem.net/ documents/12/dr_2021.pdf

V-Dem (2022) Democracy Report 2022, v-dem.net/media/ publications/dr_2022.pdf

Waller, J. (2005) What if Darwin had not sailed on the Beagle, *New Scientist*, 17 Aug

Weigard, A., et al. (2021) Little evidence for sex or ovarian hormone influences on affective variability, *Scientific Reports*, doi.org/10.1038/s41598-021-00143-7

Zhang, D., et al. (2020) Apparent emotional expression explains the effects of head posture on perceived trustworthiness and dominance, but a measure of facial width does not, *Perception*, doi.org/10.1177/0301006620909286

Part Three

Accent Bias in Britain (2020) Project Report, accentbiasbritain. org/talks-and-materials/

Albarelli, H. P. (2009) *A Terrible Mistake*, Trine Day

Al-Heeti, A. (2018) WhatsApp: 65B messages sent each day, and more than 2B minutes of calls, *CNET*, 1 May

AP (2001) American Hostage Freed in Philippines, *The New York Times*, 13 Apr

AP (2015) Fla. school settles bizarre lawsuit over hypnotized students, suicides, *CBS News*, 7 Oct

Barkman, R. C. (2021) Why the Human Brain Is So Good at Detecting Patterns, *Psychology Today*, 19 May

Becker, A. (2018) What is good science?, *Aeon*, 5 Apr

Bestelmeyer, P. E. G., et al. (2015) A Neural Marker for Social Bias Toward In-group Accents, *Cerebral Cortex*, doi. org/10.1093/cercor/bhu282

Binham, C. & Scannell, K. (2012) Trader messages reveal sprawl of Libor probe, *Financial Times*, 28 Jun

Bollen, J., et al. (2011) Twitter mood predicts the stock market, *Journal of Computational Science*, dx.doi.org/10.1016/j. jocs.2010.12.007

Brazel, J. (2022) When Do Managers Provide Non-Answers To Analyst Questions?, *Forbes*, 7 Mar

Brescoll, V. L. (2016) Leading with their hearts?, *The Leadership Quarterly*, dx.doi.org/10.1016/j.leaqua.2016.02.005

Casaponsa, A. & Athanasopoulos, P. (2018) The way you see colour depends on what language you speak, *The Conversation*, 16 Apr

Chafe, W. & Tannen, D. (1987) The Relation between Written and Spoken Language, *Annual Review of Anthropology*, www. jstor.org/stable/2155877

Clark, U. (2007) *Studying Language: English in Action*, Palgrave Macmillan, 2007

Cogliati Dezza, I., et al. (2017) Learning the value of information and reward over time when solving exploration-exploitation problems, *Sci Rep*, doi.org/10.1038/s41598-017-17237-w

Cowley-Cunningham, M. B. & Byrne, R. (2004) Chess Masters' Hypothesis Testing, *SSRN*, ssrn.com/abstract=2339588

Crawford, V. P. (2003) Lying for Strategic Advantage, *American Economic Review*, doi.org/10.1257/000282803321455197

Dahlke, R. & Hancock, J. (2022) The Effect of Online Misinformation Exposure on False Election Beliefs, *OSF Preprints*, doi.org/10.31219/osf.io/325tn

DeAndrea, D. C., et al. (2010) Online Language, *Journal of Language and Social Psychology*, doi.org/10.1177/0261927X10377989

DeAndrea, D. C., et al. (2015) How People Evaluate Online Reviews, *Communication Research*, doi.org/10.1177/0093650215573862

FBI, History: The Unabomber, www.fbi.gov/history/famous-cases/unabomber

Fernandez, M. & Alani, H. (2018) Online Misinformation, *WWW '18 Companion*, doi.org/10.1145/3184558.3188730

Fernando, J. (2022) What Was the LIBOR Scandal?, *Investopedia*, 12 Jun

Flege, J. E. (1984) The detection of French accent by American listeners, *The Journal of the Acoustical Society of America*, doi.org/10.1121/1.391256

Gow, I. D., et al. (2021) Non-answers during conference calls, *Journal of Accounting Research, Forthcoming*, dx.doi.org/10.2139/ssrn.3310360

Hamilton, P. & Hartley, L. (2004) Physiognomy and the Meaning of Expression in Nineteenth Century Culture, *The Modern Language Review*, dx.doi.org/10.2307/3738890

Hancock, J. T., et al. (2008) On Lying and Being Lied To, *Discourse Processes*, dx.doi.org/10.1080/01638530701739181

Hancock, J. T., et al. (2009) Butler lies, *Proceedings of the SIGCHI Conference on Human Factors in Computing Systems*, dx.doi.org/10.1145/1518701.1518782

Hogenboom, M. (2018) The Accents We Trust, *HD Today*, 31 Jul, hdtoday.human.cornell.edu/2018/07/31/the-accents-we-trust/

Jones, N. (2017) Do You See What I See?, *Sapiens.org*, 9 Feb

Juola, P. (2013) How a Computer Program Helped Show J.K. Rowling write A Cuckoo's Calling, *Scientific American*, 20 Aug

Juola, P. (2020) Authorship Studies and the Dark Side of Social Media Analytics, *Journal of Universal Computer Science*, dx.doi.org/10.3897/jucs.2020.009

Karan, A., et al. (2019) Meta-analytic evidence that we-talk predicts relationship and personal functioning in romantic couples, *Journal of Social and Personal Relationships*, dx.doi.org/10.1177/0265407518795336

Keila, P. S. & Skillicorn, D. B. (2005) Detecting unusual email communication, *Proceedings of the 2005 Conference of the Centre for Advanced Studies on Collaborative Research*, dx.doi.org/10.1145/1105634.1105643

Kinzer, S. (2019) *Poisoner in Chief*, Macmillan

Klimt, B. & Yang, Y. (2004) The Enron Corpus, in *Machine Learning: ECML 2004*, Springer, doi.org/10.1007/978-3-540-30115-8_22

Kuhn, G. & Land, M. F. (2006) There's more to magic than meets the eye, *Current Biology*, dx.doi.org/10.1016/j.cub.2006.10.012

Kuhn, G. (2010) Cognitive Illusions, in *New Horizons in the Neuroscience of Consciousness*, John Benjamin Publishing Company

Kuhn, G., et al. (2009) You look where I look!, *Visual Cognition*, doi.org/10.1080/13506280902826775

Larcker, D. F. & Zakolyukina, A. A. (2012) Detecting Deceptive Discussions in Conference Calls, *Journal of Accounting Research*, dx.doi.org/10.2139/ssrn.1572705

Lehrer, J. (2009) Magic and the Brain, *Wired*, 20 Apr

Levon, E., et al. (2022) Speaking Up, *The Sutton Trust*, www.suttontrust.com/our-research/speaking-up-accents-social-mobility/

Liu, B. (2010) Sentiment Analysis and Subjectivity, in *Handbook of Natural Language Processing*, Chapman & Hall

Liu, B. (2012) *Sentiment Analysis and Opinion Mining*, Springer Cham

Macknik, S. L., et al. (2008) Attention and awareness in stage magic, *Nature Reviews Neuroscience*, doi.org/10.1038/nrn2473

Macknik, S. L., et al. (2012) *Sleights of Mind*, Profile Books

Markowitz, D. M. & Hancock, J. T. (2016) Linguistic Obfuscation in Fraudulent Science, *Journal of Language and Social Psychology*, doi.org/10.1177/0261927X15614605

Martinez-Conde, S. & Macknik, S. L. (2008) Magic and the Brain, *The Scientific American*, 1 Dec

Martinez-Conde, S., et al. (2004) The role of fixational eye movements in visual perception, *Nature Reviews Neuroscience*, doi.org/10.1038/nrn1348

Mattson, M. P. (2014) Superior pattern processing is the essence of the evolved human brain, *Frontiers in Neuroscience*, doi.org/10.3389/fnins.2014.00265

McCoy, J., et al. (2018) Polarization and the Global Crisis of Democracy, *American Behavioral Scientist*, doi.org/10.1177/0002764218759576

Melton, H. K. & Wallace, R. (2019) *The Official CIA Manual of Trickery and Deception*, HarperCollins e-books

Miller, M. (2018) Canadian court awards $2.6 billion in Sino-Forest fraud case, *Reuters*, 15 Mar

Miner, G., et al. (2012) *Practical Text Mining and Statistical Analysis for Non-structured Text Data Applications*, Elsevier

Mittal, A. & Goel, A. (2011) Stock Prediction Using Twitter Sentiment Analysis

Moriuchi, E. (2021) English Accent Variations in YouTube Voice-Over Ads, *Journal of Interactive Advertising*, doi.org/10.1080/15252019.2021.1973620

Mosteller, Frederick & Wallace, David L. (1989) Deciding

Authorship, in *Statistics: A Guide to the Unknown*, Duxbury Press

Nelson, G. L., et al. (2002) Directness vs. indirectness, *International Journal of Intercultural Relations*, doi.org/10.1016/S0147-1767(01)00037-2

Newman, M. L., et al. (2003) Lying Words, *Personality and Social Psychology Bulletin*, doi.org/10.1177/0146167203029005010

Ogiermann, E. (2009) Politeness and in-directness across cultures, *Journal of Politeness Research*, dx.doi.org/10.1515/JPLR.2009.011

Olson, J. A., et al. (2015) Influencing choice without awareness, *Consciousness and Cognition*, doi.org/10.1016/j.concog.2015.01.004

Olson, J. A., et al. (2016) Simulated thought insertion, *Conscious Cognition*, doi.org/10.1016/j.concog.2016.04.010

Otero-Millan, J., et al. (2011) Stronger Misdirection in Curved than in Straight Motion, *Frontiers in Human Neuroscience*, doi.org/10.3389/fnhum.2011.00133

Parris, B. A., et al. (2009) Imaging the impossible, *NeuroImage*, doi.org/10.1016/j.neuroimage.2008.12.036

Partnoy, F. (2018) What Your Boss Could Learn by Reading the Whole Company's Emails, *The Atlantic*, 20 Nov

Pickard, J. (2019) Ferry company with no ferries stripped of Brexit contract, *Financial Times*, 9 Feb

Purnell, T., et al. (1999) Perceptual and Phonetic Experiments on American English Dialect, *Journal of Language and Social Psychology*, doi.org/10.1177/0261927X99018001002

Rakove, J. N. & Sheehan, C. A. (2020) *The Cambridge Companion to the Federalist Papers*, Cambridge University Press

Rensink, R. A. & Kuhn, G. (2015) A framework for using magic to study the mind, *Frontiers in Psychology*, doi.org/10.3389/fpsyg.2014.01508

Rice, P. (2006) Linguistic profiling, *The Source: Newsroom, Washington University in St. Louis*, 2 Feb

Rosenfeld, M. J., et al. (2019) Disintermediating your friends, *PNAS*, doi.org/10.1073/pnas.1908630116

Schmid, P. & Betsch, C. (2019) Effective strategies for rebutting science denialism in public discussions, *Nature Human Behaviour*, doi.org/10.1038/s41562-019-0632-4

Science Daily (2014) Magic tricks created using artificial intelligence for the first time, 16 Nov

Seider, B. H., et al. (2009) We can work it out, *Psychology and Aging*, doi.org/10.1037/a0016950

Sharma, D. (2019) British people still think some accents are smarter than others, *The Conversation*, 25 Nov

Shashkevich, A. (2019) Meeting online has become the most popular way U.S. couples connect, *Stanford News*, 21 Aug

Singh, M. (2020) WhatsApp is now delivering roughly 100 billion messages a day, *TechCrunch*, 30 Oct

Slepian, M. L., et al. (2013) Quality of professional players' poker hands is perceived accurately from arm motions, *Psychological Science*, doi.org/10.1177/0956797613487384

Sosik, J. J. & Megerian, L. E. (1999) Understanding Leader Emotional Intelligence and Performance, *Group & Organization Management*, doi.org/10.1177/1059601199243006

Sweney, M. & Robinson, J. (2020) Not all regions like to hear their own accents in ads, survey finds, *Guardian*, 13 May

Teller (1999) Witchcraft as Statecraft, *The New York Times Magazine*, 18 Apr

Teller (2012) Teller Reveals His Secrets, *Smithsonian*, Mar

The Canadian Press (2017) Chronicle of a collapse, *Financial Post*, 2017

Travis, L., et al. (2001) Links Between Social Understanding and Social Behavior in Verbally Able Children with

Autism, *Journal of Autism and Developmental Disorders*, doi. org/10.1023/a:1010705912731

Treaster, J. B. (1977) C.I.A. Hired Magician in Behavior Project, *The New York Times*, 3 Aug

Troy, T. F. (1993) Truman on CIA, *CIA Historical Review Program*, www.cia.gov/static/140d431d2c0e7dc2a891a4ed2 24c9991/Truman-on-CIA.pdf

Tucker, J. (2016) Here's how text analysis is transforming social-science research, *Washington Post*, 27 May

US Department of Energy, Espionage and the Manhattan Project, www.osti.gov/opennet/manhattan-project-history/ Events/1942-1945/espionage.htm

Wang, Z., et al. (2009) The Impact of Accent Stereotypes on Service Outcomes and Its Boundary Conditions, *ACR*, www. acrwebsite.org/volumes/14622/volumes/v36/NA-36

Wang, Z., et al. (2013) 'You lost me at hello', *International Journal of Research in Marketing*, doi.org/10.1016/j. ijresmar.2012.09.004

Wang, Z., et al. (2015) Effects of Employees' Positive Affective Displays on Customer Loyalty Intentions, *AMJ*, doi. org/10.5465/amj.2014.0367

Wargaming, How a Magician Made a Harbor Vanish, wargaming. com/en/news/jasper_maskelyne/

Weigard, A., et al. (2021) Little evidence for sex or ovarian hormone influences on affective variability, *Scientific Reports*, doi.org/10.1038/s41598-021-00143-7

Weiner, T. (1999) Sidney Gottlieb, 80, Dies; Took LSD to C.I.A., *The New York Times*, 10 Mar

Wiehl, L. (2002) 'Sounding Black' in the Courtroom, *Harvard Black Letter Law Journal*, harvardblackletter.org/wp-content/ uploads/sites/8/2016/10/18-JREJ-185.pdf

Wired (2021) Korean Language Professor Breaks Down *Squid Game*'s Subtitles, Youtube.com

Young, L. & Soroka, S. (2012) Affective News, *Political Communication* dx.doi.org/10.1080/10584609.2012.671234

Zadrozny, B. (2019) Fake science led a mom to feed bleach to her autistic sons, *NBC News*, 14 Jun

Zax, D. (2014) How Did Computers Uncover J.K. Rowling's Pseudonym?, *Smithsonian*, Mar

Zubeck, R. & Doyle, D. (2020) Measuring Government Policy with Text Analysis, *OxPol: The Oxford University Politics Blog*, 1 Nov

Part Four

Adbrands.net (2017) Young and Ribicam Group, 25 Jul, www. adbrands.net/archive/us/y-and-r-us-p.htm

Almashat, S., et al. (2008) Framing effect debiasing in medical decision making, *Patient Education and Counseling*, doi. org/10.1016/j.pec.2007.11.004

Angrisani, M., et al. (2002) Strategic Sophistication and Trading Profits, *SSRN*, dx.doi.org/10.2139/ssrn.4310087

Bradshaw, K. A. (2006) America Speaks, *Journalism History*, doi. org/10.1080/00947679.2006.12062689

Braverman, M., et al. (2008) Mafia: A Theoretical Study of Players and Coalitions in a Partial Information Environment, *The Annals of Applied Probability*, www.jstor.org/stable/25442651

Butler, H. A. (2017) Why Do Smart People Do Foolish Things?, *Scientific American*, 3 Oct

Camerer, C. F., et al. (2004) Behavioural Game Theory, in *Advances in Understanding Strategic Behavior*, Palgrave

Chinoy, S., et al. (2023) Zero-Sum Thinking and the Roots of U.S. Political Divides, Harvard University Working Paper, scholar.harvard.edu/files/stantcheva/files/zero_sum_us_political_divides.pdf

Christopher, B. (2016) The Spectrum Auction: How Economists Saved the Day, *Priceonomics*, 19 Aug

Davidai, S. & Ongis, M. (2019) The politics of zero-sum thinking, *Science Advances*, doi.org/10.1126/sciadv.aay3761

DeCosta-Klipa, Nik (2016) Here are 3 people who correctly predicted Donald Trump would win the election, *Boston.com*, 10 Nov

Dixit, A. K. & Nalebuff, B. J. (1993) *Thinking Strategically*, W. W. Norton

Economic Sciences Prize Committee of the Royal Swedish Academy of Sciences (2012) Stable Allocations and the Practice of Market Design, *NobelPrize.org*, 15 Oct

Florida Museum, International Shark Attack File: Risk of Death, www.floridamuseum.ufl.edu/shark-attacks/odds/compare-risk/death/

Friedman, H. H. (2017) Cognitive Biases that Interfere with Critical Thinking and Scientific Reasoning, *SSRN*, dx.doi.org/10.2139/ssrn.2958800

Gallup, G. H. (1928) An objective method for determining reader interest in the content of a newspaper, *Iowa Research Online*, doi.org/10.17077/etd.wvf7mzkt

Gallup.com, George H. Gallup, Founder, www.gallup.com/corporate/178136/george-gallup.aspx

Gass, S. I. (2003) What is game theory and what are some of its applications?, *Scientific American*, 2 Jun

Gisiger, N. (2009) Managing Uncertainty, *SSRN*, doi.org/10.2139/ssrn.1355190

Guess, A., et al. (2018) Selective Exposure to Misinformation, *Meta*, about.fb.com/wp-content/uploads/2018/01/fake-news-2016.pdf

Hansen, N. D., et al. (2019) Relationship Between Media Coverage and MMR Vaccination Uptake in Denmark,

JMIR Public Health and Surveillance, doi.org/10.2196/publichealth.9544

Ipsos (2015) Sharks: Half (51%) of Americans are Absolutely Terrified of Them and Many (38%) Scared to Swim in the Ocean Because of Them, 7 Jul

Johnson, E. J. & Tversky, A. (1983) Affect, generalization, and the perception of risk, *Journal of Personality and Social Psychology*, doi.org/10.1037/0022-3514.45.1.20

Kahneman, D. & Smith, V. L. (2002) Daniel Kahneman: Biographical, *NobelPrize.org*

Kahneman, D. & Tversky, A. (1979) Prospect Theory, *Econometrica*, doi.org/10.2307/1914185

Kolbert, E. (2017) Why Facts Don't Change Our Minds, *The New Yorker*, 19 Feb

Krakow, M. (2019) A flight attendant who contracted measles has died amid a global rise in outbreaks, *Washington Post*, 13 Aug

Lucas, G. M., et al. (2015) Against Game Theory, in *Emerging Trends in the Social and Behavioral Sciences*, John Wiley & Sons

Magistro, B. & Wittstock, N. (2020) Zero-Sum Thinking on Immigration Will Make America Poorer, *University of Washington Political Economy Forum*, 25 Jun

Marshall, W. F. (2020) Pattern Formation and Complexity in Single Cells, *Current Biology*, doi.org/10.1016/j.cub.2020.04.011

Matros, A. (2018) Lloyd Shapley and chess with imperfect information, *Games and Economic Behavior*, doi.org/10.1016/j.geb.2017.12.003

Milgrom, P. & Wilson, R. (2020) The quest for the perfect auction, *The Royal Swedish Academy of Sciences*, www.kva.se/app/uploads/2022/06/popeken20.pdf

Moltz, B. (2014) How 'Scary' Sells With Fear Based Marketing, *Small Business Trends*, 22 Apr

National Centre for Social Research, *What UK Thinks: EU*, www.whatukthinks.org

Nuhfer, E., et al. (2016) Random Number Simulations Reveal How Random Noise Affects the Measurements and Graphical Portrayals of Self-Assessed Competency, *Numeracy*, dx.doi.org/10.5038/1936-4660.9.1.4

PBS, George Gallup and the Scientific Opinion Poll, www.pbs.org/fmc/segments/progseg7.htm

Post, T., et al. (2012) Deal or No Deal? Decision Making under Risk in a Large-Payoff Game Show, *SSRN*, ssrn.com/abstract=636508

Prisner, E. (2014) *Game Theory through Examples*, Mathematical Association of America

Pullinger, J. (2013) Margins of Error presentation, Royal Statistical Society

Ritchie, H., et al. (2013) Terrorism, *OurWorldInData.org*

Roshco, B. & Crespi, I. (1996) From Alchemy to Home-Brewed Chemistry – Polling Transformed, *The Public Perspective*

Schwab, K. (2015) A Cultural History of Rock-Paper-Scissors, *The Atlantic*, 23 Dec

Sequeira, S., et al. (2020) Immigrants and the Making of America, *The Review of Economic Studies*, dx.doi.org/10.1093/restud/rdz003

Sharockman, A. (2016) The truth (so far) behind the 2016 campaign, *Politifact*, 29 Jun

Slotnik, D. E. (2018) Richard Jarecki, doctor who conquered roulette, dies at 86, *San Francisco Chronicle*, 9 Aug

Stephens-Davidowitz, S. (2013) Who Will Vote? Ask Google

Sydney Morning Herald (1969) The Gambling Professor

Tell Me More (2011) Racism As A Zero-Sum Game, *NPR.org*, 13 Jul

The Committee for the Prize in Economic Sciences in Memory

of Alfred Nobel (2020) Improvements to Auction Theory and Inventions of New Auction Formats, *NobelPrize.org*, 12 Oct

The Times (2018) Richard Jarecki Obituary, 24 Aug

Tversky, A. & Kahneman, D. (1981) The Framing of Decisions and the Psychology of Choice, *Science*, doi.org/10.1126/science.7455683

Tversky, A. & Kahneman, D. (1989) Rational Choice and the Framing of Decisions, in *Multiple Criteria Decision Making and Risk Analysis Using Microcomputers*, Springer

Tzu, S. (2009) *The Art of War*, Pax Librorum

Van Allen, S. (1999) George Gallup, Twentieth-Century Pioneer, *Gallup.com*, 29 Dec

Vanderslott, S. (2019) Skepticism to vaccines and what to do about it, *OurWorldInData.org*

Wainwright, M. (2012) Sherlock Holmes and Game Theory, *Mosaic: An Interdisciplinary Critical Journal*, www.jstor.org/stable/44030696

Weiss, D. J. & Shanteau, J. (2021) The futility of decision making research, *Studies in History and Philosophy of Science*, doi.org/10.1016/j.shpsa.2021.08.018

WHO (2019) More than 140,000 die from measles as cases surge worldwide, 5 Dec

WHO (2023) Malaria fact sheet, 19 Mar

Credits

Souvenir Press would like to thank everyone who worked on the publication of *The Truth Detective*.

Editor
Rebecca Gray

Editorial Assistant
Zara Sehr Ashraf

Copy-editor
Amber Burlinson

Proofreader
Anne Rieley

Managing Editor
Emily Frisella

Audio Editor
Audrey Kerr

Production Controller
Anna Howarth

Designer
Samantha Johnson

Marketing
Rosie Parnham
Angie Curzi

Publicity
Anna Pallai
Kate McQuaid

Contracts
Nikki Griffiths

Trade
Claire Beaumont
Elif Akar
Hannah Hyslop
Sarah Ward
Lisa Finch

Finance
Frances Ford
Catherine Clohessy-McCarthy
Rolf Hoving
Angelika Pakiry-Palmer
Pooja Patel
Farzana Sultana
Jen Tyler

Operations
Cait Davis
Edwin Laing
Alia McKellar
Christina Savidge